Land of Cotton

A Collection of Southern Recipes

LAND OF COTTON

Published by
John T. Morgan Academy
Selma, Alabama 36702

P.O. Box 1587
Selma, Alabama 36702-1587

First Printing 1988 5,412 copies
Second Printing 1989 5,286 copies
Third Printing 1990 5,224 copies
Fourth Printing 1991 7,568 copies
Fifth Printing 1992 7,500 copies
Sixth Printing 1993 7,644 copies
Seventh Printing 1994 5,400 copies
Eighth Printing 1995 7,992 copies
Ninth Printing 1996 5,154 copies
Tenth Printing 1997 5,226 copies
Eleventh Printing 1998 5,206 copies
Twelfth Printing 2000 5,280 copies
Thirteenth Printing 2001 5,328 copies
Fourteenth Printing 2001 5,232 copies
Fifteenth Printing 2002 5,137 copies
Sixteenth Printing 2003 5,388 copies
Seventeenth Printing 2004 3,414 copies
Eighteenth Printing 2005 3,000 copies

International Standard Book Number 0-9620539-0-2

WIMMER
COOKBOOKS

ConsolidatedGraphics
800.548.2537
wimmerco.com

Contents

APPETIZERS: 5

BEVERAGES: 29

SOUPS AND SANDWICHES: 41

CHEESE, EGGS, AND PASTAS: 55

SALADS AND DRESSINGS: 67

ENTREES: 97
   BEEF 98
   LAMB 116
   PORK 117
   POULTRY 123
   GAME 144
   SEAFOOD 148
   SAUCES AND MARINADES 160

VEGETABLES AND FRUITS: 169

BREADS: 193

DESSERTS: 213
   CAKES AND ICINGS 214
   PIES 232
   DESSERTS 248
   COOKIES AND CANDY 267
   ICE CREAM 293

PRESERVES AND PICKLES: 297

POTPOURRI: 303

TABLES: 310

INDEX: 315

Introduction

Way "down yonder" where cotton is king and moss-draped oak boughs offer cooling shade, good food is a great part of a gentle heritage. Family recipes are as treasured heirlooms as the family silver. Rich blackbelt soil and a generous southern sun bless us with the bounty of the land which graces our tables daily. The recipes in LAND OF COTTON have met the ultimate test—the family dinner table. From quiet, special times for family and friends to grand celebrations, these southern treasures are presented to you with pride and delight.

Appetizers

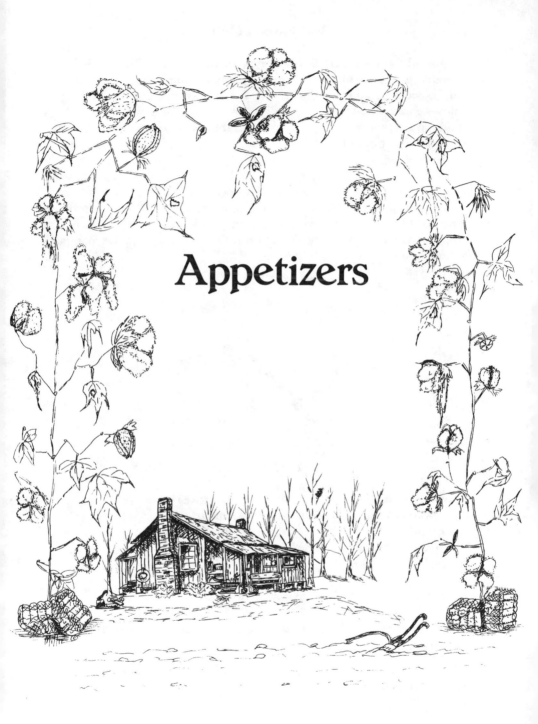

Beef Hors d'Oeuvres

1½ pounds boneless beef sirloin
1½ tablespoons soy sauce
3 tablespoons sliced fresh ginger
4 cloves garlic, sliced
1½ teaspoons sugar
3 green onion tops, sliced

4 small hot red chilies, seeded
  and crushed
2 tablespoons vegetable oil
Soy sauce
1 tablespoon sesame seed, toasted

Cut beef into ¾-inch cubes; set aside. Combine soy sauce, ginger, garlic, sugar, onion tops, and chilies for marinade. Add beef cubes and let marinate for 30 minutes, stirring once. Heat oil in electric frying pan or wok. Add drained beef cubes and cook, stirring to brown lightly on all sides. Place beef in casserole or chafing dish. Sprinkle with soy sauce, then with sesame seed. Provide toothpicks for serving.

Nellie Kate Tepper   Yield: 4 dozen

Beef Knishes

1 pound ground beef
1 (1⅜-ounce) package onion
  soup mix
½ cup bean sprouts, drain and
  reserve ¼ cup liquid

1 (4-ounce) jar chopped
  mushrooms
4 (8-ounce) packages refrigerated
  crescent rolls

Brown meat and drain. Add onion soup mix, bean sprouts, bean sprout liquid, and mushrooms; simmer for 10 minutes. Place heaping teaspoon of meat in center of crescent roll. Fold up like a diaper. Cook at 400 degrees for 10 to 12 minutes.

Note: Cut crescent rolls into 2 small triangles to make appetizers. Flash freeze on cookie sheet and place in freezer bags. Can take out as many as desired and bake. Men love these!

Edie Delp   Yield: 5 dozen

Beef Rolls

2 (3-ounce) packages cream cheese
   softened
3 teaspoons grated onion

2 teaspoons horseradish
Dash of Worcestershire sauce
1 (4-ounce) package sliced beef

Combine cream cheese, onion, horseradish, and Worcestershire. Mix well. Spread mixture on 1 slice of beef at a time. Roll beef up and refrigerate. When thoroughly chilled, the beef rolls may be cut into smaller pieces if desired.

Cookbook Committee   Yield: 8 servings

Sausage Balls

1 pound hot sausage
2 cups grated mild Cheddar cheese

3 cups biscuit mix

Mix all ingredients and shape into balls. Place on greased cookie sheet and bake at 325 degrees for 15 minutes.

Rose Mary DeRamus   Yield: 3 dozen
Gloria Sims Crump

Picadillo Dip

1 pound ground beef or venison
½ bell pepper, chopped
4 medium tomatoes, peeled and
   chopped
6 tablespoons tomato paste
½ cup tomato sauce
1 tablespoon instant minced onion

⅔ cup water
¼ teaspoon oregano
½ cup dark raisins
½ cup white raisins
Salt to taste
Pepper to taste
Slivered almonds

Sauté meat and drain fat. Add remaining ingredients except almonds. Simmer slowly until well mixed, about 30 minutes. If meat mixture is too thick to use as a dip, add water. Serve in a chafing dish with almonds sprinkled on top. Use tostadas for dipping.

Sherry Taylor   Yield: 20 servings

Cocktail Meatballs

2 pounds ground beef
1 small onion, grated
1 clove garlic, crushed
½ cup cornflakes, crushed
2 eggs, beaten

Salt to taste
Pepper to taste
1 (12-ounce) bottle chili sauce
Juice of one lemon
1 (8-ounce) jar grape jelly

Thoroughly mix ground beef, onion, garlic, cornflakes, and eggs. Season to taste. Shape into walnut size balls. Combine chili sauce, lemon juice, and grape jelly in a heavy skillet. Simmer 5 minutes. Place meatballs in sauce. Cook slowly for 1 hour. Cool, refrigerate until fat hardens, skim off, and discard. Reheat to serve.

Note: May be frozen for use later.

Rosemary Harris   Yield: 5 dozen

Creamy Beef Cheese Dip

1 (8-ounce) package cream cheese
1 (2½-ounce) jar sliced dried beef,
   finely chopped
¼ cup chopped walnuts
¾ teaspoon pepper
¼ cup sour cream

2 tablespoons finely chopped
   onion
2 tablespoons milk
Melba toast, rice crackers, or
   toast points

Place cream cheese in a 1-quart glass casserole. Microwave at HIGH 45 seconds to 1 minute, or until cheese is softened. Add remaining ingredients and stir until well blended. Cover and microwave at HIGH 1½ minutes. Stir. Microwave at MEDIUM 2 to 2½ minutes. Serve with toast or crackers.

Note: Can be baked at 350 degrees for 15 minutes instead of microwave.

Kay Foster   Yield: 12 to 15 servings
Ginger Wilson

Pizza Dip

1 (8-ounce) package cream cheese, softened
1 (12-ounce) bottle chili sauce
Parmesan cheese
1 (12-ounce) package shredded Mozzarella cheese

1 (3½-ounce) package sliced pepperoni
1 small onion, chopped
1 small green pepper, chopped
1 (4-ounce) jar sliced mushrooms, optional

Spread cream cheese on bottom of serving tray. Cover with chili sauce. Sprinkle with Parmesan and Mozzarella cheese. Layer other ingredients. Serve with corn chips.

Variation: Various toppings may be added such as shrimp, olives, sausage, etc.

Cheryl Watts   Yield: 12 to 15 servings

Bourbon Franks

1 (14-ounce) bottle catsup
1 cup bourbon
1 cup dark brown sugar

4 (8-ounce) packages miniature cocktail frankfurters

In large saucepan, mix all ingredients except frankfurters. Cover and simmer 2 hours. Add franks and simmer 5 minutes. Serve in chafing dish. This can be made in advance.

Cookbook Committee   Yield: 70 to 80 servings

Ham and Cheese Puffs

½ cup margarine, softened
1½ cups grated sharp Cheddar cheese
⅓ cup finely chopped ham or cooked and crumbled sausage

¼ teaspoon Worcestershire sauce
Dash of cayenne pepper
1 cup sifted flour

Preheat oven to 350 degrees. Combine all ingredients except flour and mix. Blend in flour and shape into small balls. Place on ungreased baking sheet and bake for 15 to 20 minutes.

Adrienne DeRamus   Yield: 3 dozen

9

Bacon and Tomato Spread

1 (8-ounce) package cream cheese, softened
1 tablespoon mayonnaise

Garlic salt to taste
1 tomato, peeled and chopped
6 to 8 slices of bacon

Blend cream cheese and mayonnaise until smooth. Add garlic salt and tomatoes. Cook bacon until crispy and blend in bacon when ready to serve. Spread on dark party bread.

Note: This makes a delicious dip with stiff chips.

Mary Ann Norris

Yield: 1 cup

Corndog Bites

1 cup flour
2/3 cup cornmeal
1 tablespoon sugar
1 1/2 teaspoons baking powder
1 teaspoon salt
1 tablespoon melted bacon drippings

1 egg, beaten
1 to 1 1/4 cups buttermilk
1/2 teaspoon baking soda
1 pound frankfurters
Vegetable oil
Mustard, catsup, picante sauce, optional

Combine flour, cornmeal, sugar, baking powder, and salt. Stir in bacon drippings. Combine egg, buttermilk, and baking soda; mix well. Stir into flour mixture, mixing well. Cut frankfurters into bite-size pieces. Dip frankfurter sections into batter, covering completely. (Wooden toothpicks inserted in one end works well). Drop into hot oil (375 degrees), and cook until golden, turning once; drain on paper towels. Serve warm with condiments.

Faye Messer

Yield: 4 dozen

Chicken Nut Bites

1 cup canned chicken broth	¾ teaspoon celery seed
½ cup butter	½ teaspoon paprika
1 cup flour	⅛ teaspoon cayenne
1 tablespoon parsley	4 eggs
2 teaspoons seasoned salt	1 (5-ounce) can boned chicken
2 teaspoons Worcestershire sauce	¼ cup toasted almonds

Combine broth and butter; bring to a boil. Stir in flour and seasonings. Cook, beating rapidly, until mixture leaves sides of pan and forms a smooth compact ball. Remove from heat. Add eggs one at a time, beating well until mixture is shiny. Stir in chicken and almonds. Drop by rounded teaspoon onto two greased baking sheets. Bake at 400 degrees for 15 minutes.

Note: If freezing, bake before freezing, take out as many as needed and reheat.

Variation: May use 2 chicken breasts or ¾ cup diced chicken in place of canned chicken.

Cookbook Committee   Yield: 6 dozen

Delicious Chicken Wings

2 eggs	8 tablespoons cornstarch
5 tablespoons soy sauce	1 clove garlic, minced
4 tablespoons flour	2 green onions, chopped
1½ teaspoons monosodium glutamate	3 pounds chicken wings

Mix eggs and soy sauce; add remaining ingredients. Chop wing tips off, split into 2 pieces. Soak wings overnight. Deep fry.

Note: Very good for cocktail hors d'oeuvres.

Cookbook Committee   Yield: 45 servings

Hot Shrimp Dip I

1 (10½-ounce) can cream of
   shrimp soup
1 (10½-ounce) can cream of
   chicken soup
1 (8-ounce) bag small frozen
   shrimp

1 cup sour cream
1 cup grated sharp cheese
1 tablespoon minced onion
Salt to taste
Pepper to taste

Combine all ingredients. Simmer in chafing dish. Serve with Melba toast.

Christine Moore

Yield: 20 servings

Hot Shrimp Dip II

1 cup butter, melted
2 (6-ounce) tubes garlic cheese
   spread
3 (8-ounce) cans shrimp, drained

½ (2¼-ounce) jar black olives,
   drained
1 (8-ounce) can mushrooms,
   drained and chopped

Mix all the ingredients well. Heat and serve in chafing dish. Serve with Melba Rounds or Triscuits.

Note: An easy and great hors d'oeuvre.

Wanda Bass

Yield: 10 to 12 servings

Shrimp Mold

1 (10¾-ounce) can tomato soup
1 (1-ounce) envelope unflavored
   gelatin
1 (8-ounce) package cream cheese
1 cup mayonnaise

½ cup finely chopped celery
¼ cup finely chopped onion
2 (4½-ounce) cans shrimp,
   drained; or 1½ pounds fresh
   boiled shrimp

Heat to dissolve soup and gelatin. Break up cheese and add to warm mixture. Leave on warm heat and add mayonnaise, celery, onion, and shrimp. Pour into slightly greased mold.

Beatrice Russell

Yield: 20 to 24 servings

Shrimp Celery Stuffing

1 (5-ounce) can deveined shrimp,
   drained
¼ teaspoon salt
2 teaspoons lemon juice
1 tablespoon chopped onion

½ cup mayonnaise
2 dashes of Tabasco
1 (3-ounce) package cream cheese
1 stalk celery, separated into
   individual pieces and cleaned

Mix all ingredients together and stuff one bunch of celery. Slice ribs finger length. Refrigerate until served.

Note: Tabasco is a registered trademark of McIlhenny Co., Avery Island, LA 70513.

Cheryl Watts   Yield: 36 servings

Salmon Spread

1 (5½-ounce) can pink salmon
1 (3-ounce) package cream cheese,
   softened

¼ cup finely chopped onion
10 shakes liquid smoke
Mayonnaise

Drain salmon and mix with cream cheese. Add onion and liquid smoke; mix well. Add enough mayonnaise to make the salmon mixture spread easily on crackers.

Jane S. Singley   Yield: 10 to 12 servings

Cream Cheese-Crabmeat Log

1 (6½-ounce) can crabmeat,
   well drained
1 (8-ounce) package cream cheese

Horseradish
Heinz 57 Sauce

Be sure no shells are in the crabmeat. Take a piece of string or thread and divide cream cheese into 3 sections, lengthwise. On the first cream cheese section spread some of the horseradish, then one half of the crabmeat. Repeat for next layer, and top with third cream cheese section. Pour steak sauce over top and down sides. Serve with crackers. Secure the layers with toothpicks.

Lillian Riddle Gilley   Yield: 12 to 15 servings
   Class of 1972

Curried Crab Meatballs

2 (7½-ounce) cans king crabmeat
¼ cup butter or margarine
¼ cup flour
1 cup milk
1 teaspoon salt
¼ teaspoon pepper

1 teaspoon Worcestershire sauce
1 teaspoon curry
⅛ teaspoon Tabasco
Flour
1 egg
¾ cup dry bread crumbs

Drain and flake crabmeat, removing any cartilage. Melt butter in medium saucepan, stir in flour, and gradually add milk, stirring until smooth. Bring to a boil, stirring constantly. Reduce heat, and simmer 1 minute. Remove from heat. Add salt, pepper, Worcestershire sauce, curry, and Tabasco. Mix well. Stir in crabmeat, refrigerate until completely cooled. Shape into small balls. Roll in flour to coat lightly. Dip each into beaten egg in shallow dish, roll in crumbs to coat completely. Deep fry balls until golden brown, about 1 minute. These can be done ahead and put in the freezer. To reheat, bake at 350 degrees for 10 to 15 minutes.

Cookbook Committee   Yield: 2 to 3 dozen

Party Crab Mold

2 (1-ounce) envelopes unflavored
  gelatin
½ cup cold water
½ cup boiling water
3(8-ounce) packages cream cheese
  softened
¾ cup lemon juice
1 teaspoon salt

1 teaspoon Worcestershire sauce
½ teaspoon hot sauce
½ teaspoon grated onion
4 (6-ounce) cans lump crabmeat,
  drained
Pimento stuffed olive slices
Chopped fresh parsley
Crackers

Sprinkle gelatin over cold water, let stand 5 minutes. Add boiling water, stir until gelatin dissolves. Combine gelatin mixture with cream cheese, lemon juice, salt, Worcestershire sauce, hot sauce, and onion in a mixing bowl. Beat on medium speed of electric mixer until smooth. Stir in crabmeat, pour into a lightly oiled 5½ cup mold and chill until firm. Unmold and garnish with sliced olives and parsley. Serve with crackers.

Christine Moore   Yield: 15 to 20 servings

Oyster Roll

2 to 3 tablespoons mayonnaise
2 (8-ounce) packages cream cheese
2 teaspoons Worcestershire sauce
Garlic salt to taste or 1 to 2 cloves
   garlic, pressed
½ small onion, pressed
⅛ teaspoon salt
2 to 3 (3¾-ounce) cans smoked
   oysters

Cream enough mayonnaise into cream cheese to hold it together. Add Worcestershire sauce, garlic, onion, and salt. Combine well. Spread about ½-inch thick (rectangle shape) on piece of waxed paper. Chop oysters and spread on top of cheese mixture. Place in refrigerator for a few minutes to harden cheese a little. Roll as if for jelly roll. Seal ends. Chill for 12 hours. Slice and serve with toast rounds or crackers.

Paula Vardaman   Yield: 12 to 15 servings

Oysters in Mexican Blankets

1 pint select oysters, drained
12 slices bacon
Salt to taste
Pepper to taste
Paprika to taste
2 tablespoons chopped parsley
1 to 2 drops Tabasco

Lay each oyster across ½ slice bacon. Add salt, pepper, and paprika to taste. Add parsley and Tabasco. Roll bacon blankets around oysters and place on rack in shallow pan. Bake at 450 degrees for 10 minutes or until bacon is crisp.

Note: Toothpicks can be used to hold all together until they are ready to be served.

Terry Hunter   Yield: 6 to 8 servings

Olive Pimento Cheese Spread

2 cups grated Cheddar cheese
½ cup mayonnaise
½ cup green olives with pimentos,
   diced
1 tablespoon mustard
1 teaspoon sugar
Salt to taste
Pepper to taste

Mix ingredients well; serve on crackers or as sandwiches.

Becky Bailey   Yield: 3 cups

Cheese Wafers

2 cups grated sharp Cheddar
  cheese
1 cup margarine
2 cups flour

Dash salt
Dash red pepper
2 cups crispy rice cereal

Cream cheese and margarine together. Add flour, salt, pepper, and cereal. Form small balls and place on ungreased cookie sheet. Press into wafers with floured fork. Bake at 350 degrees for 10 to 15 minutes or until light brown.

Faye Carter
Fran Pearce
Joanne Dillingham

Yield: 12 dozen

Fondue Cheese Dip

1 pound bulk sausage
1 (10-ounce) can tomatoes with
  chilies

1 pound pasteurized processed
  cheese

Brown sausage and drain. Drain tomatoes and chop in blender. Place tomatoes, sausage, and cheese in fondue pot. Blend as cheese melts.

Fran Pearce

Yield: 15 to 20 servings

Cheese Straws I

1 (5-ounce) jar sharp cheese
1 (11-ounce) box pie crust sticks,
  2 in a box

1 tablespoon margarine
Cayenne pepper to taste

Preheat oven to 325 degrees. Mix ingredients by hand. Spoon mixture into a cookie press; squeeze onto an ungreased cookie. Bake for 10 to 12 minutes. Store in airtight container.

Betty Schroeder
Sally Swink

Yield: 3 to 4 dozen

Cheese Straws II

1 (16-ounce) package sharp
  Cheddar cheese
½ cup margarine

1¾ cups flour
½ teaspoon baking powder
½ teaspoon cayenne pepper

Grate cheese. Melt margarine and pour over cheese. Add all dry ingredients. Mix well. Spoon mixture into cookie press and squeeze onto greased cookie sheet. Bake at 400 degrees for 12 to 15 minutes or until light brown. Sprinkle lightly with salt while hot.

Rose Mary DeRamus

Yield: 6 to 7 dozen

Famous Cheese Ring

1 pound sharp cheese, grated
1 cup chopped pecans
¾ cup mayonnaise
1 small onion, grated

1 medium clove garlic, minced
½ teaspoon Worcestershire sauce
1 cup strawberry preserves

Mix all ingredients except preserves together and press into a 1-quart mold. Chill. Serve with strawberry preserves in center of ring.

Susie Kirkpatrick
Sally H. Swink

Yield: 20 servings

Cheese Puffs

1 (8-ounce) package cream cheese
1 (8-ounce) package sharp
  Cheddar cheese

1 cup butter
4 egg whites, beaten stiff
1 loaf white bread, unsliced

Combine cheese and butter. Cook over low heat, stirring constantly, until cheese and butter melt and mixture is thick and smooth. Remove from heat and cool. Fold in egg whites. Trim crusts from bread; cut into 1 inch slices and quarter each slice. Dip bread cubes until saturated. Place on cookie sheet and chill in refrigerator overnight. Bake at 400 degrees for about 5 minutes. Squares may be frozen.

Edie Delp

Yield: 6 dozen

Cheese Ball

2 (8-ounce) packages cream cheese
1 (8-ounce) can crushed
   pineapple, drained
1 small onion, finely chopped
¼ green pepper, finely chopped

2 cups chopped pecans, divided
1 tablespoon garlic seasoned salt
½ teaspoon onion powder
1 teaspoon garlic powder, optional

Soften cream cheese at room temperature; add remaining ingredients, using ½ cup of chopped pecans. Refrigerate until firm. Roll into 2 balls and cover with remaining pecans. Store in plastic food wrap in refrigerator.

Note: May also be frozen.

Variation: Parsley may be substituted for chopped nuts.

Patty Sexton
Adrienne DeRamus
   Class of 1985
Dickie Phillips

Yield: 20 to 24 servings

Cheese Rolls

1 (8-ounce) package grated
   Cheddar cheese
1 (8-ounce) package cream cheese,
   softened

1 cup crushed pecans
¼ teaspoon garlic salt
1 teaspoon Tabasco
Paprika

Mix above ingredients. Roll into 2 rolls about size of quarter when sliced. Roll in paprika. Wrap in waxed paper and refrigerate. Will keep for several weeks in refrigerator. Can also be made into single cheese ball.

Betty Schroeder
Sally Swink

Yield: 15 to 20 servings

Baked Brie

1 large round Brie cheese, about
   2¼ pounds

1 jigger brandy
½ cup slivered almonds, toasted

Remove outer skin from Brie. Place cheese in shallow casserole or baking dish of similar size. Pour brandy over cheese and top with almonds. Bake at 250 degrees for 30 minutes. Serve with unsalted crackers, French bread, and/or apples.

Judy Oxford

Yield: 36 servings

Cream Cheese-Olive Dip

1 (8-ounce) package cream cheese,
   softened
1 (3-ounce) bottle pimento stuffed
   olives

1 tablespoon mayonnaise
Salt to taste
Pepper to taste
Dash of garlic salt

Combine all ingredients. Serve with crackers.

Grace Henry

Yield: 4 to 6 servings

Holladay's Cream Cheese Puffs

1 (3-ounce) package cream cheese
1 (2-ounce) can sliced mushrooms,
   drained
2 tablespoons chopped pimento
1 tablespoon minced onion

2 drops hot sauce
1 (8-ounce) package refrigerated
   crescent rolls
½ cup finely chopped pecans

Soften cheese and chop mushrooms. Combine and mix well with pimento, onion, and hot sauce. Unroll crescent rolls and separate to make 4 rectangles. Spread each rectangle with ¼ of mixture, carefully spreading to edges. Beginning with long end, roll up each rectangle jelly roll style. Refrigerate until firm. Slice each roll into 6 pieces. Coat with pecans. Place on ungreased cookie sheet. Bake at 375 degrees about 15 minutes.

Kay Traylor

Yield: 24 servings

Cheese and Olive Croquettes

1 ¹⁄₃ tablespoons butter, melted
¹⁄₈ cup flour
¹⁄₃ cup milk
Salt to taste
Pepper to taste
Cayenne to taste

2 egg yolks
¹⁄₄ cup sharp cheese, grated
¹⁄₂ cup mild cheese, cubed
Stuffed olives, sliced
Bread crumbs

Combine and cook butter, flour, milk, salt, pepper, and cayenne stirring until thick and smooth. Add 1 unbeaten egg yolk, mix well. Add grated cheese; melt and remove from heat. Fold in cheese cubes and olives. Spread in shallow pan; chill. Turn onto board; cut into small rectangles or shape into small balls. Dip in crumbs, then in remaining egg yolk (beaten and diluted with water), then back in crumbs. Fry in deep fat (390 degrees). Should brown slightly.

Faye Bailey   Yield: 1½ dozen

Stuffed Snow Pea Pods

50 snow pea pods
1 (8-ounce) package cream cheese
6 tablespoons fresh tomato purée
6 teaspoons mayonnaise

¹⁄₂ teaspoon dry mustard
¹⁄₄ teaspoon powdered coriander
Salt to taste
White pepper to taste

Pour boiling salted water over snow pea pods and let soak for one minute. Drain and dry the pods. While they are still warm make an incision ¼ inch long across the width in the flat side of each pod. Using a sharp pointed knife, cut through just to the inside of the pod. The opposite side must not be cut. Cool the pods. Blend softened cream cheese with tomato purée, mayonnaise, mustard, coriander, and salt and pepper to taste. Using a metal cake decorator fitted with a small plain tube, pipe the cheese mixture into the pea pods through the incision. Chill the pods for at least one hour before serving.

Edie Delp   Yield: 20 to 25 servings

Greek Spinach Triangles

2 eggs beaten
1 medium onion, chopped
1 (8-ounce) package cream cheese,
  softened cut in chunks
1/4 teaspoon pepper
1/2 pound Feta cheese or 3/4 cup
  Ricotta cheese

2 (10-ounce) packages frozen
  chopped spinach, cooked and
  drained well
1 cup butter, melted
1 package phyllo Greek pastry
  leaves

Mix all ingredients except butter and pastry. Refrigerate mixture at least one hour. Open package of dough and cut a strip 2 inches wide the length of dough cutting through all layers of dough. Cover remaining dough with damp cloth to keep from cracking. Take apart dough so that you have 2 sheets for each triangle. Brush the 2 sheets with melted butter and put 1 rounded teaspoon of the mixture at the top of the strip. Fold pastry over like folding a flag. Place on well buttered sheet and brush top with butter. To freeze and cook later, butter both sides of triangle and wrap well. Bake at 375 degrees for 20 minutes. Serve warm.

Edie Delp

Yield: 4 dozen

Spinach Dip

1 (10-ounce) package frozen
  spinach
1 cup mayonnaise
1 (8-ounce) carton sour cream
1 medium onion, chopped

1 (8-ounce) can sliced water
  chestnuts, chopped
1 (1 3/8-ounce) envelope dried
  vegetable soup mix

Thaw spinach and press out excess water. Combine all the ingredients and stir well. Chill for several hours before serving.

Jackie Woodfin
Joy Beers

Yield: 10 to 12 servings

Second Lady Spinach Dip

1 (10-ounce) package frozen
 chopped spinach
1 (8-ounce) carton sour cream

½ cup mayonnaise
1 (³⁄₈-ounce) package buttermilk
 dressing mix

Thaw spinach thoroughly and drain. Mix all ingredients together. Refrigerate 4 to 6 hours.

Barbara Bush
 Wife of Vice President George Bush

Yield: 8 to 10 servings

Mushroom Turnovers

Pastry:
1 (3-ounce) package cream cheese,
 softened

½ cup butter, softened
1½ cups flour

Cream together cheese and butter. Stir in flour and blend well. Chill.

Filling:
1 onion, minced
3 tablespoons butter
½ pound fresh mushrooms,
 minced
¼ teaspoon thyme

½ teaspoon salt
Pepper to taste
2 tablespoons flour
¼ cup sour cream

Sauté onion in butter until golden. Add mushrooms and cook 3 minutes. Add seasonings. Sprinkle flour over mixture. Add sour cream. Cook until thickened. DO NOT BOIL! Roll chilled dough very thin on floured board. Cut 3-inch rounds and place 1 teaspoon filling on each. Fold edges over and press together. Prick with fork. Bake on ungreased sheet at 450 degrees for 15 minutes.

Note: May be frozen before baking. Allow more time for baking.

Edie Delp

Yield: 4 dozen

Mushroom Sandwiches

½ teaspoon grated onion
1 tablespoon chopped parsley
1 teaspoon lemon juice
1 (3-ounce) package cream cheese, softened

1 tablespoon mayonnaise
1 (8-ounce) can sliced mushrooms, chopped
Bread of your choice

Combine first five ingredients. Add mushrooms. Remove crusts from bread and spread with mushroom mixture. Top with another slice of bread and cut into finger sandwiches.

Dickie Phillips

Yield: 1 cup

Stuffed Mushrooms

2 cups whole fresh mushrooms
2 tablespoons butter
¼ cup chopped almonds
2 tablespoons chopped onion or 1½ teaspoons instant minced onion

½ teaspoon salt
1 teaspoon lemon juice
½ cup breadcrumbs
1 tablespoon sherry

Wash mushrooms and remove stems (save and use in sauces, soups, or with vegetables). Arrange mushroom caps, hollow side up in a shallow baking dish. In small saucepan, combine butter and almonds. Cook until golden brown. Add remaining ingredients. Mix well. Spoon into mushroom caps. Bake at 375 degrees until hot, about 5 minutes.

Cookbook Committee

Yield: 12 to 15 servings

Cherry Tomato Appetizers

1 pint cherry tomatoes
⅓ pound blue cheese, mashed
⅓ cup sour cream
1 teaspoon lemon juice

Salt to taste
Dash of Tabasco
Paprika
Parsley

Wash tomatoes, cut off tomato tops and scoop out pulp. Drain well. Mix remaining ingredients. Stuff tomatoes with mixture. Garnish with paprika and parsley. Serve chilled.

Cookbook Committee

Yield: 2 dozen

Crispy Fried Artichoke Hearts

2 tablespoons grated Parmesan
cheese
2 tablespoons garlic and parsley
salt
2 cups breadcrumbs

1 (14-ounce) can artichoke hearts,
drained and quartered
2 eggs, beaten
½ cup butter
1 lemon

Combine cheese, salt, and breadcrumbs. Dip quartered hearts in breadcrumb mixture, eggs, and breadcrumbs again. Fry in deep oil until golden brown. Drain. In skillet, sauté fried hearts in butter with juice of one lemon. Serve warm.

Helen Shivers   Yield: 8 to 10 servings

Hot Artichoke Spread

1 (14-ounce) can artichoke hearts,
drained and chopped
1 cup mayonnaise

1 cup Parmesan cheese
Garlic powder to taste

Mix all ingredients and put into ramekin. Heat at 350 degrees for 20 minutes or until mixture bubbles. Serve warm with crackers or chips.

Nell Mooney   Yield: 8 to 10 servings

Cucumber Dip

1 (8-ounce) package cream cheese
2 tablespoons mayonnaise
½ cup grated cucumber
Dash of salt

Dash of pepper
Dash of Worcestershire sauce
Dash of garlic powder

Mix all ingredients together and serve with crackers, chips, or spread onto finger sandwiches.

Bonnie Bryant Fitts   Yield: 1½ cups
   Class of 1980

Guacamole Dip

1 cup mashed avocado
1 small onion, finely chopped
Dash of Worcestershire sauce
½ teaspoon olive oil

Dash of paprika
Juice of ¼ lime
Salt to taste
Pepper to taste

Blend all ingredients until smooth in electric blender. Serve with tostada chips or crackers.

Jerry Goodwin

Yield: 6 to 8 servings

Hot Broccoli Dip

3 (10-ounce) packages frozen
  chopped broccoli
1 medium onion, finely chopped
3 ribs celery, finely chopped
1 cup sliced mushrooms
½ cup margarine

2 (6-ounce) tubes garlic cheese
1 (10¾-ounce) can cream of
  mushroom soup
Tabasco to taste
Red pepper to taste

Cook broccoli according to package directions and drain. Sauté onion, celery, and mushrooms in margarine. Melt cheese and soup in double boiler. Combine all ingredients in a chafing dish and season with Tabasco and pepper.

Mae Bruner Morgan

Yield: 15 to 20 servings

Raw Vegetable Dip

1 cup mayonnaise
1 cup sour cream
1 tablespoon parsley flakes

1 teaspoon dill weed
1 tablespoon finely chopped onion

Mix together and chill. Serve with raw cut vegetables of your choice.

Gloria Sims Crump

Yield: 8 to 10 servings

Nut Roll

1 (8-ounce) package cream cheese, softened
½ cup chopped green onion
½ cup bacon bits

1 teaspoon dill weed
1 teaspoon pepper
½ cup mayonnaise
Chopped pecans

Mix all ingredients except pecans. Form into a ball and roll in finely chopped pecans.

Kate Himes   Yield: 8 to 10 servings

Orange Sugar Pecans

2 cups sugar
⅓ cup orange juice
⅔ cup water

1 teaspoon grated orange peel
2 cups pecan halves

Combine sugar, orange juice, and water; boil to soft ball stage (240 degrees). Remove from heat; stir in orange peel and pecans. Stir until creamy. Pour out on waxed paper in big or little circles and as quickly as possible separate glazed nuts, using two forks.

Margaret Wilson   Yield: 2 cups

Pecans Worcestershire

2 teaspoons butter
⅓ cup Worcestershire sauce
2 dashes Tabasco

Salt to taste
2 cups large pecan halves

Melt butter; add remaining ingredients except pecans. Remove from heat; add pecans, stirring for about 5 minutes so that each nut is coated and all sauce is absorbed. Line cookie sheet with paper towels. Pour nuts out and spread evenly on cookie sheet. Bake at 300 degrees for 15 minutes.

Cookbook Committee   Yield: 2 cups

Toasted Pecans

2 cups pecan halves
½ cup butter

Salt to taste

Place pecans in a 12x17-inch pan in a 250 degree oven. Toast at least 30 minutes to dry and add sliced butter. Let pecans get completely greasy, stirring once or twice. After pecans and butter have mixed well, sprinkle with salt generously and stir very often sprinkling with salt each time as all the salt does not stick to the pecans. Toast pecans one hour or more to desired taste until butter has been absorbed and pecans are crisp.

Cookbook Committee

Yield: 2 cups

Garlic Rounds

5 tablespoons butter
½ teaspoon garlic powder

¼ cup Parmesan cheese
27 bread rounds

Mix together butter, garlic powder, and cheese. Spread on bread rounds. Bake at 200 degrees for one hour on cookie sheet. Check often.

Variation: ½ teaspoon garlic salt may be substituted for garlic powder.

Marjorie Anderson

Yield: 12 to 15 servings

Marinated Oyster Crackers

1 (11-ounce) box oyster or soup
  crackers
½ cup vegetable oil

1 (³/₈-ounce) package buttermilk
  dressing mix
2 tablespoons dill weed

Mix all ingredients together and let marinate for a couple of days before serving. Crackers will stay crisp for days if they are stored in an airtight container.

Carolyn Weissinger

Yield: 4 cups

South of the Border Appetizer Platter

3 ripe avocadoes, peeled and mashed
Juice from 1/2 lemon
1/2 teaspoon salt
1/4 teaspoon pepper
1 (8-ounce) carton sour cream
1/2 cup mayonnaise
1 (1 1/4-ounce) envelope taco
  seasoning mix
2 (10 1/2-ounce) cans bean dip

1 large bunch green onions, sliced
3 medium sized tomatoes, chopped
1 (15-ounce) can ripe olives, sliced
1/2 head of lettuce, chopped
1 (8-ounce) packaged shredded
  Cheddar cheese
1 (10-ounce) bag of plain tostada
  chips

Mash avocadoes; add lemon juice, salt, and pepper and set aside. Mix together in a small bowl sour cream, mayonnaise, and taco mix; set aside. On large platter, layer bean dip, avocado mixture, and sour cream mixture. Decorate the top with onions, tomatoes, sliced olives, and lettuce. Sprinkle the top with shredded cheese. Chill or serve immediately at room temperature. Serve with the tostada chips.

Lynnie Kopp
Carolyn Breeman

Yield: 12 to 15 servings

Oriental Dip

5 green onions
1 (8-ounce) can water chestnuts,
  drained

1 cup sour cream
1 cup mayonnaise
2 tablespoons soy sauce

Chop green onions and water chestnuts. Mix all ingredients. This is very good served with dip size corn chips.

Wyn Wadsworth Minor
  Class of 1972

Yield: 2 cups

Beverages

Citrus Cooler

2½ cups sugar
2½ cups water
1 (46-ounce) can pineapple juice
1 (46-ounce) can orange juice

1½ cups lemon juice
1½ quarts ginger ale
Pineapple, lime or lemon wedges

Combine sugar and water in a medium suacepan; bring to a boil, stirring until sugar dissolves. Pour sugar mixture into a 4½-quart freezer container. Stir in fruit juices and freeze until firm. Remove from freezer several hours before serving (mixture should be slushy). Stir in ginger ale. Garnish with fruit slices.

Vickie Baldwin   Yield: 30 cups

Easy Punch

1 package lime flavored drink mix
1 cup sugar
2 quarts water

1 (46-ounce) can pineapple juice
1 quart ginger ale

Dissolve drink mix and sugar in water; add pineapple juice. Pour into a container and freeze. Stir mixture before it freezes. When punch is served, it should be slushy; add ginger ale before serving.

Variation: Another flavor of drink mix may be used depending on the color needed.

Cheryl Watts   Yield: 1 gallon

Fruit Crush Punch

3 cups water
2 cups sugar
1 (46-ounce) can pineapple juice
1½ cups orange juice

¼ cup lemon juice
3 bananas, mashed
3 quarts ginger ale

Mix water and sugar in saucepan; bring to a boil. Remove from heat and stir in fruit juices and mashed bananas. Pour into container and freeze. To serve, let stand at room temperature to soften. Break into small chunks and mix with ginger ale.

Rosemary Harris   Yield: 24 servings

Rita Boyd's Fruit Punch

6 cups water
4 cups sugar
1 (16-ounce) can frozen orange
   juice
1 (16-ounce) can water

1 (16-ounce) can frozen lemonade
1 (46-ounce) can pineapple juice
Juice of 2 lemons
1 (2-liter) bottle lemon-lime
   carbonated beverage, chilled

Make a syrup by boiling water and sugar in large saucepan; add remaining ingredients except carbonated beverage. Mix well. Pour into freezer container and freeze. Before serving allow to thaw to a slushy state. Add chilled carbonated beverage.

Mary McMilion Hansell

Yield: 50 to 60 servings

Party Punch

1 (3-ounce) box strawberry
   gelatin
2 cups boiling water
1 cup sugar

4 cups cold water
1 (6-ounce) can frozen lemonade
1 (46-ounce) can pineapple juice
2 quarts ginger ale

Dissolve gelatin in boiling water; add sugar, stir until it dissolves. Add cold water and lemonade; mix well. Pour in pineapple juice. Freeze punch in a gallon container until slushy. Add ginger ale when ready to serve.

Helen S. Stewart

Yield: 1½ gallons

Slush Fruit Punch

2 (48-ounce) cans unsweetened
   orange juice
2 (48-ounce) cans unsweetened
   apple juice
2 (48-ounce) cans unsweetened
   pineapple juice

1 (12-ounce) can frozen lemonade,
   thawed
½ cup sugar
2 cups water
2 (2-liter) bottles ginger ale,
   chilled

Combine juices in large plastic container. Dissolve sugar in water and add to juices, stirring to blend well. Freeze until ready to use. Take out of freezer 5 to 6 hours before serving or thaw in microwave being careful not to thaw too much. May use mixer to blend slushy juice at serving time. Pour into punch bowl and pour chilled ginger ale over juices, stirring to blend well.

Joy Beers

Yield: 20 to 25 servings

Tomato Juice Cocktail

1 green pepper, chopped
1 large onion, chopped
1 cup chopped celery
1 (46-ounce) can tomato juice
3 tablespoons sugar

1 tablespoon salt
2 bay leaves
Dash of cayenne or Tabasco
½ cup vinegar

Mix all ingredients together. Pour into a container, cover, and store in refrigerator for 24 hours. Strain and keep cold until ready to serve.

Edie Delp   Yield: 1½ quarts

Sarah's Fruit Tea Punch

2 cups sugar
1 cup water
2 cups strong tea
1 cup lemon juice

1½ cups orange juice
2 cups pineapple juice
1 gallon water, approximately
1 quart ginger ale

Make a syrup of sugar and water in large saucepan. Add tea, fruit juices, and enough water to make 1½ gallons. Stir in ginger ale just before serving.

Kaye Plummer   Yield: 50 servings

Mother's Fruit Icee

1 cup orange juice
½ cup lemon juice
½ cup crushed pineapple
½ cup mashed banana

¼ to ¾ cup sugar, according
   to taste
¾ cup water

Mix all ingredients together; freeze. Beat with mixer or blender before serving. May be served as a beverage or in a sherbet dish as a dessert with cake or cookie.

Joy Beers   Yield: 4 servings

Mint Drink Frappé

1 (6-ounce) can frozen orange
   juice
3 cups sugar

3 cups water
1 cup mint leaves
¾ cup lemon juice

Mix frozen orange juice with water according to directions and set aside. Mix sugar and water together and bring to a boil. Then add mint leaves and steep for 30 minutes and strain. To the syrup mixture add orange juice and lemon juice. Either freeze to make a frappé drink or serve over finely crushed ice.

Sarah Turner James   Yield: 4 cups

Orange Blend

1 (6-ounce) can frozen orange
   juice
¼ cup sugar
1 cup water

1 cup milk
1 teaspoon vanilla
Ice

Put all ingredients into a blender. Fill to top with ice and blend until fluffy. Serve immediately.

Note: *Kids like it.*

Kim Cammack Cogle   Yield: 4 servings
  Class of 1974

Orange Blush

1 (6-ounce) can frozen orange
   juice
1 cup cranberry juice

4 tablespoons sugar
1 pint club soda

Combine undiluted orange juice, cranberry juice, and sugar. Chill thoroughly. Just before serving stir in club soda and pour over crushed ice.

Note: *Perfect for a brunch!*

Faye W. Bailey   Yield: 4 servings

Hot Chocolate Mix

1 (32-ounce) box powdered
   chocolate drink mix
2 (16-ounce) boxes powdered
   sugar

1 (11-ounce) jar non-dairy
   creamer
1 (8-quart) box powdered milk

Mix all ingredients together and store in an airtight container. To serve, stir 3 tablespoons in a cup of hot water.

Randy Henderson

Yield: 40 servings

Tropical Tea

3 cups water
4 family size tea bags
1¼ cups sugar

1 (12-ounce) can frozen lemonade
1 (6-ounce) can pineapple juice

In a teapot bring 3 cups of water to a boil. Add tea bags and let steep 35 minutes. Pour into a gallon jar with other ingredients. Finish filling jar with water to make 1 gallon.

Anne Williamson

Yield: 1 gallon

Purple Cow

2 scoops vanilla ice cream

Grape soda

Put 2 scoops of vanilla ice cream in a tall glass. Fill the glass to the top with grape soda. Stir until it mixes to a lovely purple.

Variation: To make an orange cow, use orange soda. To make brown cow use root beer or cola.

Amy Clower
   Fourth Grade

Yield: 1 serving

Guaranteed Good Coffee

4 scoops coffee   8 cups water

Put coffee in filter. Place filter in coffee basket. Place basket in automatic coffee maker. Pour water into automatic drip coffee pot and turn switch on. Sweeten to taste.

Note: 1 scoop coffee = 2 tablespoons. For best results use drip or fine grind coffee.

Mike Wood   Yield: 8 cups
  Class of 1972

Cafe Viennese

1 cup instant coffee granules $^{2}/_{3}$ cup non-fat dry milk
1 cup sugar $^{1}/_{2}$ teaspoon ground cinnamon

Mix in blender or food processor. For each serving use $2^{1}/_{2}$ to 3 tablespoons of mix to 1 cup of boiling water.

Beth Henry   Yield: $2^{2}/_{3}$ cups mix

Percolator Hot Punch

1 (5-ounce) package cinnamon   1 (48-ounce) jar cranberry juice
  candies   1 (46-ounce) can pineapple juice
$^{1}/_{2}$ cup boiling water   1 teaspoon ground cloves
1 (48-ounce) jar apple juice

Dissolve candy in boiling water. Combine juices in large container with dissolved candy. Sprinkle cloves on top of punch. Put in electric percolator and heat. Store leftover punch in refrigerator. Use microwave to heat a cup. Tastes good on cold nights.

Susan Hand Alsobrook   Yield: 30 servings

Russian Tea I

2 single tea bags
1 tablespoon cloves in a bag
2 to 3 cinnamon sticks
4½ quarts water

Juice of 6 lemons
3 cups orange juice, frozen or fresh
1 to 1½ cups sugar

Simmer tea, cloves, and cinnamon sticks in water until water is fairly dark in color and has a strong flavor from spices. Remove spices. Add juices and sugar. Serve hot or cold.

Faye W. Bailey

Yield: 25 servings

Russian Tea II

3 lemons
3 oranges
2 teaspoons whole cloves
Rind of 1 lemon

4 quarts water
⅓ cup tea leaves
2 cups sugar
1 (46-ounce) can pineapple juice

Squeeze juice from lemons and oranges and set aside. Boil cloves and rind of 1 lemon in water and pour over tea leaves. DO NOT boil mixture once tea is added. Add sugar to tea mixture while it is hot. Strain, cool, and add juices.

Faye W. Bailey

Yield: 25 servings

Stan's Bloody Marys

1 (46-ounce) can tomato juice, chilled
1 (12-ounce) can tomato juice, chilled
12½ ounces vodka
½ teaspoon salt

5 ounces lemon juice
2 teaspoons garlic salt
4 heavy dashes Tabasco
5 ounces Worcestershire sauce
2½ ounces lime juice

Mix above ingredients in the order they come in a plastic container with a plastic spoon. Stir vigorously 100 times. Chill overnight and serve cold in the AM.

Carolyn Sikes

Yield: 8 cups

Amaretto Frappé

2 ounces amaretto
2 ounces brandy

2½ cups vanilla ice cream
Handful of ice

Mix in blender on pureé until smooth. Serve as after dinner drink or dessert.

Betsy Pearce   Yield: 4 servings

Margaritas

Lime juice and salt for glass rims
½ cup fresh lime juice
2 cups crushed ice
½ cup triple sec

1 cup tequila
Pinch salt
Lime slices, optional

Prepare glasses by dipping rims in lime juice and salt. Place in freezer to chill. Place ½ cup lime juice in blender and add ice to top of blender. Cover and mix until ice is thoroughly crushed. Add triple sec, tequila, and a pinch of salt. Blend for 5 seconds. Put mixture in freezer until slightly frozen. Pour into chilled glasses. Add a slice of lime to rim for garnish.

Cookbook Committee   Yield: 8 to 10 servings

Mimosa

1 quart orange juice, chilled

1 fifth champagne, chilled

Just before serving, mix orange juice and champagne in large pitcher. Serve over ice. May be mixed individually.

Cookbook Committee   Yield: 2 quarts

Southern Comfort Punch

1 fifth Southern Comfort
1 (6-ounce) can frozen orange
  juice concentrate
1 (6-ounce) can frozen
  lemonade

3 quarts lemon-lime carbonated
  beverage
Red food coloring
Fresh fruit

Mix liquor, juice, and lemonade. Chill. Add carbonated beverages. Add a few dops of red food coloring. Add ice and cut up fruit.

Cookbook Committee   Yield: 1½ gallons

Eggnog

8 eggs, separated
1 cup sugar
1 pint bourbon
1 jigger rum

1½ cups milk
3 cups heavy cream
Nutmeg to taste

Eggs should be at room temperature. All other ingredients should be chilled. Beat egg whites until stiff; gradually add ½ cup sugar. Beat egg yolks until almost white (10 minutes with electric mixer); gradually add remaining sugar. Add bourbon and rum. Combine the egg yolk mixture with the egg white mixture. Combine milk and cream, and add egg mixture. Refridgerate. Make at least 2 days before using. This improves greatly with age. Sprinkle with nutmeg when ready to serve.

Cookbook Committee   Yield: 1½ quarts

Never Fail Blackberry Wine

2 quarts blackberries
1 envelope yeast

3 pounds sugar
Water

Wash berries and put in a gallon jar. Add yeast and sugar and finish filling jar with water. Cover and let stand 3 weeks. Strain the berries and put juice in jar and let stand 3 weeks longer. Strain and put in bottles.

Louise Nolen   Yield: 1 gallon

Hot Buttered Rum

2 cups butter
1 (16-ounce) box dark brown sugar
1 (16-ounce) box powdered sugar
1 quart vanilla ice cream, softened

1 teaspoon nutmeg
2 teaspoons cinnamon
1 jigger rum
Boiling water

Cream butter, brown sugar, and powdered sugar together. Add ice cream, nutmeg, and cinnamon. Mix and freeze. Place 1 or 2 teaspoons of mixture in mug, add 1 jigger rum (or more to taste). Fill with boiling water. Enjoy.

Cookbook Committee   Yield: 2 quarts frozen mix

Homemade Kahlúa

3 cups water
3 cups sugar
10 teaspoons instant dark
   roasted coffee

4 teaspoons vanilla
1 quart vodka

Simmer water, sugar and coffee 1 hour. Let cool. Add vanilla and vodka. Age in cool dark place for 30 days.

Beth Henry   Yield: 1½ quarts

Mint Julep

Powdered sugar
4 sprigs of fresh mint
½ teaspoon sugar

Dash of water
1½ ounces bourbon
Maraschino cherries with stems

Place mint julep cup in freezer to frost. Ring top with powdered sugar. Crush 4 sprigs of mint and place in frosted mint julep cup. Add sugar and dash of water. Pack mint julep cup with shaved ice and add 1½ ounces of bourbon. Garnish with fresh sprigs of mint and stemmed maraschino cherry. Add straw for sipping front porch style!

Cookbook Committee   Yield: 1 serving

Peach Fuzz Buzz

1 large peach with peeling,
   pitted
1 (6-ounce) can frozen pink
   lemonade

1 lemonade can vodka
2 cups crushed ice or more

Process peach, lemonade, and vodka in blender until smooth. Gradually add ice until mixture is slushly.

Diane Randall Chappell
                    Yield: 4 servings

Milk Punch

1¼ ounces bourbon or
   brandy
3 ounces light cream or milk
1 teaspoon powdered sugar

Dash of vanilla
Nutmeg

Shake thoroughly bourbon or brandy, cream, sugar, and vanilla in a closed container; strain into 8 ounce highball glass, and top with nutmeg.

Cookbook Committee
                    Yield: 1 serving

Soups And
Sandwiches

Split Pea Soup

1 (1-pound) bag dry green split
  peas
2 quarts water
1 meaty ham bone
1 cup chopped onion
¼ teaspoon garlic salt

¼ teaspoon dried marjoram,
  crushed
Dash of pepper
1 cup chopped celery
1 cup sliced carrots
Salt to taste

In large saucepan, cover peas with water and soak overnight. Add ham bone, onion, garlic salt, marjoram, and pepper to pea mixture. Bring to a boil; reduce heat and simmer, covered for 2 hours stirring occasionally. Remove ham bone, cut off meat. Dice meat; add to soup, along with celery and carrots. Cook slowly 45 minutes. Add salt.

Note: For quick cooking peas may be added to water, brought to a boil, cooked for 2 minutes, and soaked for 1 hour rather than overnight.

Joy Davis

Yield: 1½ quarts

French Onion Soup

2 medium onions, thinly sliced
2 tablespoons margarine, melted
4 cups beef broth
½ cup water

Salt to taste
Pepper to taste
Parmesan croutons
½ cup shredded Swiss cheese

Cook onions in margarine in a large covered skillet until tender (about 5 minutes). Uncover and cook until well browned; stir occasionally. Stir in broth and water. Cover and simmer 30 minutes. Add salt and pepper. Ladle soup into individual ovenproof dishes. Place Parmesan croutons on each and sprinkle with Swiss cheese. Bake at 400 degrees for 15 minutes.

Note: Parmesan crouton recipe is found in bread section.

Carolyn Weissinger

Yield: 4 servings

Cabbage Patch Soup

1½ pounds ground beef
1 small onion, chopped
1 small bell pepper, chopped
2 to 3 cups shredded cabbage

1 (14½-ounce) can tomatoes
Salt to taste
2 (16-ounce) cans kidney beans
1 tablespoon chili powder

Brown ground beef; add onion and bell pepper. Cover with water and cook on high for 10 minutes. Add other ingredients, cover, and cook for 30 minutes.

Kay Traylor   Yield: 6 to 8 servings

Hurry-Up-Broccoli Soup

1 (10-ounce) package frozen
   chopped broccoli
1 (10¾-ounce) can cream of
   mushroom soup
1½ cups milk

2 tablespoons butter
¼ teaspoon crushed dried whole
   tarragon
Dash of pepper

Cook and drain broccoli. Add soup, milk, butter, tarragon, and pepper. Cook over medium heat, stirring constantly until heated thoroughly.

Carolyn Weissinger   Yield: 4 servings

Broccoli Soup

2 tablespoons grated onion
½ cup butter
¼ cup flour
1 cup milk
1 cup half and half

2 cups chicken broth
½ teaspoon salt
⅛ teaspoon garlic powder
¼ teaspoon dried basil
3 cups chopped broccoli

Sauté onion in butter. Add flour, stirring until smooth. Cook 1 minute, stirring constantly. Gradually add milk, half and half, and broth. Cook over medium heat stirring constantly until thickened. Stir in salt, garlic powder, and basil. Add broccoli; cover and cook over medium heat for 15 minutes or until broccoli is tender.

Pat Labbe   Yield: 4 to 6 servings

Cheesy Vegetable Chowder

1/2 cup chopped onion
1 clove garlic, minced
1 cup sliced celery
3/4 cup sliced carrots
1 cup cubed potatoes
3 1/2 cups chicken broth
1 (17-ounce) can creamed corn
1/4 cup margarine or butter

1/4 cup flour
2 cups milk
1 tablespoon mustard
1/4 teaspoon white pepper
1/8 teaspoon paprika
2 tablespoons diced pimento
2 cups shredded Cheddar cheese

Combine onion, garlic, celery, carrots, potatoes, and chicken broth in a large Dutch oven; bring to a boil. Cover, reduce heat and simmer 15 to 20 minutes or until potatoes are tender. Stir in corn, remove from heat. Melt butter in a heavy saucepan over low heat; add flour, stirring until smooth. Cook 1 minute stirring constantly. Gradually add milk; cook over medium heat, stirring constantly until thickened and bubbly. Stir in remaining ingredients; cook until cheese melts, stirring constantly. Gradually stir cheese mixture into vegetable mixture. Cook over medium heat, stirring constantly until thoroughly heated. Serve immediately.

Martha Keith   Yield: 4 to 6 servings

Chicken-Cheese Soup

1 chicken breast
2 cups water
1/2 cup chopped onions
1/3 cup chopped carrots
1/3 cup chopped celery

1 (10 1/2-ounce) can cream of
   chicken soup
1/2 cup milk
1/2 cup shredded sharp cheese

Simmer chicken until tender. Remove chicken, cool, and dice. Boil broth uncovered until reduced to one cup. Add onion, carrots, and celery. Simmer until tender, about 10 minutes. Gradually stir in soup and milk. Add chicken and cheese; heat and stir until cheese melts. Garnish with shredded cheese if desired.

Peggy Striplin   Yield: 4 to 6 servings

Governor's Seafood Gumbo

6 tablespoons bacon drippings
6 tablespoons flour
1 quart chicken broth
5 tomatoes, peeled and quartered
1 cup chopped onion
2 pounds fresh okra, cut in
   1/4 inch slices
1/2 cup chopped green onion
1 cup chopped green pepper
1 clove garlic, minced
1/2 teaspoon salt
1 teaspoon parsley
1/2 teaspoon crushed thyme leaves

1/4 teaspoon red pepper
1 bay leaf
3 drops Tabasco
1 quart water, use as needed
1 lemon, sliced
1 pound fresh shrimp, peeled and
   deveined
1 pint raw oysters
1 pound fresh crabmeat
2 pounds fresh fish, preferably salt
   water fish, skinned and boned
3 cups cooked rice

Melt drippings in a heavy Dutch oven; blend in flour. Cook, stirring constantly, over medium heat until medium brown in color (approximately 10 to 15 minutes). Roux should be smooth and the color brown, but is easily burned. Gradually stir in chicken broth, keeping roux smooth. Add tomatoes, onion, okra, green onion, green pepper, garlic, salt, parsley, thyme, red pepper, bay leaf, and Tabasco. Simmer for 1 hour, adding water, if needed up to 1 quart to prevent burning or scorching. Add lemon slices, shrimp, oysters, crabmeat, and fish. Cover and simmer 10 minutes or until shrimp are pink and tender, and fish is white and flakey. Remove lemon slices and bay leaf. Ladle over mounds of cooked rice.

Note: Ingredients that may be disagreeable may be omitted without damaging the flavor. Gumbo should be thick and delicious.

Bobbie James
   First Lady of Alabama 1978-1982

Yield: 1 gallon

Crab Gumbo

½ cup butter
4 tablespoons flour
2 onions, diced
6 ribs celery, diced
2 (16-ounce) cans tomato and
okra
2 (15-ounce) cans tomato sauce
2 quarts beef stock or beef
Consommé
Juice of 3 lemons
2 tablespoons steak sauce

2 tablespoons Worcestershire
sauce
2 tablespoons dry mustard
2 tablespoons soy sauce
Tabasco to taste
Salt to taste
Pepper to taste
2 pounds crab meat
1 whole crab, optional
Gumbo filé to taste, optional

Combine butter and flour to make a roux. Slowly brown until mixture reaches a chocolate color being careful not to burn. Add all ingredients, except crab meat, and cook on low heat all day. Stir occasionally. One hour before serving add crab meat and whole crab. Add gumbo filé if desired.

Doll and Reyndy Wilkinson   Yield: 6 to 8 servings

Clam Chowder

1 (8-ounce) can clams, reserve
juice
5 medium potatoes, peeled and
chopped
1 small onion, chopped
2 tablespoons flour

¼ cup cold water
2 teaspoons salt
Dash of pepper
2 tablespoons butter
1 cup evaporated milk, scalded

Drain liquid from clams into a pan and add water to make 3 cups. Bring liquid to a boil, add potatoes and onions. Simmer 15 minutes. Blend flour and cold water, add to potato mixture slowly. Boil until thickened. Add salt, pepper, butter, and clams. Bring to a boil. Add heated milk to clam mixture. Serve with crusty cheese toast slices.

Beth Henry   Yield: 4 servings

Easy Brunswick Stew

2 large potatoes
1 large onion, chopped
2 tablespoons margarine
3 (5-ounce) cans white chunk
  chicken

2 (15-ounce) cans barbecue pork
2 (17-ounce) cans white cream
  style corn
1 (16-ounce) can whole tomatoes

Dice potatoes and boil. Set aside. Sauté onion in margarine. In Dutch oven combine chicken, pork, corn, and tomatoes; add onions. Simmer for 45 minutes. To keep potatoes firm add just before serving.

Carolyn Sikes   Yield: 6 to 8 servings

Uncle Clifford's Brunswick Stew

1 large hen, reserve stock
2 pounds fatback, reserve stock
5 pounds potatoes
3 (28-ounce) can tomatoes
5 pounds onions
2 (14½-ounce) cans cut okra

2 (16-ounce) cans whole kernel
  corn
Cayenne pepper to taste
Black pepper to taste
Salt to taste

In Dutch oven cover hen with water and cook until meat falls off the bone. In another boiler cover fatback with water and cook 30 minutes. Cool both meats. Peel and dice potatoes, cover with water and cook until tender. Bone chicken. Using a meat grinder grind hen, fatback, tomatoes, and onions. In a large stock pot add all ground meats and vegetables, stock from hen and fatback, okra, corn, and seasonings. Simmer until thick.

Note: This recipe will feed a small army so be prepared to freeze some, or can some, or give some away.

James Morgan   Yield: 1 gallon

V-8 Beef Stew

1½ pounds boneless stew meat
Flour
2 tablespoons vegetable oil
1 (1⅜-ounce) envelope dry onion
  soup mix
1 (46-ounce) can V-8 vegetable
  juice

1 (46-ounce) can water
2 carrots, sliced
4 to 5 potatoes, peeled and
  quartered

Roll beef in flour and brown in hot oil. Place in a large boiler. Add soup mix, juice, water, and carrots. Simmer for 2 hours. Add potatoes and cook 30 minutes longer.

Note: May be cooked in a slow cooker while you are at work.

Nellie Kate Tepper   Yield: 6 to 8 servings

Old-Time Beef Stew

2 tablespoons vegetable oil
2 pounds chuck, cut in 1½ inch
  cubes
1 large onion, sliced
1 clove garlic, on toothpick
4 cups boiling water
1 tablespoon salt
1 tablespoon lemon juice
1 teaspoon sugar
1 teaspoon Worcestershire sauce

½ teaspoon pepper
½ teaspoon paprika
1 or 2 bay leaves
Dash of allspice or cloves
6 carrots, quartered
1 pound small white onions
6 medium potatoes, diced
½ cup cold water
¼ cup flour

Heat oil in Dutch oven. Add chuck and brown on all sides. Add onion, garlic, boiling water, salt, lemon juice, sugar, Worcestershire sauce, pepper, paprika, bay leaf, and allspice. Cover and simmer 2 hours, stir occasionally to prevent sticking. When meat is almost done, add vegetables. Simmer stew about 30 minutes until all ingredients in Dutch oven are tender. Discard bay leaves and garlic clove. Pour cold water into a shaker; add flour. Blend well. Remove from heat; stir in flour mixture. Cook, stirring constantly, until gravy boils and thickens. Cook gently about 5 minutes.

Cookbook Committee   Yield: 6 to 8 servings

Real Texas Chili

3 pounds cubed stew meat
2 tablespoons vegetable oil
4 to 6 tablespoons chili powder
2 teaspoons cumin
3 tablespoons flour
2 to 3 cloves garlic, finely chopped

1 tablespoon oregano
2 (10¾-ounce) cans beef broth
1 teaspoon salt
2 to 3 (16-ounce) cans hot chili
   beans

Brown meat in oil; drain and add chili powder, cumin, and flour. Stir to coat well. Add garlic, oregano, broth, and salt. Simmer 1½ hours until meat is very tender. Add beans and simmer for 30 minutes. Best if refrigerated overnight to enhance flavors.

Note: Venison may be substituted for stew meat.

Helen Shivers   Yield: 6 to 8 servings

Elephant Stew

1 elephant
Salt
Pepper

Brown gravy
2 rabbits, optional

Cut elephant into bite-size pieces. This should take about 2 months. Cover with brown gravy. Cook over kerosene fire about 4 weeks at 465 degrees. This will serve 3,800 people. If more are expected, 2 rabbits may be added, but do this only if necessary as most people do not like to find hare in their stew.

Martha Washington   Yield: 3,800 servings

Puff-Topped Asparagus Sandwiches

¾ cup mayonnaise
1 tablespoon lemon juice
2 egg whites
½ teaspoon salt

6 slices buttered toast
6 slices baked or boiled ham
1 (16-ounce) can chopped
   asparagus

Combine mayonnaise and lemon juice. Beat egg whites with salt until stiff, fold into mayonnaise mixture. Toast bread well, buttered if desired. Place 1 slice ham on each piece of toast. Arrange asparagus on ham. Spoon egg white mixture over asparagus. Broil as far from heat as possible until puffed and browned.

Elaine Walton   Yield: 6 servings

Tuna Puffs

4 English muffins, split
Mayonnaise
8 thick slices tomato
1 (9¼-ounce) can white tuna,
   drained

1 (8-ounce) cold pack Cheddar
   cheese
⅔ cup mayonnaise
2 tablespoons dried minced onion
Paprika

Spread muffin halves lightly with mayonnaise. Place tomato slices on muffins.
Divide tuna equally among muffins. In medium bowl mix cheese, mayonnaise,
and onion. Spoon on top of tuna, covering well. Sprinkle with paprika. Bake at
325 degrees for 15 minutes or until lightly brown. Serve hot.

*Note: Delicious served with Suttle's Church Salad recipe found in Salad section. Even
my men like this.*

Jackie Hines   Yield: 4 servings

Madras Tuna Sandwiches

1 (9¼-ounce) can white tuna
   packed in water, drained
¼ cup minced celery
1 tablespoon minced green onions
¼ cup unpeeled chopped apple
2 tablespoons raisins

2 tablespoons chopped toasted
   almonds
1 teaspoon turmeric
½ teaspoon curry powder
1 teaspoon lemon juice
Mayonnaise to taste

Mix all ingredients and serve on dark whole grain bread.

Debe Henry   Yield: 4 servings

Pimento Sandwiches

1 pound New York State sharp
   cheese, grated
4 slices bacon, cooked and
   crumbled
1 cup chopped pecans

1 to 2 teaspoons Worcestershire
   sauce
1 (2-ounce) jar olives, chopped
Onion to taste
Mayonnaise, enough to spread

Mix all ingredients together. Spread on rye bread and broil.

Note: Good served on party rye as an appetizer.

Paula Vardaman   Yield: 6 to 8 sandwiches

Shrimp Burgers

4 hamburger buns, split
2 tablespoons butter, melted
1 cup mayonnaise
3 tablespoons chopped green
   pepper
1 tablespoon chopped onion
1 tablespoon Worcestershire sauce

1 teaspoon dry mustard
1 tablespoon lemon juice
4 ounces pasteurized processed
   cheese, chopped
2 (4½-ounce) cans shrimp,
   drained and washed

Open buns and dip in melted butter. Toss together mayonnaise, green pepper, onion, Worcestershire, mustard, lemon juice, cheese, and shrimp; spoon on buns. Broil 6 inches from heat for 6 minutes or until cheese melts and bubbles.

Helen Shivers   Yield: 4 servings

Baked Sandwiches

16 slices bread, buttered
8 slices chicken
8 slices ham
8 slices sharp cheese

4 eggs
3 cups milk
Salt to taste
Paprika to taste

In a rectangular pan, three inches deep, place half of the bread slices, buttered side up. Place slice of chicken, ham, and cheese on buttered bread. Top with remainder of bread, buttered side down. In mixing bowl, beat eggs and milk; add salt and paprika to taste. Beat well. Pour egg mixture over sandwiches. Place in refrigerator overnight. Bake at 300 degrees for 1½ hours.

Note: This is good served with a mushroom sauce.

Helen Yow   Yield: 8 servings

Chili-Cheese Rolls

1½ pounds Longhorn cheese,
  grated
1 (2¼-ounce) can ripe olives,
  chopped
2 cloves garlic, minced
6 small onions, chopped
6 hard cooked eggs, chopped

1 cup chili sauce
1 (4½-ounce) can roasted green
  chilies, chopped
6 ounces vegetable oil
Rolls—French, Italian, or
  Sourdough

Mix together cheese, olives, garlic, onions, eggs, chili sauce, green chilies, and oil. Slice off one end of rolls and scoop out crumbs. Stuff cheese mixture into hollowed out individual rolls. Replace end and wrap each tightly in aluminum foil. Bake at 350 degrees for approximately 45 minutes. The rolls will stay warm until unwrapped. This recipe can be made ahead and frozen.

Note: This recipe won $500.00 for me in the Birmingham News/Southern Living Cooking Contest.

Carolyn Breeman   Yield: 24 rolls

Ham-Pita-Wiches

1 (8-ounce) can sliced pineapple,
  drained and cut up
1 (6¾-ounce) can chunk ham,
  chopped
1 small tart apple, chopped
¼ cup chopped walnuts
⅓ cup plain yogurt

1 tablespoon mustard
1 tablespoon honey
Dash ground cinnamon
Dash ground allspice
Dash ground cloves
Bean sprouts or shredded lettuce
3 large pita bread rounds, halved

Combine all ingredients, except pita bread. Cover and chill. Spoon into pita rounds and serve.

Linda Hollingsworth   Yield: 6 servings

Bacon Sandwiches

2 (8-ounce) packages cream
    cheese, whipped
6 tablespoons mayonnaise
8 green onions, chopped
8 slices bacon, cooked and
    crumbled

1 cup Parmesan cheese
1 teaspoon Worcestershire sauce
5 to 6 dashes Tabasco sauce
2 loaves, white bread

Mix together cream cheese, mayonnaise, onions, bacon, Parmesan cheese, Worcestershire, and Tabasco. Cut bread into thirds. Do not cut the crust off. Toast one side of bread, turn over and spread mix on the other side. May freeze or refrigerate at this stage. When ready to serve, broil until bubbly.

Lillian Riddle Gilley
   Class of 1972

Yield: 5 dozen

Reuben Turnovers

1 (4-ounce) finely diced Kielbasa
   or Polish sausage
1 (8-ounce) can sauerkraut, rinsed
   and drained
1/2 cup shredded Swiss cheese

1/2 teaspoon caraway seed
1 (10-ounce) package refrigerated
   biscuits
Hot mustard

Combine sausage and sauerkraut in medium skillet, cook over medium low heat about 5 minutes stirring occasionally. Remove from heat. Stir in cheese and caraway seed. Cool slightly. Separate biscuits and roll each into a 4½-inch circle. Place 3 tablespoons filling in center of each. Fold dough over and seal edges with tines of fork. Place on ungreased cookie sheet. Bake at 375 degrees for 12 to 14 minutes. Serve with mustard.

Janice Stapp

Yield: 10 servings

Yumbos

¼ cup margarine or butter, softened   Ham slices
2 tablespoons mustard   Swiss cheese
2 tablespoons chopped onion   Poppy seed buns

Mix margarine, mustard, and onion together and spread on inside of buns. Pile on thinly sliced ham and cheese. Wrap each sandwich in aluminum foil and heat in 350 degree oven for 20 minutes.

Anna Speir   Yield: 6 sandwiches

Mini Pizzas

1 (10¾-ounce) can tomato soup   4 hamburger buns
¼ teaspoon instant minced garlic   1 (12-ounce) package shredded
1 teaspoon oregano   Mozzarella cheese

Heat soup, garlic, and oregano. Spread mixture on halves of hamburger buns. Sprinkle with cheese. Broil until cheese melts.

Cheryl Watts   Yield: 8 servings

Cheese, Eggs,
And Pastas

Glorified Eggs

2 tablespoons butter
2 tablespoons flour
1/2 teaspoon salt
1/8 teaspoon pepper
1 cup milk

2 teaspoons minced onion
1 tablespoon chopped pimento
1/3 cup thinly diced celery
1/3 cup English peas, cooked
3 hard cooked eggs, quartered

Melt butter; blend in flour, salt, and pepper. Slowly add milk and bring to a slow boil. Add onion, pimento, celery, and peas just before serving. Fold in eggs. Serve over biscuit halves or toast.

Faye Bailey   Yield: 2 to 4 servings

Deviled Eggs

6 hard cooked eggs
Mayonnaise, as needed
1/4 teaspoon garlic salt

1/4 cup sweet relish
Paprika

Cut eggs in half. Mash yolks. Add mayonnaise, salt and relish. Mix well. Stuff egg halves and sprinkle with paprika. Chill and serve.

Joy Beers   Yield: 12 servings

Scotch Eggs

6 hard cooked eggs
1 pound pork sausage

1 egg
1 cup breadcrumbs

Cook and peel eggs. Wrap each egg with sufficient sausage to make a ball around the egg. Brush with beaten raw egg and roll in breadcrumbs. Place in refrigerator to chill; will keep overnight. Place eggs in a heavy skillet with 1 inch of hot grease. Fry until sausage is done. Drain and cut eggs in half lengthwise. Serve immediately.

Note: Great for a brunch, supper, or hors d'oeuvre.

Cookbook Committee Selection   Yield: 6 to 8 servings

Brunch Eggs Supreme

½ to ¾ pound fresh mushrooms,
  sliced
4 tablespoons butter
1 dozen hard cooked eggs,
  quartered or chopped
1 (8-ounce) package frozen
  English peas, cooked
1 (8-ounce) can sliced water
  chestnuts, drained

1 (10½-ounce) can cream of
  chicken soup
1 cup sour cream
1 teaspoon grated onion
1 (2-ounce) jar chopped pimento,
  drained
Salt to taste
Pepper to taste
1½ cups buttered breadcrumbs

Sauté mushrooms in butter and spread in a 9x13-inch baking dish. Layer eggs, peas, and water chestnuts. In a small saucepan heat soup, sour cream, onion, pimento, salt, and pepper. Pour over layers. Sprinkle breadcrumbs over top. Bake at 375 degrees for 20 minutes.

Dickie Phillips   Yield: 6 to 8 servings

Spinach Pie Parma

2 cups seasoned croutons, coarsely
  crushed
¼ cup margarine, melted
¼ cup grated Parmesan cheese
1 (10-ounce) package frozen
  chopped spinach, thawed
  and drained
1 cup small curd cottage cheese
4 ounces Monterey Jack cheese,
  cut into ½-inch cubes

3 eggs, beaten
¼ cup chopped onion
2 tablespoons sour cream
1 clove garlic, minced
½ teaspoon salt
2 tablespoons grated Parmesan
  cheese

Combine croutons and margarine; mix well. Press into bottom of a 9-inch pie plate. Combine ¼ cup Parmesan cheese and remaining ingredients; mix well. Spoon over crust. Bake at 350 degrees for 35 minutes or until set. Sprinkle with 2 tablespoons Parmesan cheese; let stand 5 minutes.

Carolyn Breeman   Yield: 6 to 8 servings

Spinach Quiche

2 (9-inch) deep dish pie shells
½ pound fresh torn spinach
1 medium onion, chopped
1 tablespoon margarine
6 slices bacon, fried and crumbled
1 cup shredded Mozzarella or
  Swiss cheese

4 eggs
2 cups milk
½ teaspoon salt
¼ teaspoon pepper

Prick pie shells with a fork and bake at 400 degrees for 3 minutes. Cook spinach 8 to 10 minutes in salted water. Drain well and squeeze with paper towel. Sauté onion in margarine and add spinach. Sprinkle bacon and cheese in pie shell, top with spinach mixture. Beat eggs and add milk, salt, and pepper. Mix well and pour over other ingredients in pie shells. Bake at 350 degrees for 1 hour. Let stand a few minutes before cutting.

Variation: 1 (10-ounce) package frozen chopped spinach and 1 (10-ounce) package frozen leaf spinach may be substituted for fresh spinach.

Paula Vardaman

Yield: 12 servings

Quiche Lorraine

3 eggs, lightly beaten
1 cup half and half
1 cup grated Swiss cheese
¼ cup minced onion
5 slices bacon, fried and crumbled

¼ teaspoon salt
⅛ teaspoon pepper
3 tablespoons spicy mustard
1 (9-inch) pie shell

Mix all ingredients together and pour into pie shell. Bake at 375 degrees for 35 to 40 minutes.

Note: Freezes well.

Joy Green

Yield: 4 to 6 servings

Sausage Quiche I

1 pound sausage
2 (9-inch) pie shells
1 cup grated Swiss cheese
1 cup grated Cheddar cheese
4 large eggs, beaten

⅔ cup milk
1 teaspoon dry mustard
Dash salt
1 (8-ounce) carton sour cream

Cook and crumble sausage; drain. Line pie shells with sausage. Sprinkle cheese over sausage. Beat together eggs, milk, dry mustard, salt, and sour cream. Pour over sausage. Bake at 350 degrees for 1 hour.

Note: These may be frozen before baking. Cover with aluminum foil and freeze. Do not thaw before baking.

Lynn Moseley
Carolyn Harris

Yield: 12 servings

Sausage Quiche II

2 (9-inch) deep dish pie shells
1 pound hot sausage
1 medium onion, finely chopped
½ green pepper, finely chopped
1 teaspoon basil
1 teaspoon parsley flakes

1 (4-ounce) jar sliced mushrooms
1 (8-ounce) package grated sharp
   Cheddar cheese
4 eggs
1 (10-ounce) can evaporated milk
2 tablespoons flour

Bake pie shells at 350 degrees for 5 minutes. Cool and set aside. Cook sausage until brown; drain. Add onion, green pepper, basil, parsley, and sliced mushrooms. Divide into the 2 pie shells. Sprinkle with cheese. In blender mix eggs, milk, and flour and pour over sausage mixture. Cook at 350 degrees for 30 to 35 minutes or until knife comes out clean.

Note: Freezes well. When frozen cook 30 to 40 minutes at 350 degrees. Serve as main dish with fruit. May also be cooked and then frozen.

Joyce Hewston

Yield: 12 servings

Breakfast Sausage Casserole

8 slices bread, cubed
2 cups grated sharp Cheddar
  cheese
4 eggs
2½ cups milk

¾ teaspoon dry mustard
1 (10¾-ounce) can cream of
  mushroom soup
1½ pounds hot pork sausage
1½ pounds mild pork sausage

Grease a 2-quart casserole dish. Line casserole with bread cubes. Cover with grated cheese. Beat eggs with 2 cups milk and mustard. Pour into casserole and refrigerate overnight. Dilute soup with ½ cup milk. Brown sausage and drain. Sprinkle sausage into dish and pour soup mixture over sausage. Bake at 300 degrees for 1½ hours.

Note: Can be made ahead and frozen.

Wanda Bass   Yield: 8 servings

Cheese Sandwich Casserole

12 slices bread, crust removed
6 slices American cheese
3 eggs, beaten
2 cups milk
1 teaspoon salt

1 teaspoon minced onion
1 teaspoon mustard
1 medium tomato, peeled and
  sliced
6 slices bacon, crispy fried

Grease a 9x13-inch casserole. Make sandwiches with bread and cheese. Line casserole with sandwiches. Combine eggs, milk, salt, onion, and mustard; mix well. Pour over sandwiches and let stand 2 hours. Bake at 350 degrees for 30 minutes. Place a tomato slice and piece of bacon over each sandwich and cook an additional 3 minutes.

Dickie Phillips   Yield: 6 servings

Never Fail Cheese Soufflé

Butter
8 slices white bread, crust removed
1 pound sharp Cheddar cheese,
    grated
6 eggs, beaten

3 cups milk
Dash cayenne pepper
3/4 teaspoon salt
3/4 teaspoon dry mustard

Butter both sides of bread. Place alternate layers of bread and cheese in a buttered 8-inch square pan. Combine eggs, milk, pepper, salt, and mustard; pour over bread. Refrigerate overnight. Bake at 350 degrees for 1 hour.

Iler Walden

Yield: 8 servings

Make Ahead Breakfast Casserole

1 pound sausage
6 eggs
2 cups milk or half and half
1/2 teaspoon salt

4 slices white bread, crust removed
    and cubed
1 cup grated cheese

Brown and drain sausage; set aside. Beat eggs; add milk and salt. Into a greased 9x13-inch baking dish layer bread, sausage, and cheese. Pour egg mixture over bread. Refrigerate overnight. This is an easy breakfast dish. Bake at 350 degrees for 45 minutes.

Ann Edwards
Vickie Baldwin

Yield: 8 to 10 servings

Pasta Prima

1/2 cup milk
1/2 cup mayonnaise
2 eggs, beaten
1 (10-ounce) package fettuccini
    noodles, cooked and drained

8 slices bacon, crispy fried and
    crumbled
1/2 cup grated Parmesan cheese
1/4 cup chopped parsley

Gradually add milk to mayonnaise, cook over low heat until warm. Remove from heat. Stir in eggs. Toss with noodles until well coated. Add bacon, cheese, and parsley; toss lightly. Serve with additional cheese.

Geri Craig

Yield: 6 servings

Herb Fettuccini

½ pound fettuccini noodles
8 tablespoons butter
2 cups sour cream
1 tablespoon flour
1 cup freshly grated Parmesan
   cheese
¼ cup dry vermouth

1 tablespoon lemon juice
2 cloves garlic, crushed
Pinch of each: oregano, basil,
   thyme, and marjoram
Salt to taste
Pepper to taste

Cook noodles according to package directions and drain. Melt butter, combine with noodles, and add remaining ingredients. Mix well. Pour into a 2-quart casserole dish. Bake at 350 degrees for 20 minutes or until thoroughly heated. Serve immediately.

Judy Oxford   Yield: 6 servings

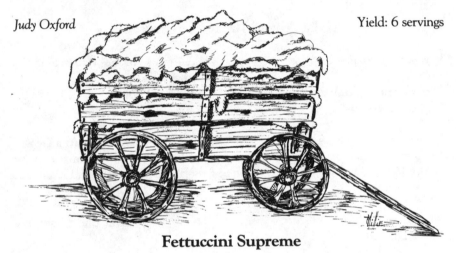

Fettuccini Supreme

1 (8-ounce) package cream cheese,
   softened
¼ cup margarine
2 tablespoons parsley flakes
1 teaspoon dried whole basil
¼ teaspoon pepper

⅔ cup boiling water
1 (8-ounce) package fettuccini
1 clove garlic, minced
¼ cup margarine
½ cup Parmesan cheese

Beat cream cheese and ¼ cup margarine. Add parsley, basil, and pepper. Mix well. Add boiling water and mix until smooth. Cook fettuccini, drain well and rinse. Sauté garlic in ¼ cup melted margarine. Combine garlic mixture and warm noodles, tossing gently. Add cream cheese mixture and ¼ cup Parmesan cheese. Toss gently. Place in a serving dish. Sprinkle with remaining ¼ cup Parmesan.

Judy Free   Yield: 6 to 8 servings

Healthy Pasta Primavera

1 (16-ounce) package tri-colored
   pasta, cooked
3 tablespoons safflower oil
1 bunch green onions, chopped
1 to 2 green peppers, chopped
1 cup broccoli flowerets, chopped
2 to 3 large tomatoes, chopped

¾ cup safflower oil
½ cup olive oil
⅔ cup cider vinegar
2 teaspoons spicy mustard
Dash of garlic powder
Salt to taste
Pepper to taste

Drain, rinse, and toss pasta with 3 tablespoons oil. Add vegetables. Combine oils, vinegar, add mustard; pour enough over pasta to moisten. Season. Serve hot or cold.

Peggy Striplin
Yield: 6 to 8 servings

Pasta with Cream, Ham, and Mushrooms

¾ pound fresh mushrooms, thinly
   sliced
½ cup dry white wine
¼ teaspoon salt
5 tablespoons butter
6 ounces sour cream
6 ounces heavy cream or half and
   half

5 tablespoons freshly grated
   Parmesan cheese
1½ cups chopped ham
Dash freshly ground nutmeg
1 pound spinach fettuccini,
   slightly undercooked

In a large skillet simmer mushrooms in wine for 25 minutes. Stir in remaining ingredients except fettuccini. Cook until thoroughly heated over medium heat. Toss with fettuccini in a large bowl. Serve immediately with additional grated Parmesan cheese.

Variation: English peas can also be added.

Judy Oxford
Yield: 8 to 10 servings

Noodle Ring

¼ cup butter
1½ cups milk
½ pound pasteurized processed
  cheese
1 tablespoon grated onion
1 tablespoon chopped parsley

1 (2-ounce) jar diced pimento
1 cup soft breadcrumbs
3 eggs, beaten well
1 cup broken noodles, cooked and
  rinsed
1 (16-ounce) can English peas

Melt butter with milk and cheese in saucepan. Add onion, parsley, pimento, and breadcrumbs; stir. Add a little warm mixture to beaten eggs; slowly add eggs to mixture and cook until thick. Fold in cooked noodles. Pour into buttered ring mold or an 8x12-inch casserole. Let set at room temperature. Bake at 350 degrees for 30 minutes. Cool and turn out of mold. Serve with English peas in center of mold.

Helen Shivers   Yield: 4 to 6 servings

Macaroni and Cheese

1 (8-ounce) package macaroni

Cook macaroni in salted water for 15 minutes. Drain and rinse.

Cheese Sauce:
3 tablespoons butter
2½ tablespoons flour
2 cups milk
½ pound sharp cheese

1 tablespoon chopped pimento
Dash Tabasco
1 teaspoon vinegar

Melt butter; stir in flour, milk, and cheese. Cook over low heat until cheese melts; add pimento, Tabasco, vinegar, and cooked macaroni. Pour into a greased 2-quart casserole. Chill for several hours or until firm. Bake at 350 degrees for 30 minutes.

Note: Freezes well.

Carolyn Weissinger   Yield: 4 to 6 servings

Macaroni and Cheese Deluxe

1 (8-ounce) package elbow
   macaroni
2 cups creamed cottage cheese
1 (8-ounce) carton sour cream
3 eggs, slightly beaten

¾ teaspoon salt
4 cups shredded cheese
Dash of pepper
Paprika

Cook macaroni according to directions on package; drain, rinse and set aside. Combine cottage cheese, sour cream, eggs, salt, 2 cups cheese and pepper; add to macaroni and stir well. Pour into a 2-quart casserole and top with 2 cups shredded cheese and sprinkle with paprika. Bake at 350 degrees for 45 minutes.

Sara Adams
                                       Yield: 8 servings

Garlic Rice

½ teaspoon garlic powder
1 small onion, chopped
1 cup uncooked rice
1 (4-ounce) jar sliced mushrooms
¾ cup grated American cheese

1 (10¾-ounce) can cream of
   mushroom soup
Cracker crumbs
Butter

Cook garlic powder and onion with rice according to directions. Combine rice, mushrooms, cheese, and soup. Pour into a greased 1½-quart baking dish. Cover with cracker crumbs and dot with butter. Bake at 350 degrees for 1 hour or until brown. Very good with barbecued chicken.

Rosemary Harris
                                       Yield: 6 servings

Sour Cream Rice Casserole

2 cups uncooked rice
3 cups sour cream
3 (4-ounce) cans chopped green
   chilies

12 ounces Muenster cheese
Black pepper to taste
Parmesan cheese
Butter or margarine

Cook rice according to directions on box; mix with sour cream. In a 2½-quart casserole dish place a 1-inch layer of rice, a layer of chilies, a layer of cheese, and black pepper. Repeat layers until ingredients have been used. Top with Parmesan cheese and pats of butter. Bake at 350 degrees for 30 minutes.

Milly Noah
                                    Yield: 8 to 10 servings

Brown Rice

½ cup butter
1 onion, chopped
1 (10½-ounce) can beef
  consommé

1 (10½-ounce) can beef broth
1 cup uncooked rice
1 (4-ounce) can mushrooms,
  optional

Melt butter and sauté onion. Add consommé, broth, and rice to onion mixture. Place in a 9x13-inch casserole dish. Add mushrooms to top. Cover and bake at 350 degrees for 1 hour.

Lynn Moseley
Emily Jones

Yield: 6 to 8 servings

Garlic Grits

1 cup quick cooking grits
4 cups water
1 teaspoon salt
1 (6-ounce) tube garlic cheese

½ cup margarine
2 eggs
½ cup milk
Garlic salt to taste

Preheat oven to 350 degrees. Cook grits in salted water. Cut cheese into small pieces and stir into hot grits; add margarine. Cool. Beat eggs with milk. Stir slowly into grits. Add garlic salt to taste. Pour into a 1½-quart greased casserole. Bake for 1 hour.

Variation: 1 (8-ounce) package Cheddar cheese may be substituted for tube garlic cheese.

Carolyn Weissinger

Yield: 4 to 6 servings

Nassau Grits

1 pound bacon
2 green peppers, chopped
2 medium onions, chopped
1½ cups ham, finely ground

1 (28-ounce) can whole tomatoes,
  chopped
1½ cups white grits

Fry bacon; drain and set aside. Sauté peppers and onions in ¼ cup bacon drippings until soft. Add ham and stir well. Sauté over low heat for 15 minutes. Add tomatoes and simmer 30 minutes. In separate saucepan, cook grits according to package directions. When grits are cooked, add ham mixture and bacon, reserving enough bacon to crumble on top. Stir well before serving.

Milly Noah

Yield: 10 to 12 servings

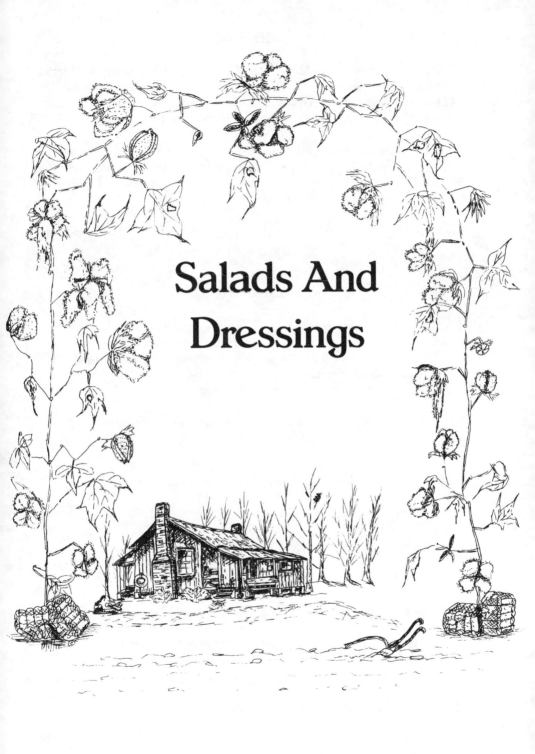

Salads And Dressings

Fruit Salad

2 (20-ounce) cans pineapple
    chunks, reserve juice
2 (11-ounce) cans mandarin oranges,
    reserve juice

2 (16½-ounce) cans sweet cherries
1 (4¾-ounce) package vanilla
    pudding, not instant
4 bananas, sliced

Drain fruit; reserve 2 cups pineapple juice (add juice from mandarin oranges if needed to equal the 2 cups). Cook pudding according to directions using juice for liquid. Let pudding cool for 5 minutes. Add drained fruit and refrigerate. Add sliced bananas just before serving.

Faye Carter   Yield: 8 servings

Paradise Salad

1 (20-ounce) can strawberry pie
    filling
1 (20-ounce) can crushed pineapple
1 (14-ounce) can sweetened
    condensed milk

2 cups miniature marshmallows
½ cup chopped pecans
1 (12-ounce) carton whipped
    topping
Lettuce

Mix all ingredients together. Place in a 9x13-inch pan and refrigerate at least 1 hour before serving. Slice and serve on lettuce. May be frozen for future use. May be used for dessert.

Variation: Favorite pie filling may be substituted for strawberry filling.

Debbie Moore   Yield: 8 to 10 servings

Snow Ball Salad

1 cup sour cream
2 (12-ounce) cartons whipped
    topping
2 tablespoons lemon juice
1 to 1½ cups sugar

3 or 4 mashed bananas
1 (15¼-ounce) can crushed
    pineapple, drained
1 cup chopped nuts
½ cup chopped cherries

Mix all ingredients together in a bowl and refrigerate.

Nadine Hain   Yield: 8 to 10 servings

Rosie Pink Salad

1 (17-ounce) can pears in heavy syrup
1 (20-ounce) can pineapple chunks in heavy syrup, reserve half the juice
1 (16-ounce) or 2 (10-ounce) packages frozen strawberries in heavy syrup

1 (20-ounce) can peach pie filling
3 or more bananas, sliced
1 cup chopped pecans

Drain and cut up pears. Mix all ingredients and add reserved juice. Let sit in refrigerator for at least 2 hours before serving. Delicious!

Helen Stewart   Yield: 8 servings

Mama's Cranberry Salad

1¾ cups orange juice
1 (3-ounce) package cherry gelatin
1 (1-ounce) package unflavored gelatin

1 cup chopped pecans
1 (14-ounce) jar cranberry-orange relish

Heat orange juice and dissolve gelatins. Add pecans and relish. Pour into mold to congeal.

Ellen Traylor   Yield: 4 to 6 servings

Here's Lookin' At Ya Kid

1 (8-ounce) package cream cheese, softened
2 tablespoons honey
Nutmeg to taste
¼ cup milk

Lettuce
12 pineapple slices, well drained
12 slices kiwi, peeled
12 black or red grapes

Blend together cream cheese, honey, and nutmeg; gradually add milk. Chill. Arrange lettuce leaves to cover six salad plates. Spoon 2 tablespoons of cream cheese mixture over lettuce. Arrange pineapple slices over each tablespoon of dressing and top with kiwi. Add grapes in center to make eyes.

Terry Hunter   Yield: 6 servings

Magnolia Room Frozen Fruit Salad

1 (8-ounce) package cream cheese, softened
½ cup powdered sugar
⅓ cup mayonnaise
2 teaspoons vanilla
1 (6½-ounce) can sliced peaches, drained
½ cup marashino cherries, drained

1 (26-ounce) can fruit cocktail, drained
1 (13-ounce) can crushed pineapple, drained
2 cups miniature marshmallows
½ cup whipping cream, whipped
Few drops food coloring, if desired

In mixing bowl cream cheese, add sugar, and blend in the mayonnaise. Add vanilla and blend in the fruit and marshmallows gently. Fold in whipped cream. Pour into large paper-lined muffin tins; freeze. Remove from freezer 10 to 15 minutes before serving but do not allow to become too soft. Remove paper-liners and serve with dollop of whipped cream.

Faye Bailey

Yield: 20 to 24 servings

Party Pear Salad

1 (29-ounce) can pear halves
⅓ cup cinnamon candies
1 (3-ounce) package cream cheese, softened
1 tablespoon lemon juice

2 tablespoons almonds, toasted
1 (8-ounce) can crushed pineapple, drained
Lettuce
Watercress

Drain pears and combine syrup with candies; heat until dissolved. Add pears and bring to boil. Chill in syrup several hours or overnight. Blend cream cheese and lemon juice. Add almonds and pineapple. Drain pears thoroughly on paper towels. Place cream cheese filling in center. Serve on lettuce and garnish with watercress.

Virginia Moseley

Yield: 6 servings

Deluxe Waldorf Salad

2 large tart red apples, unpeeled
    and diced
1 large green apple, unpeeled and
    diced
Lemon juice
½ pound seedless green grapes,
    halved
½ cup coarsely chopped pecans

½ cup finely diced celery
⅓ cup raisins
2 tablespoons sliced marashino
    cherries
¼ cup plus 2 tablespoons
    mayonnaise
Lettuce

Toss apples with lemon juice. Add remaining ingredients; mix well. Spoon into a lettuce-lined bowl.

Faye Bailey   Yield: 6 to 8 servings

Fresh Fruit Compote

¼ watermelon
½ cantaloupe
1 pint strawberries
2 peaches

2 pears
1 cup seedless green grapes
1 banana

Remove seeds from watermelon and cantaloupe and cut into bite-sized pieces. Clean strawberries and halve. Peel and slice peaches and pears. Rinse and drain grapes and slice banana. Mix fruit in serving bowl and refrigerate for 2 hours. Before serving, drizzle with fruit dressing.

Fruit Dressing:
¾ cup vegetable oil
¼ cup red wine vinegar
1 tablespoon lemon juice
1 tablespoon catsup
1 clove garlic
¼ teaspoon dry mustard

1 teaspoon salt
1¼ teaspoons sugar
2 dashes Tabasco sauce
1 cup mayonnaise
2 teaspoons poppy seed

In a blender, combine all ingredients except mayonnaise and poppy seed and beat for 2 minutes. Fold in mayonnaise and poppy seed and refrigerate.

Gigi Campbell   Yield: 10 to 12 servings

Suttles "Church" Salad

1 (15¼-ounce) can crushed
  pineapple, reserve juice
1 (3-ounce) box lemon gelatin
2 (3-ounce) packages cream cheese,
  softened

1 (4-ounce) jar diced pimento
⅔ cup chopped pecans, toasted
½ cup chopped celery
½ pint whipping cream

Drain pineapple. Heat juice to dissolve gelatin. Chill well in refrigerator before blending in cream cheese and pimento. Blend in pecans and celery and fold in whipped cream. Pour salad into greased mold. Tastes different and good!

Helen Holmes   Yield: 10 to 12 servings

Thanksgiving Salad

1 (20-ounce) can crushed
  pineapple
2 (3-ounce) packages raspberry
  gelatin
2 cups hot water
1 (11-ounce) can mandarin
  oranges or 2 to 3 fresh oranges

1 (14-ounce) jar cranberry-orange
  relish
1 cup broken pecans
1 cup miniature marshmallows

Drain pineapple and reserve juice adding enough water to equal 1 cup. Mix gelatin, water, and juice together. Add remaining ingredients. Place in a 2-quart casserole and congeal in refrigerator.

Mary Drue Wheeler   Yield: 8 to 10 servings

Orange Sherbet Salad

2 (3-ounce) packages orange
  gelatin
1 cup boiling water
1 pint orange sherbet
1 (8-ounce) can crushed
  pineapple, drained

1 cup miniature marshmallows
1 (11-ounce) can mandarin oranges,
  drained
½ pint whipping cream

Dissolve gelatin in boiling water. Add orange sherbet and chill. When partially set, add other ingredients folding in whipped cream last. Pour into a 9x13-inch pan and chill until firm.

Vickie Baldwin   Yield: 8 to 10 servings

Pretzel Congealed Salad

2½ cups coarsely crushed pretzels
⅓ cup margarine
3 tablespoons sugar
1 (8-ounce) package cream cheese, softened
1 cup sugar
1 (12-ounce) carton whipped topping

2 (3-ounce) packages strawberry gelatin
2 cups boiling water
2 (10-ounce) packages frozen strawberries

Preheat oven to 350 degrees. Combine pretzels, margarine, and 3 tablespoons sugar and mix well. Bake in a 9x13-inch pan for 10 minutes; cool completely. Cream the cheese and blend in 1 cup sugar. Add the whipped topping; mixing well. Spread over the cooled pretzels. Dissolve the gelatin in the boiling water. Add the frozen strawberries, breaking up with a fork as you stir. Chill until slightly thickened. Pour over whipped topping layer; chill until set.

Note: This is also delicious as a dessert!

Meg Smith
Cindy Yeager
Kathryn Hardy

Yield: 8 to 10 servings

Tea Room Salad

1 (20-ounce) can crushed pineapple
½ cup sugar
1 (6-ounce) package peach gelatin

2 cups buttermilk
1 (8-ounce) carton whipped topping
Chopped nuts, optional

Combine crushed pineapple and sugar in saucepan and bring to a boil. Add gelatin and mix well. Remove from heat. Add buttermilk and fold in whipped topping. Blend well. Pour in a 9x13-inch dish. May sprinkle chopped nuts on top. Chill overnight.

Helen S. Stewart
Sis Wood
Linda Hill

Yield: 8 to 10 servings

Crème de Menthe Salad

1 (3-ounce) package lemon gelatin
1 (3-ounce) package lime gelatin
2 cups boiling water
1 (16-ounce) carton cottage cheese, drained

1 (20-ounce) can crushed pineapple
4 tablespoons crème de menthe
1 (5-ounce) can evaporated milk

Mix gelatin in boiling water. Let cool. Stir together cottage cheese, pineapple, crème de menthe, and evaporated milk. Add to gelatin and let congeal in a 9x13-inch pan.

Dressing:
4 ounces sour cream
3 tablespoons salad dressing
1 to 3 tablespoons crème de menthe

1 tablespoon sugar
1 teaspoon poppy seeds

Mix together and serve over crème de menthe salad.

Cecile Youngblood

Yield: 8 to 12 servings

Fresh Apple Salad

2 (3-ounce) packages lemon gelatin
20 large marshmallows
2 cups hot water

½ cup cold water
3 apples, finely chopped
1 cup chopped pecans

Dissolve gelatin and marshmallows in hot water. Add cold water. Let thicken and add apples and pecans. Congeal in a 2½-quart dish.

Topping:
2 eggs
½ cup sugar

1 (8-ounce) carton whipped topping

Cook eggs and sugar until thick. Cool. Add whipped topping to egg mixture and pour over congealed salad.

Sandra Todd
  Class of 1981

Yield: 8 servings

Peach Pickle Salad

1 (17-ounce) jar peach pickle,
    cut up
1 (8-ounce) can chunk pineapple
Orange juice, if needed
1 (6-ounce) package orange-
    pineapple gelatin

1 (1-ounce) envelope unflavored
    gelatin
½ cup broken pecans
2 tablespoons orange marmalade

Drain fruit and reserve juice adding enough orange juice to make 4 cups of liquid. Dissolve gelatin in ¼ cup of liquid. Heat remaining liquid and add other ingredients. Chill in an 8-inch square dish.

Mary Drue Wheeler   Yield: 8 servings

Mandarin Orange Salad

1 (3-ounce) package orange gelatin
1 (3-ounce) package lemon gelatin
1 cup boiling water
2 (8-ounce) cans crushed
    pineapple
3 (11-ounce) cans mandarin
    oranges

1 (6¼-ounce) package miniature
    marshmallows
1 cup sour cream
1 cup mayonnaise
Grated cheese

In a 9x13-inch baking dish, dissolve gelatin in boiling water. Add pineapple and oranges, plus juices to gelatin. Top with marshmallows and refrigerate until congealed. Combine sour cream and mayonnaise; spread over marshmallows. Top with desired amount of cheese.

Kathy Jones   Yield: 8 to 10 servings
Joyce Hewston

Blueberry Salad

1 (16½-ounce) can blueberries
1 (8½-ounce) can crushed
  pineapple

1 (6-ounce) package black cherry
  gelatin
2 cups boiling water

Drain blueberries and pineapple and reserve juices. Dissolve gelatin in water and mix with juices. Add fruit and congeal. When congealed, add topping.

Topping:
1 (8-ounce) package cream cheese,
  softened
1 (8-ounce) carton sour cream

½ cup sugar
½ teaspoon vanilla
½ cup chopped pecans

Cream the cheese, sour cream, sugar, and vanilla. Spread on top of gelatin. Sprinkle pecans on top.

Peggy Raybon
Carolyn Sikes

Yield: 6 servings

Olive Mold

1 (15¼-ounce) can crushed
  pineapple
1 (3-ounce) package lime gelatin
1 (1-ounce) envelope unflavored
  gelatin
½ cup grated cheese
½ cup chopped pimento

½ cup chopped celery
⅔ cup chopped walnuts
¼ teaspoon salt
1 cup whipping cream
1 (4¼-ounce) jar stuffed
  olives

Drain pineapple and reserve juice. Heat juice to a boil, add gelatins, and cool. When mixture begins to thicken, add cheese, pimento, celery, walnuts, and salt. Fold in whipped cream. Line bottom of mold with sliced olives before pouring in salad.

Carolyn Weissinger

Yield: 6 to 8 servings

Mom Bryant's Carrot Salad

6 carrots
Sugar to taste
1 (3-ounce) package orange gelatin
1 (3-ounce) package lemon gelatin

2 cups hot water
¾ cup cold water
1 (8-ounce) can crushed pineapple
Mayonnaise

Cook carrots, mash, sprinkle with sugar, and set aside. Dissolve gelatins in hot water. Add cold water, carrots, and pineapple. Pour into mold and congeal. Top with a dollop of mayonnaise. Um good!

Kay Traylor   Yield: 6 to 8 servings

Carrot Salad

1 cup golden raisins
½ cup water
¼ to ½ cup cooking sherry,
    wine or bourbon
2 pounds carrots, grated
1 cup chopped pecans

1 (6-ounce) can crushed pineapple
1 (3-ounce) can coconut
1 (6-ounce) package miniature
    marshmallows
Mayonnaise to taste

Boil raisins in water and wine until raisins are soft and puffed up. Drain and add other ingredients. Add mayonnaise to taste. Refrigerate several hours before serving.

Myrna Todd   Yield: 6 to 8 servings

Easy Corn Salad

1 (16-ounce) can whole kernel
    corn
1 small onion, chopped
1 medium tomato, chopped

⅓ cup mayonnaise
Salt to taste
Pepper to taste

Drain corn. Add chopped onion and tomato. Mix in mayonnaise. Salt and pepper to taste. Cover and refrigerate at least 4 hours. Especially good when tomatoes are in season.

Cheryl Watts   Yield: 4 servings

Tomato Soup Salad

1 (1-ounce) envelope unflavored
gelatin
1/3 cup cold water
1 (10¾-ounce) can tomato soup
1 (3-ounce) package cream cheese,
softened

1/2 cup chopped celery
1/2 cup chopped bell pepper
1/4 cup chopped onion
2/3 cup mayonnaise
Olives, optional
Avocado, optional

Soften gelatin in cold water. Add to soup, simmer, and stir until gelatin is dissolved. Remove from heat and cool. Add cream cheese, celery, bell pepper, onion, and mayonnaise. Pour into mold and chill. Garnish with olives and avocado.

Variation: May add lump crabmeat or white tuna for main dish.

Carolyn Weissinger
Iler Walden
Yield: 6 to 8 servings

Mystery Salad

1 (10½-ounce) can chicken
noodle soup
1 (3-ounce) package lemon gelatin
1/2 cup boiling water
1 (6-ounce) can white chunk tuna
1/2 cup chopped celery

1/2 cup evaporated milk
2 teaspoons finely chopped green
pepper
2 teaspoons finely chopped onion
1/2 cup mayonnaise

Refrigerate soup and skim off fat when solid. Dissolve gelatin in boiling water. Rinse tuna in hot water and drain. Mix all ingredients and pour into an 8x8-inch pan. Refrigerate.

Note: This recipe tripled will fill a 9x13-inch pan and will serve 24.

Iler Walden
Yield: 6 to 8 servings

Cauliflower Salad

1 large head cauliflower, broken
1 cup sliced radishes
¼ cup sliced onions
1 cup sliced squash
1 bunch broccoli, cut into
   flowerets

1 cucumber, diced
1 (8-ounce) can sliced water
   chestnuts, drained

Wash and drain all vegetables. Mix all ingredients in large bowl.

Dressing:
1 cup mayonnaise
1 cup sour cream

1 (1-ounce) package dry cheese
   Italian salad dressing

Mix all dressing ingredients together and store in covered container. Pour dressing over vegetables and cover. Store at least 2 hours before serving. May be made 24 hours in advance of serving.

Variation: 1 (1-ounce) package dry Italian salad dressing and the addition of Parmesan cheese may be substituted for the package of dry cheese Italian salad dressing mix.

Smyly Kirkpatrick
Anna Speir

Yield: 8 to 10 servings

Broccoli Salad

1 bunch fresh broccoli
Cherry tomatoes
Fresh mushrooms, sliced
¼ cup Italian salad dressing

¼ cup creamy cucumber dressing
6 slices of bacon, fried and broken
   into bits

Cut flowerets from broccoli and discard stems. Add cherry tomatoes and sliced mushrooms. Mix a marinade of Italian dressing and creamy cucumber dressing. Pour over vegetables and refrigerate for at least 6 hours. Add bacon bits before serving.

Eady McCormick

Yield: 4 to 6 servings

Nutty Broccoli Salad

4 cups chopped tender broccoli
1/2 pound bacon
1 cup white raisins
1 medium red onion, chopped

1 (4-ounce) package salted
   sunflower seeds
1 (2-ounce) package almonds,
   sliced or slivers

Wash broccoli and drain. Fry bacon and crumble. Combine all ingredients and refrigerate. One hour before serving add dressing.

Dressing:
2 tablespoons red wine vinegar
2 tablespoons sugar

1 cup mayonnaise

Mix and pour over broccoli salad. Delicious!

Variation: 1 cup unsalted roasted peanuts may be substituted for sunflower seeds.

Elsie Randall
Elna Scales

Yield: 8 servings

Marinated Broccoli Ring

2/3 cup vegetable oil
1/3 cup tarragon vinegar
1 teaspoon salt
1/2 teaspoon mustard
1/4 teaspoon pepper
1 tablespoon sugar
2 tablespoons grated Parmesan
   cheese

1 1/2 pounds fresh broccoli,
   cut into pieces
Escarole
2 tomatoes, sliced
1/2 pound fresh mushrooms,
   sliced

Mix first 7 ingredients in a jar. Shake well. Cook broccoli in a small amount of salted water for 9 minutes. Drain. Place broccoli in a large shallow dish. Drizzle 1/2 cup dressing over top. Chill for 24 hours. Line a serving platter with escarole. Layer broccoli and sliced tomatoes. Pile mushrooms in the center. Drizzle remaining dressing over the tomatoes and mushrooms.

Cecile Youngblood

Yield: 6 to 8 servings

English Pea Salad

2 (17-ounce) cans English peas, drained
2 hard cooked eggs, chopped
1 small red onion, finely chopped

½ cup chopped pecans
½ cup mayonnaise
Salt to taste
White pepper to taste

Mix all ingredients together and chill.

Gigi Campbell   Yield: 6 to 8 servings

Spinach Salad

2 (10-ounce) bags fresh spinach
2 (8-ounce) cans water chestnuts, thinly sliced
4 hard cooked eggs, diced

1 (16-ounce) can bamboo shoots
½ pound bacon, fried crisp and crumbled
Sweet and Sour Dressing

Wash spinach and chill well. Toss together spinach, water chestnuts, eggs, and bamboo shoots. Top with bacon crumbs. Pour dressing on salad to suit taste and toss well.

Note: Sweet and Sour Dressing recipe found in Dressing section.

Edie Delp   Yield: 8 servings

Layered Salad

1 head of lettuce, washed and torn
1½ cups chopped celery
1½ cups chopped green pepper
1½ cups chopped onion
1 (17-ounce) can English peas, drained
1 cup mayonnaise

1 cup ranch dressing
6 ounces grated Cheddar cheese
2 hard cooked eggs, chopped
1 (4-ounce) can sliced water chestnuts, optional
8 slices bacon, fried and crumbled

Layer ingredients as listed, except bacon, into a 4-quart bowl. Cover and refrigerate overnight. Just before serving top with bacon and toss.

Gigi Campbell   Yield: 6 to 8 servings
Ruth Moore
Lula Wood

Vegetable Salad

1 (16-ounce) can shoe-peg corn
1 (16-ounce) can French style
   green beans
1 (16-ounce) can English peas

1 (2-ounce) jar diced pimento
1 onion, chopped
1 cup chopped celery
1 small bell pepper, chopped

Sauce:
1 cup sugar
1 cup vinegar
½ cup vegetable oil

1½ teaspoons pepper
1 teaspoon salt
½ cup water

Drain vegetables and combine. Heat sauce but do not boil. Mix sauce with vegetables. Refrigerate and drain before serving.

Kathy Jones
Gladys Stephens Elliot
Carolyn Sikes

Yield: 8 to 10 servings

Oriental Salad

1 (17-ounce) can English peas,
   drained
1 (14-ounce) can bean sprouts,
   drained
1 (12-ounce) can white shoe peg
   corn, drained
1 (8-ounce) can sliced water
   chestnuts, drained

1 (4½-ounce) jar chopped
   pimento, drained
1 large green pepper, thinly sliced
1 large onion, thinly sliced
1 cup sliced celery

Mix all ingredients and marinate overnight in dressing.

Dressing:
1 cup sugar
1 cup vegetable oil
½ cup vinegar
½ cup water
2 tablespoons red wine vinegar

1 tablespoon soy sauce
¼ teaspoon pepper
1 teaspoon dry mustard
½ teaspoon salt
½ teaspoon paprika

Mix and pour over vegetables. Refrigerate.

Edna Ledyard

Yield: 10 to 12 servings

Mandarin Orange-Almond Salad

1 (10-ounce) package fresh
  spinach
1 head lettuce
1 (11-ounce) can mandarin
  oranges, drained

1 (2-ounce) package slivered
  almonds

Wash, drain, and tear spinach and lettuce. Add oranges and almonds.

Dressing:
1 cup vegetable oil
1 medium onion, finely chopped
1 tablespoon Worcestershire sauce

¼ cup cider vinegar
¼ cup sugar
⅓ cup catsup

Combine all dressing ingredients in blender. Pour over salad and toss.

Beth Henry Yield: 8 to 10 servings

Picnic Potato Salad

8 potatoes, peeled, diced, and
  cooked
4 hard cooked eggs, finely chopped
4 green onions, finely chopped
2 slices bacon, crispy fried and
  crumbled
1 large dill pickle, finely chopped
1 tablespoon pickle juice

½ small green pepper, finely
  chopped
Salt to taste
Pepper to taste
4 heaping tablespoons mayonnaise
  or salad dressing
1 tablespoon mustard

Combine ingredients in bowl and add mayonnaise and mustard.

Peggy Striplin Yield: 15 servings

83

Lots O' Macaroni Salad

2 (8-ounce) packages elbow
   macaroni
1 medium bell pepper, chopped
1 medium onion, finely chopped
4 large carrots, grated

1 (14-ounce) can sweetened
   condensed milk
1 cup apple cider vinegar
2 cups mayonnaise

Cook macaroni and drain; mix with pepper, onion, and carrots. Combine milk, vinegar, and mayonnaise; pour over mixture and let sit overnight without stirring. Mix well before serving.

Kay Randall Eddins   Yield: 16 servings

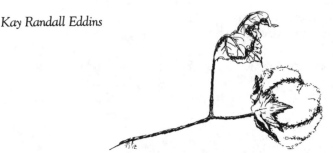

Pasta Salad with Parmesan Mayonnaise

1 (8-ounce) package rainbow pasta,
   cooked and drained
1 bunch green onions, sliced
1 (10-ounce) package frozen green
   peas, thawed

1 (4-ounce) can black olives,
   chopped
1 cup finely chopped ham, optional
1 (2-ounce) jar pimento, minced

Mix all ingredients together and carefully fold in Parmesan mayonnaise.

Parmesan Mayonnaise:
1 large egg
1 tablespoon lemon juice
1/2 teaspoon Louisiana hot sauce
1 teaspoon dry mustard
1/2 teaspoon salt

1/2 teaspoon white pepper
1 1/2 cups vegetable oil
1/2 to 3/4 cup freshly grated
   Parmesan cheese

Place all ingredients except oil and cheese in food processor; turn on and off to blend well. Turn on processor again and add oil very slowly. When mayonnaise forms, add cheese and process a little longer.

Judy Oxford   Yield: 12 servings

Jill's Pasta Salad

1 head of fresh broccoli, cut into
  flowerets
1 pound fresh mushrooms
1 (2¼-ounce) can black olives,
  sliced

1 red onion, chopped
1 (16-ounce) bottle Italian dressing
1 cup shell macaroni
2 fresh tomatoes
¼ cup Parmesan cheese

Combine broccoli, mushrooms, olives, and onion. Pour Italian dressing over ingredients and marinate overnight. Cook shell macaroni and let cool. Chop tomatoes and add Parmesan cheese. Combine all ingredients and toss.

Beth Williams   Yield: 8 to 10 servings

Mexican Salad

1 pound ground chuck
1 head lettuce
1 cup chopped onions
1 cup chopped tomatoes
1 cup chopped bell pepper
½ cup shredded carrots

1 (15-ounce) can kidney beans,
  drained
1 cup grated mild Cheddar cheese
1 (⅜-ounce) package ranch
  dressing
1 (11-ounce) package corn chips

Brown chuck; drain and cool. Wash lettuce, drain, and tear. Combine lettuce, onion, tomatoes, bell pepper, carrots, kidney beans, and cheese together. Prepare ranch dressing according to directions on package. Mix all ingredients together, adding broken corn chips last. Serve immediately!

Debbie Moore   Yield: 8 to 10 servings

Chicken Salad

1 tablespoon lemon juice
1 cup mayonnaise
2 cups diced cooked chicken
1 cup shredded carrots
¾ cup finely chopped celery

½ cup slivered almonds or
  chopped pecans
2 tablespoons chopped onion
Salt to taste

Combine lemon juice and mayonnaise. Mix with other ingredients. Chill.

Virginia Moseley   Yield: 8 servings

Don's Chicken and Rice Salad

1½ cups raw instant rice
1½ teaspoons salt
1½ cups boiling water
⅔ cup mayonnaise
⅓ cup French dressing

⅛ teaspoon pepper
1½ cups diced cooked chicken
1 cup diced celery
1 cup diced orange sections
1 cup chopped pecans

Combine rice, ½ teaspoon salt, and boiling water. Mix just enough to moisten rice; cover and remove from heat. Cool to room temperature. Combine mayonnaise, French dressing, pepper, and remaining salt; mix well. Combine chicken, celery, orange sections, and pecans. Stir in mayonnaise mixture. Add rice; mix lightly. Chill for 1 hour before serving.

Don Yelverton   Yield: 6 to 8 servings

Shrimp and Artichoke Salad

1 tablespoon crab boil
2 pounds medium shrimp
2 cups fresh broccoli flowerets
2 green onions
1 (14-ounce) can water-packed
   artichoke hearts, drained

2 cups Sherry Mayonnaise
Salt to taste
Freshly ground pepper to taste

In a large pot, bring 4 quarts salted water with crab boil to a boil and cook shrimp 1 minute. Drain shrimp; cool, peel, and devein. Cook broccoli for 3 to 5 minutes. Drain broccoli, cool in ice water and drain again. Slice onions and cut artichokes in halves or quarters. combine all ingredients with mayonnaise, seasoning to taste.

Note: Sherry Mayonnaise recipe found in Dressing section.

Marly Thomas   Yield: 6 servings

Shrimp Salad

1 cup chopped boiled shrimp
1 cup cottage cheese
3 ribs celery, chopped
½ cup mayonnaise
2 tablespoons mustard

Chopped green onions to taste
2 hard cooked eggs, chopped
Salt to taste
Pepper to taste

Combine all ingredients and refrigerate 2 hours before serving.

Bonnie Bryant Fitts
  Class of 1980

Yield: 4 to 6 servings

New Orleans Shrimp Salad

2 cups shrimp
1 cup raw cauliflower
⅓ cup chopped green pepper
2 tablespoons finely chopped onion
12 pimento stuffed olives, sliced
½ cup mayonnaise

Juice of ½ lemon
¼ teaspoon paprika
Dash of hot sauce
Salt to taste
Pepper to taste
Lettuce

Cook shrimp, peel, and devein. Combine remaining ingredients, mix well, and chill. Serve on lettuce leaves.

Iler Walden

Yield: 6 servings

Seafood Salad

1 pound shrimp
¼ to ½ pound crab meat
1 (8½-ounce) can English peas
¼ head shredded cabbage,
   optional

1 (8-ounce) package shell
   macaroni, cooked and drained
1 teaspoon mustard
Mayonnaise to moisten
Lettuce

Cook shrimp; peel and devein. Mix all ingredients and chill for at least 2 hours. Serve on lettuce leaf with crackers.

Marian Carter

Yield: 4 servings

Bay Salad

1 pint cherry tomatoes, halved
1 (6-ounce) bag frozen shrimp,
    thawed
1/3 cup coconut

1 (11-ounce) can mandarin
    oranges, drained
Romaine or iceberg lettuce, torn

Combine all ingredients in a large salad bowl. When ready to serve, top with dressing.

Dressing:
1/2 cup sugar
1 teaspoon dry mustard
1/4 teaspoon curry powder
1 teaspoon salt
3 tablespoons grated onion

1/3 cup vinegar
1 tablespoon lemon juice
2 tablespoons chutney
1 cup vegetable oil

In a blender combine sugar, mustard, curry powder, salt, onion, vinegar, lemon juice, and chutney. Mix on high; slowly adding oil. Chill.

Joy Beers   Yield: 6 to 8 servings

West Indies Salad

1 pound lump crabmeat
1 medium onion, chopped
Salt to taste
Pepper to taste

1 cup vegetable oil
1 cup cider vinegar
1 cup ice cold water

Place layer of crabmeat in bottom of stainless steel or glass mixing bowl. Add a layer of onion and repeat layers. Add salt and pepper to taste. Combine oil, vinegar, and water; pour over crabmeat. Make sure salad is completely covered with liquid; add more vinegar if needed. Cover and let marinate 24 hours. Serve ice cold and do not freeze.

Senator Earl Goodwin   Yield: 6 to 8 servings

Crab Louis Salad

1 cup mayonnaise
¼ cup chili sauce
¼ cup whipping cream
¼ cup chopped green pepper
1 bunch green onions, chopped
1 teaspoon lemon juice

Salt to taste
6 tomato wedges
6 hard cooked eggs
Lettuce
1½ pounds crabmeat

Combine first seven ingredients, and chill 6 hours or overnight for more flavor. Arrange tomatoes and eggs around outer edges of lettuce leaf with crabmeat in center. Pour dressing over top and serve with crackers.

Marian Carter   Yield: 6 servings

Mariners' Salad

4 tablespoons unflavored gelatin
⅔ cup lemon juice
½ cup horseradish
2 cups thinly sliced crosswise
  celery
2 teaspoons salt

½ cup sliced ripe olives
2 teaspoons pepper
4 (7-ounce) cans tuna
5 cups tomato juice
Lettuce

Soften gelatin with lemon juice. Mix together remaining ingredients with the exception of tomato juice. Heat tomato juice and add to gelatin mixture. Combine with other mixed ingredients and pour into mold. Chill until set; unmold on lettuce. Serve with Mariner's Spicy Sauce.

Mariner Spicy Sauce:
1 cup mayonnaise
2 teaspoons horseradish
2 teaspoons mustard
2 tablespoons pickle relish

1 tablespoon chopped parsley
2 teaspoons grated lemon peel
¼ lemon juice

Combine all ingredients and mix well. Delicious on any fish or meat salad.

Note: Makes 1½ cups salad dressing.

Edie Delp   Yield: 10 servings

Marinated Slaw

1 cup vinegar
½ cup sugar
2 teaspoons celery seed
1 teaspoon dry mustard
1 teaspoon salt
¼ teaspoon pepper

1 cup vegetable oil
1 large head cabbage, shredded or
   chopped
1 onion, chopped
1 green pepper, chopped

Bring vinegar, sugar, celery seed, mustard, salt, and pepper to a boil. Remove from heat and add oil. Pour over cabbage, onion, and green pepper. Cover tightly and refrigerate over night. Will keep for several days.

Joy Green
Peggy Christian

Yield: 10 to 12 servings

Cornbread Salad

¼ cup white cornmeal
¾ cup yellow cornmeal
3 tablespoons flour
¼ teaspoon soda
1½ teaspoons baking powder
1 teaspoon salt
1 teaspoon sugar
2 tablespoons vegetable oil
1 cup buttermilk

1 beaten egg
1 jalapeño pepper, finely chopped
1 (10-ounce) can diced tomatoes
   with chilies
2 cups mayonnaise
1 cup chopped onions
2 ribs celery, chopped
1 (2-ounce) jar diced pimento

Mix together the first twelve ingredients and bake in an iron skillet at 425 degrees for 25 to 35 minutes. Crumble cornbread and add remaining ingredients.

Variation: 1 cup self rising cornmeal may be substituted for first 6 ingredients.

Eloise Anderson

Yield: 8 to 10 servings

Kraut Salad-Relish

1 (16-ounce) can chopped kraut
½ cup chopped bell pepper
½ cup chopped onion
½ cup chopped celery

½ cup chopped olives, optional
½ cup vegetable oil
½ cup vinegar
½ cup sugar

Mix kraut, pepper, onion, celery, and olives together. Mix together oil, vinegar, and sugar; pour over vegetables to marinate. Cover and chill at least two hours. Toss again and drain before serving. Keeps well in refrigerator for at least two weeks.

Patty Sexton   Yield: 6 to 8 servings

Sherry Mayonnaise

1 whole egg
2 egg yolks
1 tablespoon Dijon mustard
¼ cup sherry vinegar

Salt to taste
Freshly ground pepper to taste
1½ to 2 cups vegetable oil

Combine eggs, mustard, and vinegar in food processor fitted with steel blade. Add salt and pepper. Process for 1 minute. With motor running, add oil in a slow steady stream. When oil is incorporated, shut off machine and scrape down sides of bowl; add correct seasoning to taste. Transfer to storage jar. Cover and refrigerate.

Marly Thomas   Yield: 2½ cups

Blender Mayonnaise

1½ tablespoons lemon juice
1 teaspoon spicey mustard
½ teaspoon salt

1 egg
1 cup vegetable oil
Paprika

Place first 4 ingredients in blender; add ⅓ cup oil. Blend at low speed for 30 seconds. Turn blender to high, and very slowly add remaining oil until mayonnaise is thick. Sprinkle a dash of paprika for color.

Note: Quick and easy.

Norma Friday   Yield: 1½ cups

Tomato Honey Dressing

1 cup vegetable oil
1/2 cup catsup
1/2 cup honey
1/3 cup salad vinegar

1/2 teaspoon paprika
1/2 teaspoon onion juice
1/4 teaspoon salt, optional
1/4 teaspoon garlic salt

Blend together. Chill. Delicious on summer fruit.

Terry Hunter

Yield: 2 cups

Lemon Dressing

1 cup vegetable oil
4 tablespoons wine vinegar
4 tablespoons lemon juice

4 teaspoons sugar
2 teaspoons dry mustard
1 teaspoon salt

Mix well and chill. Good over spinach salad.

Mary Drue Wheeler

Yield: 1 1/4 cups

Mother's Honey Dressing

2/3 cup sugar
1 teaspoon dry mustard
1 teaspoon paprika
1 teaspoon celery seed
1/4 teaspoon salt

1/2 cup honey
5 tablespoons vinegar
1 tablespoon lemon juice
1 tablespoon grated onion
1 cup vegetable oil

Mix all ingredients except oil. While processing, slowly add oil.

Note: Use either a processor or blender. Good on fresh fruit.

Lois Sanford

Yield: 2 cups

Poppy Seed Dressing

1½ cups sugar
2 teaspoons mustard
2½ cups vegetable oil

1 cup vinegar
2 teaspoons salt
2 teaspoons poppy seeds

Mix all ingredients except poppy seeds. Blend well with a beater. Add poppy seeds, pour in a covered quart container, and refrigerate.

Margie Swift   Yield: 1 quart

Sweet and Sour Dressing

1 cup vegetable oil
¼ cup cider vinegar
1 medium onion, finely chopped

¾ cup sugar
1 tablespoon Worcestershire sauce
⅓ cup catsup

Combine all ingredients in blender and blend well. Dressing may be refrigerated in tightly closed jar for a week.

Note: Delicious on spinach salad.

Edie Delp   Yield: 1 pint
Dickie Phillips

Bleu Cheese Salad Dressing

¼ cup chopped onion
2 tablespoons vegetable oil
2 tablespoons flour
1 teaspoon sugar
½ teaspoon salt

¼ teaspoon pepper
¾ cup milk
1 tablespoon vinegar
¼ cup bleu cheese

Sauté onion in oil. Combine flour, sugar, salt, and pepper; add to onions. Add milk, vinegar, and bleu cheese. Mix well.

Susan Brinkley   Yield: 1 cup

Mrs. Baen's Ranch Dressing

2 cups mayonnaise
1 cup milk
1 cup sour cream
2 tablespoons chopped parsley

1 tablespoon minced onion
1 tablespoon garlic salt
1 tablespoon garlic powder
1 teaspoon monosodium glutamate

Mix with wire wisk thoroughly. Refrigerate in covered container. Keeps 3 weeks. Makes a great salad dressing or dip for raw vegetables.

Fran Pearce   Yield: 3½ to 4 cups

Mr. B's House Dressing

2 cups mayonnaise
1 cup Zatarain's or Creole mustard
¼ cup prepared mustard
¼ cup white vinegar

½ teaspoon Worcestershire sauce
Salt to taste
Pepper to Taste
Tabasco to taste

Mix all ingredients together. Stir well.

Note: This dressing comes from "Mr. B's Restaurant" in New Orleans. It is wonderful.

Wanda Bass   Yield: 3½ cups

Granny's Salad Dressing for Green Salad

2 cloves garlic, pressed
1 cup mayonnaise
¼ cup catsup
¼ cup chili sauce
1 tablespoon mustard
½ cup vegetable oil

1 tablespoon Worcestershire sauce
1 tablespoon black pepper
Juice of one grated onion
2 tablespoons water
Dash Tabasco sauce
Dash paprika

Mix all ingredients well and refrigerate. Keeps well.

Jerry Goodwin   Yield: 2 cups

Thousand Island Dressing

1 cup mayonnaise
¼ cup chopped relish or
   sweet pickle
1 or 2 hard cooked eggs, chopped

1 tablespoon chopped parsley
1 teaspoon grated onion
1 tablespoon chili sauce or catsup
2 pimentos, finely chopped

Mix and store in refrigerator.

Dickie Phillips

Yield: 1½ cups

French Dressing

1 (10¾-ounce) can tomato soup
1 cup vegetable oil
¼ cup sugar
1 tablespoon garlic salt
1 tablespoon black pepper

1 tablespoon Worcestershire sauce
1 tablespoon mustard
1 teaspoon salt
½ cup vinegar

Mix ingredients together adding vinegar last. Refrigerate in a covered jar. Shake well before using.

Aileen Wadsworth

Yield: 1½ pints

Kay's Famous Birmingham Slaw Dressing

1 cup sugar
2 cups mayonnaise
½ cup catsup
¼ to ½ cup white vinegar

1 tablespoon mustard
1 teaspoon Worcestershire sauce
½ teaspoon salt

Mix well and serve over finely shredded cabbage.

Kay Randall Eddins

Yield: 4 cups

95

Cabbage Salad Dressing

½ cup water
¾ cup sugar
1 (12-ounce) bottle chili sauce
¾ cup vegetable oil
1 tablespoon tarragon vinegar

Dash paprika
Juice of ½ lemon
½ onion, chopped
1 tablespoon Worcestershire sauce
Dash onion powder

Mix water and sugar; bring to a boil. Cool slightly and add other ingredients. Mix well. Cover in a airtight container and refrigerate. Shake well before serving. Serve over finely chopped cabbage.

Note: Delicious served as a salad.

Millie Thomas   Yield: 3 cups

Entrees

Best Steak in Alabama

4 steaks: ribeye, T-bone, or
   hamburger

Southern Flavor

Cover steak on both sides with Southern Flavor and let marinate for 30 minutes. Place on grill and cook to preferred doneness. Best steak you will ever eat!

Note: Southern Flavor can be ordered with form in back of book.

Leonard Ingram
Fred McCormick

Yield: 4 servings

Chateaubriand

1 (4 to 5 pound) beef tenderloin,
   fat trimmed off
1 clove garlic, cut in half
¼ cup Worcestershire sauce

Juice of 1 lime
1 to 2 teaspoons salt
½ teaspoon pepper

Rub meat all over with cut side of garlic; discard garlic. Combine Worcestershire sauce, lime juice, salt, and pepper; brush over meat. Let stand 1 hour. Grill about 5 inches from heat for about 30 to 35 minutes for rare, or 40 to 45 minutes for medium.

Peggy Striplin

Yield: 12 servings

Beef Scraps

4 pounds beef tenderloin
½ cup margarine
Greek seasoning
2 lemons

Green peppers
Red onions
Rice

Cut beef into bite-size pieces. In an electric skillet, brown beef in margarine. Sprinkle generously with seasoning. Squeeze juice of both lemons and drop the lemons into the skillet. Simmer 5 minutes. Serve over rice. Garnish with green peppers and red onions.

Geri Craig

Yield: 8 servings

Herb Marinated Tenderloin

1 cup soy sauce
½ cup olive oil
1 cup port wine
1 teaspoon thyme
1 bay leaf
4 cloves garlic

1 teaspoon salt
1 teaspoon coarsely ground black
  pepper
½ teaspoon hot sauce
1 (5 to 6 pound) tenderloin

Mix all of the ingredients. Marinate the meat for at least 24 hours. Bake in marinade at 425 degrees for 45 minutes for rare. For medium well, bake at 425 degrees for 45 minutes and reduce heat to 325 degrees for 45 minutes.

Variation: 1 cup burgundy and 2 tablespoons sugar may be substituted for 1 cup port wine.

Brenda Maske   Yield: 8 to 10 servings

Filet of Beef Wellington

4 pounds beef filet
½ cup butter
Salt to taste
Ground pepper
½ cup sliced celery
1 cup sliced carrots
½ cup sliced onion
⅓ cup chopped parsley
1 bay leaf

½ teaspoon crumbled dried
  rosemary
Paté de fois gras, canned
1 (8-ounce) package frozen
  crescent rolls
Milk
1 cup veal stock
¼ cup additional paté de fois gras
¼ cup chopped mushrooms

Spread meat generously with butter. Sprinkle with salt and pepper. Spread vegetables, bay leaf and rosemary over bottom of a shallow baking pan and place roast on top. Cook in a preheated 450 degree oven for 40 to 50 minutes. Remove from oven and allow to cool completely. When cold spread paté de fois gras over entire roast. Roll pastry ⅛-inch thick and wrap around roast. Trim edges of pastry, moisten and seal edges together. Place in a baking dish with sealed side down. Brush milk on crust and prick. Bake until browned about 15 to 20 minutes. Remove to platter to keep warm. Add veal stock, ¼ cup of fois gras and chopped mushrooms to roasting pan. Simmer to sauce consistency about 10 to 15 minutes. Slice beef and serve with sauce.

Joy Beers   Yield: 6 servings

Beef Piquant

1 (3-pound) chuck roast
1 lemon
2 tablespoons mustard
Salt to taste
Pepper to taste
2 tablespoons Worcestershire
  sauce

2 tablespoons brown sugar
3 dashes Tabasco
2 medium onions, sliced
1 tablespoon capers
2 tablespoons butter

Place roast on a large piece of heavy duty aluminum foil. Fold up around sides. Rub roast with cut surface of lemon. Spread one side of roast with 1 tablespoon mustard and brown under broiler. Spread other side with 1 tablespoon mustard and brown. Remove from oven and sprinkle with salt, pepper, and rest of lemon. Sprinkle with Worcestershire, brown sugar, and Tabasco. Add onions and capers which have been sautéed in butter. Close aluminum foil on top of meat and seal edges so no juice escapes. Place in shallow pan. Bake at 300 degrees for 3 hours. Serve with natural juices.

Sandy Stewart   Yield: 6 to 8 servings

Sunday Dinner Roast Beef

4 pounds eye of the round roast
Salt to taste
Pepper to taste

Crab apples, optional
Parsley, optional

Have roast at room temperature. Season with salt and pepper. Preheat oven to 500 degrees until light goes off. Bake roast 8 minutes per pound. Turn oven off and do not open door until cool, about 2½ hours. Slice, arrange on platter, and garnish with apples and parsley. This is excellent for Sunday dinner as it will finish cooking while the cook is at church with no fear of the roast burning. This is my family's favorite.

Nellie Kate Tepper   Yield: 8 servings

Hearty Steak and Onions

2 pounds round steak,
  cut into bite-size pieces
2 tablespoons vegetable oil
3 large onions, sliced
1 teaspoon salt

$\frac{1}{2}$ teaspoon thyme
$\frac{1}{4}$ teaspoon pepper
2 cups red wine
1$\frac{1}{3}$ cups hot water
Potatoes or rice

In a large skillet brown beef in hot oil. Add onions and cook until tender. Season with salt, thyme, and pepper. Add the wine and water; cover and simmer for 1 hour or until meat is tender. Serve over potatoes or rice.

Note: This may be made ahead and frozen. Take out the morning before serving. Heat until hot. Easy and good!

Wanda Bass   Yield: 4 to 6 servings

Stir-Fry Beef and Vegetables

$\frac{3}{4}$ pound boneless sirloin steak
$\frac{1}{2}$ cup water
1 tablespoon cornstarch
1$\frac{1}{2}$ teaspoons sugar
$\frac{1}{4}$ cup plus 1 tablespoon soy sauce
1$\frac{1}{2}$ to 2 tablespoons oyster
  flavored sauce
3 tablespoons peanut oil
$\frac{1}{4}$ teaspoon salt
1 large onion, thinly sliced and
  separated into rings

3 ribs celery, diagonally sliced
4 ounces fresh mushrooms, sliced
$\frac{1}{2}$ cup coarsely chopped water
  chestnuts
1 (6-ounce) package frozen
  Chinese pea pods, thawed and
  drained
Hot cooked rice

Partially freeze steak; slice across grain into 2x$\frac{1}{4}$-inch strips. Set aside. Combine water, cornstarch, sugar, soy sauce, and oyster sauce; set aside. Pour peanut oil around top of preheated wok, coating sides; allow to heat at medium high (325 degrees) for 2 minutes. Add steak and salt; stir-fry about 3 minutes. Push meat up sides of wok, forming a well in center. Place onion, celery, mushrooms, and water chestnuts in well; stir-fry 2 to 3 minutes. Add pea pods; cover and reduce heat to medium (275 degrees). Simmer 2 to 3 minutes. Stir in soy sauce mixture. Cook on medium high heat (325 degrees), stirring constantly, until thickened and bubbly. Serve over rice.

Veronica Chesnut   Yield: 4 to 6 servings

Chinese Beef in Oyster Sauce

1 pound round steak
3 tablespoons soy sauce
2 tablespoons dry sherry
2 tablespoons steak sauce
1 tablespoon cornstarch

1 tablespoon vegetable oil
1 (15-ounce) can Chinese
   vegetables
Rice

Slice steak into thin strips and set aside. Combine the soy sauce, sherry, steak sauce, and cornstarch. Set this mixture aside. Heat the oil in a wok or skillet. Add steak slices and stir fry quickly until the meat loses its red color, approximately 5 minutes. Drain the vegetables and add to the meat. Add the soy sauce mixture. Cook and stir until the mixture thickens and the meat and vegetables are bubbly hot. Serve with hot rice.

Gale Bedgood   Yield: 4 servings

Alabama's Pepper Steak

2 pounds beef round steak
2 tablespoons vegetable oil
1 teaspoon salt
Black pepper to taste
2 cups diced or sliced bell pepper
   rings
2 cups chopped celery

1 medium onion, sliced
1 (10-ounce) can beef consommé
4 tablespoons flour
$\frac{1}{2}$ cup water
4 tablespoons soy sauce
3 cups cooked yellow rice

Cut beef into slices. Heat oil in a large skillet. Cook and stir beef over high heat about 5 minutes or until meat is browned. Add salt, pepper, bell pepper, celery, onion, and consommé. Cover and cook over low heat until meat and vegetables are tender. Blend flour, water, and soy sauce. Stir into mixture. Cook and stir until mixture is slightly thickened. Serve over bed of yellow rice.

Nellie Kate Tepper   Yield: 4 to 6 servings

Beef Burgundy Stroganoff

½ pound fresh mushrooms, sliced
½ cup chopped onion
1 clove garlic, minced
¼ cup margarine, melted
1 pound sirloin tips
2 tablespoons flour
1 (10½-ounce) can beef
  consommé

3 tablespoons lemon juice
3 tablespoons burgundy or red
  wine
¼ teaspoon pepper
1 (8-ounce) carton sour cream
Noodles

Sauté mushrooms, onions, and garlic in margarine until onion is tender. Cover meat with flour. Add beef; cook until browned. Stir to brown all sides. Reduce heat and add consommé, lemon juice, wine, and pepper. Simmer for 15 to 20 minutes. Stir in sour cream and heat thoroughly. Serve over hot cooked noodles.

Karim Plummer Oaks
  Class of 1979

Yield: 4 servings

Hamburger Stroganoff

½ cup minced onion
1 clove garlic, minced
¼ cup margarine
1 pound ground beef
1 teaspoon salt
½ teaspoon pepper
2 tablespoons flour

1 (8-ounce) can sliced mushrooms,
  drained
1 (10¾-ounce) can cream of
  chicken soup
1 cup sour cream
Parsley, optional
Rice

Sauté onion and garlic in margarine over medium heat. Stir in meat and brown. Add salt and pepper and cook for 5 minutes. Stir in flour, mushrooms, and soup; simmer uncovered 10 minutes. Stir in sour cream. Heat thoroughly. Garnish with parsley. Serve over rice.

Peggy Christian

Yield: 4 to 6 servings

Three Way Meat Loaf

1 pound beef or veal
1 pound lean pork
1 pound smoked ham
4 eggs
1 teaspoon salt
1 teaspoon pepper

1½ cups crushed saltine crackers
1½ cups milk
½ cup southern style barbecue
   sauce
Celery seed

Preheat oven to 325 degrees. Grind all three meats through food grinder. In a large bowl combine meats, eggs, salt, and pepper. In a small bowl combine crackers and milk, and add to meat mixture. Mix well by hand and form into loaf. Place in 9x13-inch baking dish. Coat top of meat loaf with barbecue sauce and sprinkle with celery seed. Bake uncovered for 45 minutes or until well done.

Gigi Campbell   Yield: 8 servings

Barbecue Meat Loaf

2 pounds ground beef
Salt to taste
Pepper to taste
1½ cups catsup
¼ teaspoon chili powder
4 teaspoons vinegar

4 teaspoons sugar
2 teaspoons diced onion
¼ teaspoon cayenne
½ cup water
4 teaspoons Worcestershire

Season ground beef with salt and pepper to taste. Form uncooked beef into small individual loaves. Place in casserole dish. Mix remaining ingredients and pour over meat loaves. Bake at 375 degrees for 45 minutes.

Frances Woodfin Kelly   Yield: 6 to 8 servings

Meat Loaf

2 eggs
¾ cup minced onion
¼ cup minced green pepper
2 cups cracker crumbs or
   breadcrumbs
1½ pounds lean ground chuck
½ pound pork sausage
¼ teaspoon horseradish

1 tablespoon salt
1 teaspoon dry mustard
¼ cup milk
1 teaspoon Worcestershire sauce
½ teaspoon sweet basil
½ teaspoon oregano
½ teaspoon dry celery leaves
¼ cup catsup

In a large bowl, beat eggs slightly; add onion, pepper, cracker crumbs, ground meat, and sausage. Add other ingredients, except catsup. Shape meat into an oval loaf in a greased baking pan. Spread catsup on top. Bake at 375 degrees for 45 to 50 minutes.

Louise Nolen   Yield: 8 to 10 servings

Stuffed Green Peppers

1½ pounds ground chuck
1 small to medium onion,
   chopped
½ cup rice
1 (16-ounce) can tomatoes,
   chopped

1 (6-ounce) can tomato paste
6 ounces water
1 teaspoon Worcestershire
4 to 6 green peppers
Grated cheese

Brown meat and onion; drain. Add remaining ingredients except peppers and cheese and simmer 20 to 30 minutes. Halve and clean peppers. Cook until tender in small amount of salted water. Drain. Place peppers on plate, cover with meat mixture, and top with grated cheese as desired.

Teri Beck   Yield: 4 to 6 servings

Quick Manicotti

8 to 9 manicotti shells
1 pound ground beef
1 clove garlic, crushed
1 cup cottage cheese
1 cup shredded Mozzarella cheese

½ teaspoon salt
¼ cup mayonnaise
1 (15½-ounce) jar spaghetti sauce
½ teaspoon oregano
⅓ cup grated Parmesan cheese

Cook manicotti shells according to package directions. Drain. Rinse in cold water; drain and set aside. Sauté ground beef and garlic, stirring until beef is no longer pink. Drain. Add cottage cheese, Mozzarella cheese, salt, and mayonnaise to skillet; stir well. Stuff manicotti shells with meat mixture and arrange in a lightly greased 9x13-inch baking dish. Combine spaghetti sauce and oregano; pour over manicotti. Sprinkle with the Parmesan cheese. Cover and bake at 350 degrees for 15 minutes. Uncover and bake for 10 additional minutes.

Janice Stapp   Yield: 8 servings

World Famous Spaghetti

1 onion, chopped
1 cup chopped celery
1 (4-ounce) can mushrooms
1 pound ground beef
1 (6-ounce) can tomato paste
3 (15-ounce) cans special tomato
  sauce

1 (16-ounce) can stewed tomatoes
2 bay leaves
Salt to taste
Pepper to taste
Garlic powder to taste

Sauté onion, celery, and mushrooms until tender; lightly brown ground beef. Add all tomato ingredients and bay leaves. Add salt, pepper, and garlic powder to taste. Simmer for 2 hours and hope that it is as good as mine.

Tom Sommerville   Yield: 6 servings
  Class of 1976

Aunt Jean's Lasagna

Sauce:

1 pound Italian sausage or ground
beef
1 clove garlic, minced
1 tablespoon whole basil

1½ teaspoons salt
1 (16-ounce) can tomatoes or
tomato sauce
2 (6-ounce) cans tomato paste

Preheat oven to 375 degrees. Brown meat and drain. Add garlic, basil, salt, tomatoes, and tomato paste. Simmer uncovered for 30 minutes stirring occasionally.

Lasagna Filling:

1 (10-ounce) package of lasagna or
wide noodles
3 cups ricotta or creamy cottage
cheese
½ cup grated Parmesan or
Romano cheese

2 tablespoons parsley flakes
2 eggs, beaten
1 teaspoon salt
½ teaspoon pepper
1 pound Mozzarella cheese, sliced
very thin

Cook noodles in large amount of boiling salty water until tender. Drain and rinse with hot water. Combine ricotta cheese, Parmesan cheese, parsley flakes, eggs, salt, and pepper. Place noodles in bottom of 9x13-inch baking dish. Spread with about ½ cheese filling mixture. Add meat sauce then layer with sliced Mozzarella cheese. Repeat layers. Bake for 30 to 40 minutes or until heated well. Take out of oven and let stand for 10 minutes before cutting into squares. Filling will set slightly.

Note: May assemble early and refrigerate. If refrigerated, allow 15 minutes or longer in oven.

Variation: If ground beef is used 1 pound of ground pork may be used also to add bulk and taste.

Becky Bailey
Judy Hawes

Yield: 12 servings

Tagganocci

6 ounces ¼-inch noodles
1 pound ground beef
1 medium onion, chopped
Garlic powder to taste
1 (32-ounce) jar spaghetti sauce
1 (2¼-ounce) can sliced
   mushrooms

1 (2-ounce) jar olives, sliced
1 (16-ounce) can whole kernel
   corn
½ pound grated sharp cheese,
   divided

Cook noodles according to directions on package. Brown meat with onion and a little garlic powder if desired. Drain meat mixture and add sauce, mushrooms, olives, corn, and half of cheese. Add cooked noodles and mix thoroughly. Pour into baking dish and cover with remaining cheese. Bake 1 hour at 325 degrees. Casserole freezes well. This is good served with a green salad and bread.

Nell Mooney   Yield: 4 servings

Beef Bonaparte

1 pound ground beef
1 (16-ounce) can tomatoes, drain
   and reserve juice
1 (8-ounce) can tomato sauce
2 teaspoons garlic juice
2 teaspoons sugar
2 teaspoons salt
Tabasco to taste
Cracked black pepper to taste

1 bay leaf
1 (5-ounce) package thin egg
   noodles
1 (3-ounce) package cream cheese
1 cup sour cream
6 green onions, chopped
1 cup grated Cheddar cheese
1 (6-ounce) package Mozzarella
   cheese slices

Preheat oven to 350 degrees. Brown beef in salted skillet. Drain. Add tomatoes and brown lightly. Add reserved juice and tomato sauce. Season with garlic, sugar, salt, and Tabasco. Stir and lower heat to simmer. Sprinkle with cracked pepper. Add bay leaf snapped in two. Simmer 30 minutes. Cook noodles; drain and combine with cream cheese, sour cream, and onions. Grease a 9x13-inch glass baking dish. Alternate layers of noodle mixture, meat mixture, and grated Cheddar cheese. Bake covered for 20 minutes. When ready to serve, reheat uncovered for 30 minutes. Place strips of Mozzarella cheese on top and bake until cheese melts.

Joy Green   Yield: 8 servings
Mary McDavid

Coal Miner's Pie

1 pound ground beef	1 teaspoon pepper
2 medium onions, chopped	3/4 cup corn meal
1 (15-ounce) can tomato sauce	1 tablespoon flour
2 medium green peppers, chopped	1 teaspoon baking soda
1 (12-ounce) can Mexican corn	1/2 cup buttermilk
1 to 2 tablespoons chili powder	1 tablespoon shortening
1 1/4 teaspoons salt	2 eggs, beaten

Preheat oven to 350 degrees. Brown beef and onions. Drain. Combine this mixture with tomato sauce, green peppers, Mexican corn, chili powder, salt, and pepper. Pour into a 10-inch pie plate. Mix remaining ingredients and pour over the beef mixture. Bake for 20 minutes.

Vickie Booker   Yield: 6 servings

Family Supper Casserole

1 (8-ounce) package thin spaghetti	1/8 teaspoon pepper
1 pound ground chuck	1 1/2 cups grated sharp Cheddar
3/4 cup chili sauce	cheese
1 teaspoon dried oregano leaves	1 1/2 cups milk
1/4 teaspoon salt	

Preheat oven to 350 degrees. Cook spaghetti according to package directions. Drain and set aside. Brown beef and drain. Add to meat: 1/2 cup chili sauce, oregano, salt, and pepper. In a well greased 2-quart casserole, layer half of spaghetti, half of meat mixture, and half of cheese. Add remaining spaghetti, meat, and cheese. Pour milk over all. Top with remaining 1/4 cup of chili sauce. Bake uncovered for 35 minutes or until milk is absorbed and cheese is melted.

Lori Schiffer Tolar   Yield: 6 servings
  Class of 1979

Hamburger-Can-Be-Heaven Casserole

2 pounds ground beef
1 medium onion, chopped
1/4 teaspoon salt
Dash of pepper
1 (6-ounce) box long grain wild
  rice mix
1 (10 1/4-ounce) can chicken
  with rice soup

2 (10 3/4-ounce) cans cream of
  mushroom soup
1 (8-ounce) can chopped
  mushrooms, drained
1/4 cup water
1/2 cup blanched almonds

In skillet, brown beef and onion. Add salt and pepper as browning begins. Drain off excess juice. Add seasoning packet with wild rice, chicken with rice soup, 1 1/2 cans of the cream of mushroom soup, and mushrooms; stir and simmer for 5 minutes. Place in a 9x13-inch casserole dish and bake at 350 degrees for approximately 40 minutes. For the last ten minutes, spread the top of the casserole with the remaining 1/2 can of mushroom soup diluted with 1/4 cup of water. Sprinkle with almonds.

Julie Tepper
  Class of 1983

Yield: 6 to 8 servings

Cheeseburger Pie

1 1/2 pounds ground beef
1 (8-ounce) can tomato sauce
1/2 cup cracker crumbs
1 teaspoon salt

1/2 teaspoon oregano
1/4 cup chopped onion
1/4 cup chopped bell pepper
2 (9-inch) pie shells

Preheat oven to 400 degrees. Brown meat and drain. Add other ingredients. Simmer until pepper and onion are tender. Pour mixture into 2 shallow pie crusts. Add cheese topping.

Cheese Topping:
1 (8-ounce) package mild Cheddar
  cheese, grated
1 egg
1/2 teaspoon salt

1/2 teaspoon Worcestershire sauce
1/2 teaspoon dry mustard
1/4 cup milk

Mix together and spread over pies. Bake until crust is brown and cheese melts.

Joy Davis
Barbara Rosser

Yield: 12 servings

Got It All Together

1 loaf of French bread
1 (5-ounce) can evaporated milk
1½ pounds very lean
   ground beef
½ cup cracker crumbs
1 egg

⅓ cup minced onion
Salt to taste
Pepper to taste
½ cup shredded Cheddar cheese
1 tablespoon mustard
2 tablespoons catsup

Split the loaf of bread lengthwise and remove most of the middle; discard. Mix together all the ingredients and fill the loaf. Wrap bread halves in double pieces of heavy duty aluminum foil. Rake coals from campfire and dig shallow trench. Place bread in trench and cover with coals. Bake for 35 minutes.

Note: For baking in a conventional oven brown beef and onion prior to mixing and bake at 350 degrees for 15 to 25 minutes.

Terry Hunter   Yield: 4 to 6 servings

Cherokee Casserole

1 pound ground beef
¼ cup chopped onion
1 (10¾-ounce) can cream of
   mushroom soup
1 (16-ounce) can tomatoes

1 cup instant rice
1 teaspoon Greek seasoning
Garlic powder to taste
Grated cheddar cheese

Preheat oven to 350 degrees. Brown beef and onion. Drain. Add soup, tomatoes, rice, Greek seasoning, and garlic powder. Simmer for 5 minutes. Place in a 9x13-inch casserole dish and top with grated cheese. Cook for 25 to 30 minutes until cheese is bubbly.

Vickie Booker   Yield: 4 to 6 servings

Oriental Green Casserole

3 pounds ground beef
1 cup chopped celery
1 cup chopped onion
¾ cup chopped green pepper
3 cups water
⅓ cup cornstarch
1 tablespoon sugar
¾ teaspoon ginger
¾ cup soy sauce
2 (16-ounce) cans bamboo shoots, drained

2 (6-ounce) packages frozen pea pods, thawed
2 (10-ounce) packages frozen green peas, thawed
2 (8-ounce) cans sliced water chestnuts, drained
1 (16-ounce) can bean sprouts, drained

Preheat oven to 350 degrees. Sauté beef, celery, onion, green pepper; drain. Add water, cornstarch, sugar, ginger, and soy sauce; cook and stir until bubbly. Add bamboo shoots, pea pods, peas, chestnuts, and bean sprouts; simmer. Pour into two 9x13-inch casseroles and bake for 30 minutes. To freeze, cover and label. Bake frozen at 400 degrees for 1½ hours. Serve over rice or Chinese noodles.

Helen Shivers   Yield: 18 to 20 servings

Sausage Rice Bake

1 pound beef smoked sausage
1 (10¾-ounce) can cream of mushroom soup
1 soup can water
1 medium onion, chopped

¼ green pepper, chopped
1½ ribs celery, chopped
2 tablespoons Worcestershire sauce
1 cup uncooked rice

Cut sausage in ¼-inch slices. Combine sausage with remaining ingredients in a 2-quart covered casserole. Bake at 350 degrees for 1 hour.

Variation: ½ (4-ounce) can water chestnuts, drained, may be substituted for the celery.

Faye Carter   Yield: 4 servings

Mexican Cornbread Casserole

1½ cups self-rising corn meal
1 teaspoon baking soda
1 tablespoon salt
1 (16-ounce) can yellow cream
  corn
1 cup milk

2 eggs
⅓ cup shortening
1 pound ground beef
1 medium onion, chopped
4 jalapeño peppers, finely chopped
6 ounces sharp cheese, grated

Mix together corn meal, soda, salt, corn, milk, eggs, and shortening; set aside. Brown and drain ground beef. Pour ½ corn meal mixture into greased 9x13-inch dish. Add ground beef, onion, peppers and cheese. Pour remaining corn meal mixture into pan. Bake at 350 degrees for 45 minutes.

Laura Wallace   Yield: 6 to 8 servings

Taco Casserole

2 pounds ground beef
2 (1¼-ounce) packages taco
  seasoning
1 (8-ounce) can tomato sauce
1 sauce can water
1 (11-ounce) package corn chips

1 (11-ounce) can Cheddar cheese
  soup
1 (8-ounce) carton sour cream
Chopped tomatoes
Chopped lettuce

Brown beef and drain. Add seasoning and tomato sauce plus one can of water. Simmer for ten minutes and pour over chips, which have been layered in a 9x13-inch dish. Cover with cheese soup which has been diluted with a little water. Spread with sour cream. Brown 30 minutes at 350 degrees. Then top with tomatoes and lettuce.

Nellie Kate Tepper   Yield: 8 servings

Mexican Casserole

2 pounds ground beef
1 onion, chopped
1 (4½-ounce) can green chilies
1 (8-ounce) jar taco sauce
1 (10¾-ounce) can cream of
  mushroom soup
1 (10¾-ounce) can cream of
  chicken soup
1 (11-ounce) can Cheddar cheese
  soup
1 (11-ounce) package corn tortillas
Cheese

Sauté meat and onion; drain. Add chilies, taco sauce, and soup to meat mixture. Tear tortillas in half, and place half in 9x11-inch baking dish. Pour ½ meat mixture over tortillas. Repeat layers. Sprinkle cheese over top. Bake at 350 degrees for 20 minutes,

Nellie Kate Tepper   Yield: 6 to 8 servings

Hole-In-One Peppers

3 bell peppers
1 (16-ounce) can pork and beans
3 wieners, cut up
1 tablespoon grated onion
2 tablespoons brown sugar
¼ cup catsup
1 teaspoon mustard

Remove top of bell peppers and clean out seeds. Boil pepper shells in salted water for 5 minutes; drain. Combine pork and beans, wieners, onion, brown sugar, catsup, and mustard; fill pepper shells. Bake at 350 degrees for 20 minutes.

Martha Campbell   Yield: 3 servings

Calves' Liver with Sherry

1 pound calves' liver
Salt to taste
Pepper to taste
Flour
1 large onion, sliced
Vegetable oil
¼ cup sherry
¼ cup water

Pull membrane from liver. Salt, pepper, and cover with flour; set aside. Cook onion in small amount of oil until limp; remove from pan. Sear liver on both sides in oil in which onion was cooked. When all pieces have been browned, place in pan and cover with onion. Mix sherry and water together and pour over all. Cover with lid; simmer for 15 minutes.

Faye Bailey   Yield: 4 servings

Reuben Casserole

1 pound cooked corned beef
1/4 cup thousand island salad
   dressing
1 (16-ounce) can sauerkraut,
   drained

1/2 pound Swiss cheese, shredded
6 slices rye bread, crumbled
1/4 cup butter or margarine,
   melted

Crumble corned beef into a well greased 8x12-inch baking dish. Dot with salad dressing. Spread sauerkraut over top; cover with cheese. Toss breadcrumbs with butter; sprinkle over casserole. Bake at 350 degrees for 30 minutes or until hot and bubbly.

Joy Beers   Yield: 6 to 8 servings

Veal Congealed Loaf

2 to 3 pounds veal, cooked until it
   falls apart
6 hard cooked eggs
1 cup sweet pickle relish
1 (7-ounce) jar pimento
2 ribs celery
1 cup of stock from veal

1 tablespoon unflavored gelatin
1 tablespoon mustard
1/2 cup mayonnaise
Salt to taste
Pepper to taste
Juice of 1 lemon

Run meat, eggs, pickles, pimentos, and celery through a food grinder. In a large bowl mix ground food with remaining ingredients. Form in a loaf pan and refrigerate to congeal.

Mae Bruner Morgan   Yield: 6 to 8 servings

Veal Cordon Bleu

4 boneless veal cutlets
Salt to taste
Pepper to taste

8 thin slices ham
8 slices Mozzarella cheese
2/3 cup margarine

Cut each cutlet in half lengthwise. Place on waxed paper and flatten to 1/4-inch thick with meat mallet. Salt and pepper veal. Place one slice ham and one slice cheese on each piece of veal. Fold ends of veal toward center, overlapping slightly. Secure with a toothpick. Melt margarine, pour over cutlet, and cook for 10 minutes or until golden brown.

Gigi Campbell   Yield: 8 servings

Veal Parmesan

2 tablespoons butter
4 serving size pieces of veal,
   1/2-inch thick
3/4 cup evaporated milk
3/4 cup grated Parmesan cheese

1/4 cup flour
1/2 teaspoon salt
Dash of pepper
1 (8-ounce) can tomato sauce

Preheat oven to 350 degrees. Melt butter in an 8x12-inch pan in oven. Dip veal pieces in 1/4 cup milk. Roll in 1/4 cup Parmesan cheese, flour, salt, and pepper. Place veal in pan. Bake uncovered for 30 minutes. Mix 1/2 cup milk and 1/2 cup Parmesan cheese. Take veal from oven. Pour tomato sauce over veal. Spoon cheese mixture on veal. Bake 20 to 25 minutes more, until meat is tender.

Teri Beck   Yield: 4 servings

Leg of Lamb

1 leg of lamb
Salt to taste
Pepper to taste
Garlic salt to taste

1/2 cup bold and spicy mustard
1 (12-ounce) bottle oil and
   vinegar salad dressing

Place lamb in roasting pan in rack. Sprinkle with seasonings, spread with mustard, and cover completely with salad dressing. Cook fat side up, uncovered, at 300 degrees until tender, approximately 30 minutes per pound.

Geri Craig   Yield: 8 to 10 servings

Lamb Casserole

2/3 cup cooked, diced lamb
4 tomatoes, peeled and chopped
2 onions, grated
2 cups meat stock

3 tablespoons butter
1/2 cup uncooked rice
2 tablespoons Worcestershire sauce

Heat lamb, tomatoes, onion, and stock over very low heat for about 15 minutes. In skillet melt butter, add rice, and simmer until rice browns. Add Worcestershire. Combine in a greased 2-quart casserole and bake at 350 degrees for 35 to 40 minutes.

Dorann Frazer   Yield: 4 servings

Marinated Lamb

½ teaspoon minced garlic
1 onion, chopped
2 tablespoons olive oil
½ cup lemon juice
¾ teaspoon thyme
¾ teaspoon tarragon
¾ teaspoon rosemary

¾ teaspoon marjoram
3-inch sprig of fresh mint or
   2 tablespoons mint jelly
3 tablespoons brown sugar
2 teaspoons salt
1 teaspoon black pepper
Leg of Lamb

Mix all ingredients together except lamb in saucepan and bring to a boil. Reduce heat and simmer about 10 minutes. Place leg of lamb in roasting bag and pour hot marinade over lamb. Close tightly and marinate several hours, turning occasionally. Cook in marinade using directions found on box of roasting bags.

Variation: Reduce brown sugar to 2 tablespoons if mint jelly is used.

Milly Noah

Yield: 6 to 8 servings

Ham Loaf

2½ pounds ground fresh pork
3¼ pounds ground cured ham
Salt to taste

Pepper to taste
1 cup cracker crumbs
4 eggs, beaten

When selecting meat, choose a Boston butt and piece of ham. Ask your butcher to trim fat and grind coarsely. To prepare, mix all ingredients and shape into small loaves. Preheat oven to 325 degrees. Place loaves in 9x13-inch baking pan and cook for 1 hour, basting with sauce every 20 minutes. Dip sauce from bottom of pan over the loaves. Watch carefully to make sure the sauce is not getting too brown in pan. As the loaves cool, continue to dip sauce over them.

Sauce:
¼ cup vinegar
1 tablespoon mustard

½ cup brown sugar
½ cup water

Mix and cook for 20 minutes.

Betty Buster

Yield: 10 to 12 servings

Grilled Ham with Sauce

1/4 cup mustard
1/4 cup pineapple juice
2 tablespoons sugar
1/2 teaspoon horseradish

Dash of salt
1 pound precooked ham steak,
 1-inch thick

Mix the mustard, pineapple juice, sugar, horseradish, and salt in saucepan and heat for 10 minutes. Place the ham steak on a greased grill over hot coals. Baste frequently with heated sauce. Grill 5 to 7 minutes per side, until steak is a rich brown color and heated thoroughly. Serve remaining sauce with ham.

John Christian

Yield: 4 servings

Diane's Marinated Ham Slice

1 teaspoon dry mustard
1/4 teaspoon ginger
1/8 teaspoon cloves
1 tablespoon vegetable oil
1 1/2 teaspoons wine vinegar

1/4 cup brown sugar
1/2 cup ginger ale
1/2 cup orange juice
1 (1 1/2 to 2-inch) center cut ham
 slice

Combine all ingredients for sauce; pour over ham slice in a 9x13-inch baking dish. Marinate ham overnight in refrigerator. Cook on grill for 15 to 20 minutes on each side, brushing with marinade.

Joy Beers

Yield: 8 to 10 servings

Country Ham and Red Eye Gravy

1 (1 1/2 to 2-inch) thick slice cured
 ham
1/4 cup shortening
1 teaspoon sugar

1/8 teaspoon salt
1/2 cup hot water
1/3 cup hot coffee

Fry ham in shortening in black iron skillet. Remove ham and keep warm. Pour off fat and reserve. Add to skillet sugar and salt. Brown thoroughly. Pour in hot water and coffee. Add reserved fat. Heat and pour over ham slice.

Margaret Anne Beers

Yield: 2 to 4 servings

Ham and Scalloped Potatoes

1 (10½-ounce) can cream of
   celery soup
½ cup milk
Dash of pepper
3 cups thinly sliced potatoes

1½ cups diced cooked ham
½ cup thinly sliced onion
½ cup shredded Cheddar cheese
Paprika

Preheat oven to 375 degrees. Combine soup, milk, and pepper. In 2-quart casserole, arrange alternate layers of potatoes, meat, onion, and soup sauce. Cover; bake for 1 hour. Sprinkle with cheese and paprika and bake uncovered 15 minutes longer.

Martha Campbell

Yield: 4 servings

Ham Dumbbells and Broccoli Casserole

12 small broccoli spears
2 (6-ounce) packages boiled ham
Grated Parmesan cheese

1 (8-ounce) package part-skim
   Mozzarella cheese
Swiss cheese sauce

Cook broccoli in boiling salted water 5 minutes or until tender. Take 2 slices of ham, one on top of the other, place broccoli spears on ham so that flowerets are on opposite ends of meat. Sprinkle with Parmesan cheese. Cut Mozzarella cheese into sticks and put one or two on each dumbbell. Roll up meat with broccoli and cheeses and place side by side in lightly greased 8x12-inch casserole. Cover with Swiss cheese sauce. Bake in 350 degree oven for 25 minutes.

Swiss Cheese Sauce:
3 tablespoons margarine
3 tablespoons flour

1½ cups milk
6 ounces shredded Swiss cheese

Melt margarine and blend in flour until smooth. Add milk slowly and cook until thickened. Add cheese and stir until melted. Pour over rollups.

Terry Hunter

Yield: 6 servings

119

Pork Chops and Rice

Salt to taste
Pepper to taste
6 pork chops
1 cup rice

1 (10½-ounce) can French onion
  soup
2 soup cans water

Preheat oven to 350 degrees. Salt and pepper pork chops. In a 9x13-inch baking dish mix rice, soup, and water. Add pork chops. Cover tightly and bake 1 hour and 15 minutes. Uncover and bake 15 minutes to brown pork chops.

Anna Speir   Yield: 4 to 6 servings

Pork Chops

6 to 8 pork chops
6 to 8 tablespoons brown sugar

6 to 8 tablespoons catsup
2 lemons

Spray 9x13-inch casserole with vegetable spray. Line casserole with pork chops. On each pork chop add 1 tablespoon each of brown sugar and catsup. Squeeze lemon juice over pork chops. Slice lemons and layer in casserole. Cover with foil and bake at 275 degrees for 2 to 3 hours.

Arabella Wilkinson Sheehan   Yield: 4 servings
  Class of 1973

Quick Barbecued Pork Chops

4 to 6 center cut pork chops
¾ cup water
¼ cup vinegar
1 tablespoon sugar

1 tablespoon Worcestershire sauce
½ cup catsup
1 teaspoon salt
Dash pepper

Place pork chops evenly in 9x13-inch baking dish. Combine remaining ingredients and pour over chops. Bake uncovered at 350 degrees for 1 hour.

Note: Easy and very good.

June Thomason Twiggs   Yield: 4 to 6 servings
  Class of 1972

St. Paul's Sausage and Rice

1 pound package ground hot
  sausage
4½ cups water
½ cup rice
2 (2¼-ounce) envelopes dry
  chicken noodle soup

1 green pepper, chopped
1 medium onion, chopped
1 cup chopped celery
2 (15-ounce) cans Spanish rice
Paprika

Preheat oven to 300 degrees. Brown sausage stirring to crumble; drain well and set aside. Boil water; add rice and soup mixture. Cook 7 minutes, turn off heat and let stand. Do not drain. Mix pepper, onion, celery, and Spanish rice; add to rice and soup mixture. Blend in sausage. Spoon mixture into a greased 9x13-inch casserole dish. Bake 45 minutes or until mixture sets. Sprinkle top with paprika.

Eunice Rew

Yield: 10 to 12 servings

Easy Sausage Rice Casserole

1 pound package ground sausage
¼ cup chopped onion
¼ cup chopped bell pepper

1 (16-ounce) can stewed tomatoes
1½ cups cooked rice
2 cups grated cheese

Preheat oven to 350 degrees. Brown sausage with onion and bell pepper in skillet. Drain excess fat. Add tomatoes and cooked rice. Pour in a 1½-quart casserole dish and top with cheese. Bake in oven until cheese melts, approximately 30 minutes. Serve with garlic bread or biscuits.

Bonnie Bryant Fitts
  Class of 1980

Yield: 4 servings

Day-Of-The-Wedding Sausage Casserole

1 pound package ground hot
  sausage
1 pound package ground mild
  sausage
1 small onion, finely chopped
2 cups cooked rice
4 eggs, beaten

2 (10¾-ounce) cans cream of
  celery soup
¼ cup milk
6 cups crispy rice cereal
1 (16-ounce) package sharp
  Cheddar cheese, grated

Brown sausage and onion; drain. Mix with rice. Combine eggs, soup, and milk. Layer sausage and rice, cereal, and one half cheese in a 3-quart casserole. Pour soup mixture over layers. Top with remaining cheese. Bake at 350 degrees for 35 minutes.

Myrna Todd   Yield: 8 to 12 servings

Smoked Country Style Backbones

6 pounds country style backbones
1 (46-ounce) can unsweetened
  pineapple juice

½ cup lemon juice
2 cups dry white wine

Place backbones on rack of smoker. Combine juices and wine and place in water pan of smoker. Smoke meat 3½ hours. Turn meat and baste with sauce. If water pan goes dry refill ½ full with hot water. Continue to cook 2 to 3 hours.

Sauce:
1½ cups catsup
⅔ cup vinegar
½ cup packed brown sugar
1 teaspoon celery salt
2 teaspoons liquid smoke

½ teaspoon dry mustard
¼ teaspoon paprika
Dash of Tabasco
Juice of 1 lemon
½ cup margarine

Mix and heat all ingredients until margarine melts.

Variation: Beef backbones and ribs may be cooked in same manner.

Averee Armstrong Hicks   Yield: 6 servings
  Class of 1972

Sweet and Pungent Spareribs

2 pounds spareribs, cut in pieces
¼ cup vegetable oil
½ cup chopped onion
½ cup chopped green pepper
1 cup pineapple juice
¾ cup cider vinegar
½ cup catsup

1¼ teaspoons Worcestershire
  sauce
1 medium clove garlic, minced
½ cup firmly packed brown sugar
2 tablespoons cornstarch
¾ cup water

Brown spareribs in oil and set aside. Pour off all but 2 tablespoons drippings. Add onion and green pepper and sauté until tender. Add remaining ingredients except cornstarch and water to onion and green pepper. Heat until bubbly. Mix cornstarch and water together and add to sauce; cook 5 minutes. Add ribs and simmer for 1 hour or until tender.

Terry Hunter   Yield: 4 to 6 servings

Chicken Parisienne

12 small chicken breasts
1 (2-ounce) jar currant jelly
1 tablespoon cornstarch
1 cup water
¼ cup lemon juice

2 tablespoons Worcestershire
  sauce
2 teaspoons allspice
3 teaspoons salt
1 teaspoon pepper

Preheat oven to 450 degrees. Place chicken in 9x13-inch casserole. Do not overlap. Mix rest of ingredients in saucepan and bring to boil. Simmer 5 minutes. Pour over chicken. Bake for 15 minutes; reduce heat to 375 degrees and bake one hour. Baste often. If sauce becomes too thick, add water. Serve sauce separately. Good with wild rice.

Joanie Looney   Yield: 8 to 10 servings

Chinese Chicken

4 whole chicken breasts
1/4 cup vegetable oil
1/2 cup diced celery
2 tablespoons soy sauce
1 teaspoon salt

1/4 teaspoon pepper
1 (6-ounce) can mushrooms
1 (15-ounce) can bean sprouts
1 tablespoon cornstarch

Debone chicken breasts; skin and cut into 1-inch cubes. Heat oil in a skillet or wok. Add the chicken and cook, stirring frequently for 10 minutes. Add celery and soy sauce and continue cooking for 5 minutes. Season with salt and pepper. Drain and reserve the liquid from the mushrooms and bean sprouts. Stir in mushrooms and bean sprouts into chicken mixture. Measure 1/2 cup of reserved vegetable liquid and mix with the cornstarch until smooth. Add to the ingredients in the skillet and stir constantly until the mixture is thickened and clear.

Note: *Serve over rice or Chinese noodles.*

Gale Bedgood   Yield: 4 servings

Chicken Morgan

4 chicken breast halves, skinned
1/4 cup melted margarine
1/2 cup chopped onion
1 clove garlic, minced
1/4 to 1/2 teaspoon crushed
  marjoram
Salt to taste
Pepper to taste

1 (16-ounce) can tomatoes,
  undrained
1 (3-ounce) can mushrooms
1 chicken bouillon cube
1 teaspoon sugar, optional
2 tablespoons cornstarch
2 tablespoons cold water

Brown chicken breasts in melted margarine. Remove chicken and add onion and garlic. Sauté until onion is soft. Add marjoram, salt, pepper, tomatoes, mushrooms, and bouillon cube. Break up tomatoes. Add sugar if desired. Return chicken to pan and cook covered for 30 minutes or until chicken is tender. Remove chicken and thicken sauce with cornstarch dissolved in water. Serve chicken on bed of rice or noodles with sauce.

Betty Clower   Yield: 4 servings

Poulet d'Artichoke

2 (14-ounce) cans artichoke hearts
2⅓ cups diced cooked chicken
  breasts
2 (10¾-ounce) cans cream of
  chicken soup
1 cup mayonnaise

1 teaspoon lemon juice
½ teaspoon curry powder
1¼ cups grated sharp Cheddar
  cheese
1¼ cups bread cubes
2 tablespoons butter, melted

Preheat oven to 350 degrees. Drain artichokes and arrange in 9x13-inch casserole. Spread chicken on top. Combine soup, mayonnaise, lemon juice, curry powder and pour over chicken. Sprinkle with cheese. Toss bread cubes in melted butter and pour over cheese. Bake for 25 minutes. Can be prepared in advance.

Note: *Serve with rice for a dinner or in ramekins for a luncheon.*

Sis Wood   Yield: 8 servings

Chicken Crêpes with Mushrooms

3 tablespoons butter
3 shallots or ½ yellow onion,
  chopped
½ pound mushrooms, thinly
  sliced
2 tablespoons flour
¾ cup chicken broth
½ cup Swiss cheese, grated

1 tablespoon lemon juice
¼ cup whipping cream
Salt to taste
Pepper to taste
12 prepared crêpes
6 thin slices cooked chicken
1 tablespoon butter

Preheat oven to 350 degrees. Sauté shallots or onion in butter for three minutes until softened. Add and sauté mushrooms for three minutes. Stir in flour and add chicken broth. Add cheese, lemon juice and whipping cream. Season with salt and pepper. The mixture should be very thick so that it can be rolled in the crêpe. Spread out the crêpe and cover each with half a slice of chicken. Put about 3 tablespoons of the mushroom filling over the chicken and roll the crêpes. Place crêpes in a buttered 9x13-inch oven-proof baking dish. Dot the surface of the crêpes with butter. Bake uncovered for 15 minutes or until hot.

Joy Beers   Yield: 6 servings

Pop's Chicken Curry

1 (5-pound) chicken
1 rib celery, chopped
2 large onions, chopped
1 (8-ounce) can mushrooms
$^1/_2$ teaspoon ginger
3 tablespoons vegetable oil
1$^1/_2$ teaspoons curry powder

$^1/_2$ cup flour
2 quarts chicken stock
1 (6-ounce) can tomato paste
Rice
Raisins
Salted peanuts

Cook chicken and reserve stock. Sauté celery, onions, mushrooms, and ginger in oil for 5 minutes. Add curry powder and flour, blending well. Gradually stir in stock; add tomato paste. Cook until thickened. Debone chicken and cut into bite-size pieces. Add chicken to curry mixture. Serve on rice. Garnish with raisins and salted peanuts.

Jackie Hines   Yield: 6 to 8 servings

Hot Chicken Salad I

2 cups diced cooked chicken
1 cup mayonnaise
$^1/_2$ teaspoon salt
1 cup diced celery
1 cup sliced water chestnuts
2 tablespoons lemon juice

2 tablespoons grated onion
$^1/_2$ cup sliced almonds
1 cup sliced mushrooms
1 cup crushed potato chips
$^1/_2$ cup grated sharp Cheddar
    cheese

Mix chicken, mayonnaise, salt, celery, chestnuts, lemon juice, onion, almonds, and mushrooms. Pour into a 2-quart casserole. Top with chips and cheese. Bake at 350 degrees for 30 minutes.

Margie Swift   Yield: 4 servings

Hot Chicken Salad II

3 cups chopped cooked chicken
1½ cups finely chopped celery
3 tablespoons diced onion
1 (10¾-ounce) can cream of
    chicken soup
1¼ cups mayonnaise
¼ teaspoon curry powder

¼ teaspoon salt
Pepper to taste
1 (2¼-ounce) package slivered
    almonds, toasted
1 cup crushed potato chips
1 cup shredded Cheddar cheese

Mix chicken, celery and onion. Add soup, mayonnaise, curry powder, salt and pepper and stir into chicken mixture well. Stir in almonds. Pour into a 9x13-inch casserole or divide into smaller casseroles as preferred. Cover with crushed potato chips and sprinkle with cheese. Bake at 350 degrees for 30 to 40 minutes or until toasted and bubbly.

Phyllis McCaughan

Yield: 6 to 8 servings

Italian Drumsticks

8 chicken legs
¼ cup margarine
½ cup barbecue sauce with onions
1 (8-ounce) package refrigerated
    crescent rolls
1 egg, beaten

2 teaspoons Italian seasoning,
    NOT ITALIAN DRESSING
2 teaspoons Parmesan cheese,
    grated
2 teaspoons sesame seeds

Wash chicken legs and dry. Sauté chicken in margarine and barbecue sauce; cook over medium heat for 25 minutes. Cool. Preheat oven to 375 degrees. Brush crescent rolls with egg; sprinkle with seasoning and cheese. Roll around leg. Place seam side down. Brush top with egg and sprinkle with sesame seeds. Bake 15 to 20 minutes or until golden brown.

Mary McDavid

Yield: 4 to 6 servings

Chicken Cordon Bleu

6 whole chicken breasts
12 thin slices cooked ham
12 slices Swiss cheese
12 bacon slices

½ cup melted margarine
Soft breadcrumbs
Parmesan cheese

The Day Before You Serve:
Skin, debone, and split chicken breasts. Flatten chicken, using flat side of a meat mallet. Place 1 slice of ham and 1 slice of Swiss cheese on each chicken breast half. Roll up like a jelly roll, folding in the sides to hold in the ham and cheese. Wrap a slice of bacon around each roll to hold roll together. Place rolls in a 9x13-inch casserole and pour melted margarine over rolls. Sprinkle breadcrumbs and Parmesan cheese generously over buttered chicken rolls. Cover and refrigerate (can be frozen for later cooking). Bake chicken rolls at 350 degrees for 45 minutes to 1 hour. Serve with mushroom sauce.

Mushroom Sauce:
1 (10¾-ounce) can cream of
   chicken soup
1 (4-ounce) can sliced mushrooms,
   undrained

1 cup sour cream

Heat soup and mushrooms which have been stirred until smooth; then blend in sour cream.

Ann Till
Sue Lide
Beth Hicks Baker
   Class of 1980

Yield: 12 servings

Easy Baked Chicken

1 (2-ounce) package chipped beef
4 deboned chicken breasts
4 slices of bacon

1 (10¾-ounce) can cream of
   mushroom soup
1 (8-ounce) carton sour cream

Grease a 7½x11-inch casserole dish. Line casserole with chipped beef. Wrap chicken breasts with bacon and place on chipped beef. Make a sauce of soup and sour cream and pour over chicken. Bake at 275 degrees for 3 hours.

Jackie Woodfin

Yield: 4 servings

Chinese Veggies

1 pound boneless chicken, pork,
  or beef
4 tablespoons vegetable oil
1 onion, cut in wedges
¹/₂ cup sliced mushrooms, fresh or
  canned

1 (16-ounce) package frozen
  mixed broccoli, carrots, and
  water chestnuts
1 (6-ounce) package frozen pea
  pods, thawed

Slice meat into thin strips. Heat 2 tablespoons of oil in large skillet or wok; add meat and cook 3 to 5 minutes or until done. Remove from pan. Heat remaining 2 tablespoons oil; then add onion and mushrooms. Cook for 2 to 3 minutes or until tender. Remove from pan. Add more oil if necessary; add mixed vegetables and stir-fry 3 to 4 minutes or until tender and crisp. Stir in pea pods, meat, onion, and mushrooms.

Sauce:
1 cup water
2 tablespoons cornstarch
¹/₃ cup honey
¹/₃ cup soy sauce

¹/₄ teaspoon ginger
Garlic powder to taste
¹/₈ teaspoon crushed red pepper

Mix water with cornstarch until smooth. Add remaining ingredients. Add sauce to meat and vegetable mixture; bring to a boil and boil 1 to 2 minutes, stirring constantly until thickened. Serve over rice.

Peggy Williamson   Yield: 4 to 6 servings

Chicken Strips

¹/₂ cup chopped spring onions
1 clove garlic, crushed
¹/₄ cup vegetable oil
2 whole chicken breasts,
  cut in strips

Lemon juice
Marsala wine to taste

Heat onion and garlic in oil. Add chicken. Cook 3 to 5 minutes or until chicken is done making sure chicken does not stick. Add lemon juice and wine and cook 1 to 2 minutes longer.

Margaret Wilson   Yield: 4 servings

Chicken and Broccoli

1 (3 to 3½ pound) chicken,
  cooked and deboned
1 (10-ounce) package frozen
  chopped broccoli
½ (8-ounce) package of herb-
  dressing mixture

1 (10¾-ounce) can cream of
  chicken soup
½ teaspoon curry powder
⅓ cup mayonnaise
1 tablespoon lemon juice

In a buttered 1½-quart casserole dish place the deboned chicken. Cook the broccoli according to the directions on the package. Drain and place on top of the chicken. Moisten herb-dressing mixture according to package directions and add soup, curry powder, mayonnaise, and lemon juice. Spread this mixture over the broccoli. Bake in a 350 degree oven for about 20 minutes or until the casserole is bubbly hot.

Gale Bedgood
Helen Neighbors

Yield: 4 servings

King Ranch Casserole

4 large chicken breasts or large
  fryer, cut up
1 (10¾-ounce) can cream of
  mushroom soup
1 (10¾-ounce) can cream of
  chicken soup

1 (10-ounce) can tomatoes and
  chilies
1 large onion, diced
½ cup chicken broth
1 (9-ounce) package tortilla chips
2 cups grated Cheddar cheese

Cook chicken and cut in bite-size pieces. Mix soups, tomatoes, onion, and broth for a sauce. Layer in 9x13-inch dish: chips, chicken, sauce, and cheese ending with chips and cheese for topping. Bake at 350 degrees for 1 hour.

Variation: May add jalapeño peppers for extra flavor.

Melissa Traylor
  Class of 1985

Yield: 8 servings

Mexican Chicken

5 to 6 chicken breasts
1 (11-ounce) bag tortilla chips
1 (4-ounce) can green chilies
1 (10½-ounce) can chicken with
rice soup
1 (10½-ounce) can cream of
chicken soup

1 (8-ounce) carton sour cream
1 head lettuce
2 tomatoes
Black olives
¼ pound Cheddar cheese
1 (8-ounce) jar picante sauce

Boil and bone chicken breasts. Chop into bite-size pieces. Crush ¾ bag of tortilla chips and place in bottom of 9x13-inch casserole dish. Mix green chilies, soup, sour cream, and ½ to ¾ pound of shredded cheese with chicken. Top with remaining crushed tortilla chips and bake at 350 degrees for 30 minutes. Chop lettuce, tomatoes, and black olives and place on top of tortilla chips. Sprinkle remaining cheese and jar of picante sauce over all.

Edie Delp   Yield: 6 to 8 servings

Baked Chicken Reuben

6 whole chicken breasts, halved
and deboned
¼ teaspoon salt
⅛ teaspoon pepper
1 (16-ounce) can sauerkraut,
drained

6 slices Swiss cheese
1¼ cups bottled thousand
island dressing
1 tablespoon fresh chopped
parsley

Place chicken in greased 9x13-inch baking dish. Sprinkle with salt and pepper. Place sauerkraut over chicken; top with Swiss cheese. Pour dressing evenly over cheese. Cover with foil and bake at 325 degrees for 1 and ½ hours. Sprinkle with chopped parsley.

Geri Craig   Yield: 6 servings

Cahawba Chicken

2 (7-ounce) chicken breasts
4 tablespoons flour
1/2 teaspoon seasoned salt
1/2 cup butter
2 ounces mushrooms, sliced

1 ounce chopped shallots
1 ounce ham, julienned
2 ounces chablis
6 ounces half and half

Skin chicken breasts and pound flat with meat mallet. Lightly dust chicken in flour seasoned with salt. In heavy saucepan, melt butter and sauté chicken until golden brown. Remove chicken and place in a heated serving dish. Add mushrooms, shallots, and ham to skillet and cook until heated through. Add wine. Reduce heat by half. Add half and half. Cook until it is thick and creamy. Pour sauce over chicken. Serve.

Bob Kelley
  Tally-Ho Restaurant

Yield: 2 servings

Chicken Cottage Pie

2 tablespoons butter
1/2 cup chopped onion
1/2 cup diced celery
1/2 cup sliced carrots
1 clove garlic, minced
1/4 cup wine

1 cup canned chicken gravy
2 cups cooked chicken, cut in
  bite-size pieces
1 (16-ounce) can mixed vegetables
1/2 cup instant mashed potatoes

Melt butter in saucepan. Add onion, celery, carrots, garlic; sauté. Stir in wine and gravy and simmer for 15 minutes. Combine with chicken and vegetables. Place in 8 individual crocks. Prepare potatoes according to package directions. Spread over chicken mixture. Bake at 400 degrees for 20 minutes or until potatoes are toasty.

Geri Craig

Yield: 8 servings

Chicken Teriyaki

½ cup soy sauce
¼ cup brown sugar
1 clove garlic, crushed
1 tablespoon ginger

1 tablespoon vegetable oil
1 tablespoon sherry
2 pounds deboned chicken breast

Mix all ingredients in a large bowl. Add chicken and chill 4 hours. In a shallow baking dish place chicken breasts and pour liquid into dish. Bake uncovered at 325 degrees until done.

Gigi Campbell   Yield: 4 servings

Crunchy Chicken Pie

3 chicken breasts
3 to 6 ribs celery, chopped
1 (3-ounce) package walnut pieces
1 (3-ounce) package pecan pieces
1 (8-ounce) carton sour cream

Salt to taste
Pepper to taste
1 cup grated cheese
1 (9-inch) pie shell, baked

Cook chicken and cut into bite-size pieces. Mix all ingredients except cheese and fill the pie shell. Sprinkle cheese abundantly over the top and bake for 15 to 20 minutes at 300 degrees.

Peggy Striplin   Yield: 4 to 6 servings

Ritzy Chicken Pie

1 (16-ounce) box Ritz crackers
1 pint sour cream
1 (10¾-ounce) can cream of
  chicken soup

1 (10¾-ounce) can cream of
  mushroom soup
1 chicken, cooked and deboned
½ cup margarine, melted

Preheat oven to 350 degrees. Grease a 2-quart baking dish and crumble ½ box of crackers into bottom of dish. Combine sour cream, soups, and chicken. Spread over cracker layer and cover with remaining ½ box of crackers, crumbled. Drizzle margarine over top and bake for 30 minutes.

Pat Labbe   Yield: 4 to 6 servings
Cammie DeBardeleben Barnes
  Class of 1976

Chicken Roll-Ups

1 (8-ounce) package crescent
  dinner rolls
2 cups chopped, cooked chicken
  or turkey
1 cup (4 ounces) shredded sharp
  Cheddar cheese

1 (10¾-ounce) can cream of
  celery soup
1 soup can milk
1 (2-ounce) jar diced pimento,
  drained

Separate rolls. Combine chopped chicken and cheese. Reserve half the mixture for use in the sauce. Place about 3 tablespoons of remaining chicken-cheese mixture on each individual roll, roll up. Place roll-ups seam side down (points down) in a lightly greased 7½x11¾-inch baking dish. Mix soup, milk, and pimento together. Add reserved chicken and cheese mixture. Pour over roll-ups and bake at 350 degrees for 30 minutes.

Gayle Willis   Yield: 6 to 8 servings

Foiled-Up Fowl

2½ pounds chicken breasts
Salt to taste
Pepper to taste
½ cup catsup
½ cup water
4 tablespoons vinegar

1 teaspoon salt
¾ cup light brown sugar
6 tablespoons mustard
1 (1⅜-ounce) envelope dry onion
  soup mix

Skin chicken and place in 9x13-inch dish. Salt and pepper chicken. Combine all remaining ingredients. Spoon over chicken. Secure aluminum foil tightly over dish. Bake at 350 degrees for 1 hour. Open foil and leave in oven 15 minutes more to brown.

Beth Williams   Yield: 4 servings

Crunchy Party Chicken

2 cups cubed cooked chicken
1 cup chopped celery
1/2 cup slivered almonds, toasted
2 hard cooked eggs, chopped
2 tablespoons Worcestershire sauce

1/2 cup mayonnaise
1 tablespoon onion juice
1 (10¾-ounce) can cream of
   chicken soup
Potato chips, crushed

Mix all ingredients together except potato chips and pour into a buttered 9x13-inch baking dish. Top with crushed potato chips. Bake at 350 degrees for 30 minutes.

Beth Henry   Yield: 6 servings

Skewered Chicken Livers

1 pound chicken livers
Bacon, cut in 1½-inch pieces
Salt

Seasoned pepper
Olive oil
Seasoned bread crumbs

Clean, wash, and pat livers dry. Cut in half. Alternate liver halves and bacon pieces on skewers, beginning and ending with bacon. Salt and pepper. Brush with olive oil and roll in bread crumbs. Broil about 4 minutes on each side. Check for doneness; cook until pink in center.

Joy Beers   Yield: 4 servings

Chicken Spaghetti

1 (3-pound) chicken
1 (8-ounce) skinny elbow noodles
1 (16-ounce) can tomatoes and
   juice
1 small onion, chopped
1 bell pepper, chopped
1 (10¾-ounce) can cream of
   mushroom soup

1 (10¾-ounce) can cream of
   chicken soup
Salt to taste
Pepper to taste
1 cup grated cheese

Bake chicken; debone and cut into small pieces. Cook noodles; drain. Combine remaining ingredients except cheese and place in 9x13-inch casserole. Sprinkle cheese on top and bake at 400 degrees for 30 minutes.

Susan Brinkley   Yield: 6 servings

Nine Boy Indian Curry

1 (3-pound) chicken
¼ cup vegetable shortening
1 medium onion, chopped
1 clove garlic
1 tablespoon curry powder
½ cup flour
1 cup chicken broth
1 cup milk

1 chunk of chopped crystalized
  ginger
Salt to taste
Pepper to taste
Monosodium glutamate to taste
2 cups cooked rice
1 banana per serving

Cook and chop chicken, reserving broth. Heat shortening and brown onion and garlic in large skillet. Add curry powder and flour; this will be gooky. Add broth, milk, and ginger. Add chicken, salt, pepper, and monosodium glutamate. Simmer 30 minutes. To serve: split 1 banana vertically, cover with rice, and chicken sauce. Use condiments of your choice.

Nine Boy Condiments:
Peanuts
Bacon
Eggs, chopped
Raisins
Pickle relish

Coconut
Apricot jam
Brown sugar
Olives, chopped

Joy Green   Yield: 8 servings

Mama's Fried Chicken

1 cup milk
1 egg, beaten
Salt to taste
Pepper to taste

1 (2½ to 3-pound) chicken,
  cut up
Flour
Vegetable oil

Combine milk and egg in a medium bowl. Salt and pepper chicken. Shake chicken parts in flour in plastic bag. Dip each piece in milk mixture and then back in flour. May be dipped and floured again for thick crust. Heat 1 to 2 inches of oil in an iron skillet or dutch oven to 325 degrees. Add chicken and cook covered for about 10 minutes. Uncover, turn and continue cooking 10 to 15 minutes more or until golden brown. Drain on paper towel plus one brown paper bag.

Joy Beers   Yield: 4 servings
Sherie Sherrer

Chicken and Dumplings

1 stewing hen
1½ to 2 teaspoons salt
2 cups flour
2 teaspoons baking powder

1 teaspoon salt
⅓ cup shortening
½ cup milk

Cut up hen; place in deep pot, barely cover with water, add salt and simmer until meat is tender. Debone hen and set aside; reserve the broth. Sift together the flour, baking powder, and salt; cut in shortening. Add milk to make a stiff dough. Roll out to ¼-inch thickness on floured board. Cut into 1-inch squares, and sprinkle with flour. Drop into briskly boiling chicken stock. Cover tightly (no peeking allowed); simmer gently about 40 minutes. Add meat and serve.

Bill Neighbors   Yield: 6 to 8 servings

Easy Barbecued Chicken

1 cup light corn syrup
1 cup barbeque sauce

1 chicken, split

Mix syrup and barbecue sauce together. Grill chicken until almost done. Spread sauce over chicken and cook until crispy.

Donny Buster   Yield: 4 servings
  Class of 1972

Oven Barbecued Chicken

1 (3-pound) chicken
⅓ cup catsup
2 tablespoons vinegar
1 tablespoon lemon juice
2 tablespoons Worcestershire sauce
4 tablespoons butter
2 tablespoons brown sugar

1 teaspoon dry mustard
1 teaspoon chili powder
¼ to ½ teaspoon cayenne pepper
1 teaspoon paprika
½ teaspoon salt
¼ teaspoon pepper

Preheat oven to 350 degrees. Cut chicken into pieces and set aside. Combine other ingredients; heat to blend. Cool. Dip each piece of chicken into sauce and place in an aluminum foil lined pan. Pour remaining sauce over chicken. Carefully seal edges and bake for 1½ hours. Open foil the last 30 minutes and keep chicken well basted.

Milly Noah   Yield: 4 to 6 servings

Chicken Skillet

1 frying chicken
Salt to taste

1 (6-ounce) cola
½ cup catsup

Cut chicken as for frying. Salt and place in skillet. Pour cola and catsup over chicken. Cover and simmer until chicken is done and tender. Remove lid and finish cooking until cola and catsup are a thick sauce.

Jane Singley

Yield: 4 servings.

"Paul M's" Charcoal Chicken

2 fryers, split
Salt
1½ cups vegetable oil

Juice of 3 large lemons
½ cup Worcestershire sauce

Let charcoal burn down for medium-hot fire. Rub chicken with salt. Combine oil, lemon juice, and Worcestershire sauce for a basting sauce. Baste the bony side of the chicken halves and place on grill breast side up. Baste thoroughly and often using a mop or pastry brush. Turn as needed.

Norma Friday

Yield: 4 halves

Chicken Supreme

6 chicken breasts
1 (10¾-ounce) can cream of
  mushroom soup
1 (10¾-ounce) can cream of
  chicken soup

1 cup sour cream
½ cup slivered almonds

Place chicken in 2-quart shallow pan. Mix undiluted soups together and pour over chicken. Spread sour cream on top and sprinkle with almonds. Bake at 350 degrees for 1½ hours. Serve sauce over rice.

Kathy Jones

Yield: 6 servings

Swiss Chicken

¼ cup white wine
1 (10¾-ounce) can cream of
   chicken soup
6 chicken breasts, deboned

6 slices Swiss cheese
1 cup herb stuffing
¼ cup margarine, melted

Mix wine and chicken soup together. Layer in 2-quart casserole the chicken, cheese, soup mixture, and top with herb stuffing. Pour melted margarine on top. Bake at 325 degrees for 1 hour.

Bob Armstrong
  Class of 1977

Yield: 4 servings

Sweet and Sour Chicken

1 (2-pound) fryer, cut up
¼ cup vegetable oil
1 (8-ounce) bottle Russian salad
   dressing

1 (8-ounce) jar apricot preserves
1 (1³⁄₈-ounce) envelope dry onion
   soup mix

Arrange chicken, skin side up, in a greased 8x12-inch baking pan. Combine remaining ingredients, pour over chicken. Bake at 350 degrees for 1 hour.

Emily M. Massey

Yield: 4 servings

Chicken Casserole

1 (3-pound) chicken
1 (10¾-ounce) can cream of
   mushroom soup
1 (10¾-ounce) can cream of
   celery soup

2 to 2½ cups chicken broth
½ cup margarine, melted
1 (8-ounce) package of herb
   dressing mix

Cook chicken without salt. Cool, debone and cut in bite-size pieces. Mix soups and broth together. Add chicken to soup mixture. Add margarine to herb dressing. Mix chicken mixture and herb dressing together; toss lightly. Place in 2½-quart casserole and bake at 350 degrees for 30 minutes.

Note: 1 cup grated Cheddar cheese may be added.

Sara Jones
Ann Edwards

Yield: 6 to 8 servings

Quick and Easy Chicken Casserole

5 boneless chicken breasts
1 (15½-ounce) can French style
  green beans, drained
1 (10¾-ounce) can cream of
  celery soup

1 (8-ounce) can water chestnuts,
  drained
3 tablespoons minced onion
1 cup mayonnaise
1 cup chicken broth

Boil chicken breasts in salted water; cool and cut into bite-size pieces. Combine all ingredients in a 2-quart casserole. Bake at 400 degrees for 25 to 30 minutes. Serve over rice.

Eleanor Gantt Scales
  Class of 1981

Yield: 4 servings

Chicken and Wild Rice Casserole

3 to 4 chicken breasts
1 (5-ounce) box wild rice
1 medium onion, chopped
1 (8-ounce) can sliced mushrooms,
  drained
½ cup margarine
1 (10¾-ounce) can cream of
  mushroom soup

1 (10¾-ounce) can cream of
  chicken soup
3 tablespoons flour
1½ cups milk
1 cup grated Cheddar cheese

Cook chicken breasts and debone. Cook rice according to package directions. Set aside. Sauté onion and mushrooms in margarine. Add soups and mix well. Combine flour and milk and add to mixture. Layer in casserole rice, chicken, and cheese. Bake at 350 degrees until heated through and cheese is melted.

Annie Blackwell Stinson
  Class of 1976
Faye Carter

Yield: 4 servings

Campfire Chicken

1 (3-ounce) can mushrooms
1 (8-ounce) can green beans
1 (8-ounce) can whole onions
1 (8-ounce) can corn
1 (6¾-ounce) can boned chicken

1 (10¾-ounce) can bisque of
   tomato soup
Salt to taste
Pepper to taste

Drain all vegetables, reserving liquid. Add all ingredients; then add 1 cup of the combined vegetable liquids. Mix and simmer over campfire 20 to 30 minutes. Add more vegetable juices as needed.

Terry Hunter   Yield: 4 to 6 servings

Stuffed Cornish Hens

4 Cornish hens, washed and
   drained
Salt to taste
Pepper to taste
Garlic powder to taste
3 strips bacon, cut in pieces
1 medium onion, chopped
1 green pepper, chopped

3 to 4 garlic cloves, minced
1 (6-ounce) box long grain and
   wild rice, prepared
1 (4-ounce) can sliced mushrooms,
   drained
½ cup chopped green onions
¼ cup butter

Preheat oven to 350 degrees. Sprinkle hens with salt, pepper, and garlic powder inside and out. In a frying pan, sauté bacon until soft. Add onions, green pepper, and garlic and cook over medium heat until soft, and until bacon is done. Remove with slotted spoon to a large mixing bowl. Add rice, mushrooms, and green onions and toss to mix well. Stuff into hens. Place three pats of butter on each hen and wrap with aluminum foil. Bake for 1 hour and 15 minutes; open foil and bake 15 more minutes to brown hens.

Rae Jackson   Yield: 4 servings

Daddy's Tender Turkey

1 (12 to 18 pound) turkey
Salt to taste
Pepper to taste

Garlic salt to taste
Onion salt to taste
Squeeze butter

Remove giblets and cook for gravy. Rinse turkey and cover inside and out with seasonings, finishing with the butter. Wrap tightly in a long piece of 18-inch aluminum foil. Bake at 475 degrees for three hours.

Geri Craig

Yield: 12 to 15 servings

Turkey-Noodle Casserole

1 (8-ounce) package of noodles
1/2 cup chopped green pepper
1/2 cup chopped onion
2 tablespoons butter
2 tablespoons flour
1/4 teaspoon thyme
1 (10¾-ounce) can cream of
  chicken soup

1 (10¾-ounce) can cream of
  mushroom soup
1/2 soup can of milk
2 ounces cubed Cheddar cheese
2 cups chopped cooked turkey
1 (4-ounce) can mushrooms,
  drained

Cook noodles and set aside. In a Dutch oven or large sauce pan sauté green pepper and onion in the butter. Blend in flour and thyme. Stir in soups, milk, and cheese and heat until bubbly. Fold in noodles, turkey, and mushrooms. Pour into a 2-quart casserole dish and bake at 350 degrees for 35 minutes. This freezes well in a reclosable bag.

Ginger Wilson

Yield: 6 to 8 servings

Deviled Turkey

1 chicken bouillon cube
1 cup water
1 (8-ounce) package of herb
  dressing mixture
6 cups turkey, cut into bite-size
  pieces

3 (10-ounce) jars currant jelly
3 tablespoons mustard
¾ cup relish pickle
6 tablespoons Worcestershire
6 tablespoons butter

Dissolve bouillon cube in water. Mix herb dressing with enough chicken bouillon to be moist but still crumbly. NOT SOGGY. Layer turkey and dressing in a 9x13-inch casserole; repeat layers. Combine jelly, mustard, pickle, Worcestershire, and butter in saucepan and heat until all combines well and jelly is melted. Pour on top of casserole. Make holes with knife so that sauce gets down sides and all the way through. Bake at 350 degrees for 30 minutes.

Peggy Striplin   Yield: 8 to 10 servings

Turkey Almondine

¼ cup butter or margarine
¼ cup flour
2 cups milk
¼ teaspoon salt
Pinch Pepper
2 tablespoons dry white wine
2 egg yolks, beaten
2 cups turkey, cooked and diced

1 cup English peas, cooked and
  drained
⅓ cup slivered almonds, toasted
3 tablespoons breadcrumbs
1 tablespoon butter
2 tablespoons grated Parmesan
  cheese

Make a cream sauce with butter, flour, and milk. Add salt, pepper, and wine. Add a little sauce to yolks. Rapidly stir back into sauce. Stir in turkey, peas, and half the almonds. Pour into a 1½-quart baking dish. Scatter remaining almonds and crumbs on top. Dot with butter. Sprinkle with cheese. Brown under broiler.

Cheryl Watts   Yield: 4 servings

Smoked Turkey

½ bag hickory chips or 3 sticks
10 pounds charcoal
6 quarts water
8 to 12 pound turkey

Salt, optional
Pepper, optional
Butter, optional

Soak hickory chips in water overnight. Place charcoal in bottom of smoker. Start fire and let burn 30 minutes, or until briquettes are beginning to gray. Remove hickory chips; save water. Place chips directly on hot coals. Fill water pan with hickory water plus enough to make 6 quarts. Season turkey, if desired, and place on rack. Cover and cook 8 to 10 hours. Weather conditions will affect your results. This recipe is based on a 50 degrees F. temperature or higher. Very cold weather will require a longer cooking time.

Note: *My family likes just the natural juices with no seasonings.*

John Sherrer   Yield: 10 to 12 servings

Mike's Venison Jerky

2 pounds venison
2 tablespoons Worcestershire
  sauce
2 tablespoons soy sauce
1 tablespoon salt

1 teaspoon black pepper
1 teaspoon red pepper
2 cloves garlic, sliced
1 cup whiskey
1 cup water

Slice meat ⅛-inch thick with the grain while still slightly frozen. Cut away all fat. Make marinade by combining the remaining ingredients. Marinate the strips in a glass container overnight. Pat dry and arrange side by side on oven roasting racks without overlapping. Cook at a minimum temperature like 150 degrees for 6 hours. Leave oven door ajar to allow moisture to escape. Meat should be dark, dry, and firm. If not, turn and continue drying. Store jerky in a cool airtight container.

Mike Wells   Yield: 1 pound
  Class of 1972

Hardy Eating

2 pounds venison
Garlic salt to taste
Pepper to taste
3 tablespoons self-rising flour
1 (10¾-ounce) can cream of
  celery soup
1 (10¾-ounce) can cream of
  mushroom soup

1 (8-ounce) can tomato sauce
1 (1⅜-ounce) envelope dried
  onion soup
1 teaspoon Worcestershire sauce
2 cups water

Trim fat from meat. Cut in pieces ½ to 2 inches. Season with garlic salt and pepper. Dust meat with flour and deep fry. Set meat aside. Brown flour in large pot. Combine other ingredients with flour. Add meat and simmer until meat is tender, at least one hour. Add water as needed. Serve this on rice with hot biscuits.

Allen Hardy

Yield: 6 to 8 servings

Louisiana Duck

4 ribs celery, chopped
1 large bell pepper, chopped
1 large onion, chopped
½ to ⅔ cup mustard
3 wild ducks
Garlic to taste

Black pepper to taste
Red pepper to taste
3 slices bacon
1 (10-ounce) bottle
  Worcestershire sauce

Mix together the celery, bell pepper, and onion. Add enough mustard to this mixture to thoroughly coat the vegetables. Stuff the cavity of each duck with the vegetable mustard mixture. Season each duck with garlic salt, black pepper, and red pepper. Place the ducks breast down in a roaster. Put a slice of bacon on the back of each duck. Pour in the entire bottle of Worcestershire sauce. Cover and bake in a 300 degree oven for approximately 3 hours.

Robert Beers

Yield: 3 servings

Tew's Duck Casserole

3 Mallard ducks or 4 smaller ducks
Salt to taste
Pepper to taste
1 to 2 apples, cored and cut into
    wedges

3 ribs celery, cut
2 to 3 onions, cut into wedges
1 (10½-ounce) can beef
    consommé
1 cup cooking sherry

Preheat oven to 325 degrees. Salt and pepper prepared duck. Stuff with apples, celery, and onion. Put duck breast down on aluminum foil and pour consommé over. Wrap foil tightly and bake for 2½ to 3 hours. Leave duck breast down in liquid. Pour cooking sherry over and rewrap and continue cooking for approximately 1 hour. Leave overnight. Debone duck and prepare for casserole.

Casserole:

1 pound sausage
3 onions, chopped
1½ bell peppers, chopped
¾ cup chopped celery

2 cups rice, cooked
2 (10¾-ounce) cans cream of
    mushroom soup

Preheat oven to 350 degrees. Brown sausage and drain. Sauté onion, pepper, and celery; add to sausage. In a greased 3-quart casserole layer the rice, sausage mixture, and prepared duck. Pour soup over casserole. Bake for 20 to 30 minutes or until soup gets hot.

Mike Wood

Yield: 6 servings

Fried Duck Breast

4 to 6 halves duck breast
1 egg
1 cup milk

1½ cups flour
1 teaspoon creole seasoning
Vegetable oil

Cut duck breast into finger-size strips. Beat egg and milk together. Dip each duck strip into egg mixture. Add creole seasoning to flour and coat each strip of duck breast with seasoned flour. Heat oil in a skillet and fry each strip until it is a dark golden brown.

Gale Bedgood

Yield: 4 servings

Duck Breasts

½ cup Worcestershire sauce
½ cup soy sauce
⅛ cup red wine vinegar
Juice and rind of 4 lemons
Salt to taste

Pepper to taste
Monosodium glutamate
8 whole or 16 split wild duck
    breasts, skinned, and boned
Béarnaise sauce

Combine first 6 ingredients to make marinade. Marinate breasts for 24 hours, making sure the breasts are covered in marinade. Cook, covered, on a very hot charcoal fire for 1½ minutes on each side for very rare, or continue cooking until desired degree of doneness is reached. Serve with a Béarnaise sauce. Use as an entree, or cut into bite-size pieces and serve with toothpicks as an appetizer.

Note: Béarnaise sauce recipe can be found in the sauce section.

Cecile Youngblood   Yield: 6 to 8 servings

Smothered Dove or Quail

6 dove or quail
Salt
Pepper
1 cup flour
1 teaspoon salt

½ teaspoon pepper
½ teaspoon paprika
½ teaspoon monosodium glutamate
1 cup vegetable oil
2 cups chicken stock

Wash and dry birds thoroughly. Season with salt and pepper at least one hour before cooking. Combine dry ingredients and dredge birds lightly. Heat oil in a heavy skillet and brown lightly on all sides. Remove birds and drain off all but 2 tablespoons fat. Pour seasoned flour into hot oil and stir over low heat for about 4 minutes. Slowly stir in hot stock and cook a few minutes longer stirring frequently. Add birds to gravy, cover, and bake at 325 degrees for one hour or until tender. Baste two or three times while baking; add more hot stock if gravy becomes too thick.

Grace Henry   Yield: 3 servings

Marinated Dove

⅓ cup honey
⅓ cup white wine
½ cup beer
⅔ cup soy sauce
⅓ cup lemon juice

½ cup vegetable oil
½ cup white vinegar
10 drops garlic juice
Sprinkle monosodium glutamate
10 to 12 doves

Mix all ingredients together except the doves and cook until mixture reaches a boil. Pour the mixture over the doves and marinate at least 1 hour. Broil the doves, basting frequently with the marinade.

Jimmy Bedgood, Sr.   Yield: 4 servings

Southern Quail

8 Bobwhite quail
Salt
Pepper

Water
½ cup butter or margarine

Salt and pepper quail. Place in an iron skillet that is ⅓ full of water. Cover and steam on medium heat until water is almost gone. Slice butter in skillet and brown birds until golden. Serve over toasted biscuit with grits and a fruit or green salad.

Robert Beers   Yield: 4 servings

Crabmeat Casserole

¾ cup chopped celery
¾ cup chopped onion
¼ cup margarine
1 (10½-ounce) can cream of
   mushroom soup
¼ cup milk
Juice of ½ lemon

¼ cup sherry
2 (4½-ounce) cans crabmeat
1 (4¼-ounce) can shrimp,
   drained
½ cup grated cheese
4 hard cooked eggs, sliced
8 saltine crackers

Sauté celery and onions in margarine. Add all other ingredients; pour in a greased 2-quart casserole. Bake at 300 degrees for 30 to 40 minutes.

Variation: One whole lemon may be substituted for sherry.

Susan Brinkley   Yield: 6 to 8 servings

Crabmeat au Gratin

4 tablespoons butter
4 tablespoons flour
2 cups milk or half and half
2 cups grated sharp Cheddar
  cheese
1 teaspoon salt

Tabasco to taste
1 tablespoon onion flakes
1 tablespoon parsley flakes
½ teaspoon sweet basil
1 pound crabmeat

Melt butter in saucepan over very low heat. Remove from heat and add flour. Add milk slowly, stirring constantly. Return to low heat. Stir until thickened. Fold in cheese and seasonings. Stir until cheese is melted and sauce smooth and thick. Add crabmeat. Return to heat until warmed through and serve over toast or rice or pour in a well greased 1½-quart casserole and bake at 350 degrees for 20 minutes or until bubbly and slightly browned.

Helen Neighbors
Smyly Kirkpatrick

Yield: 6 servings

Crab "Blue Moon"

4 large onions, chopped
3 large bell peppers, chopped
4 cloves garlic, chopped
1 cup olive oil
2 (6-ounce) cans tomato paste
Hot sauce to taste

2 cups water
Salt to taste
Pepper to taste
1 pound crabmeat
Rice

Sauté onions, peppers, and garlic in olive oil until tender. Add tomato paste, hot sauce, water, salt, and pepper. Cook for about 2 hours. Add flaked crabmeat about ½ hour before serving. Serve over hot rice.

Louise Nolen

Yield: 8 servings

Marinated Crabmeat

1 pound fresh lump crabmeat
1 medium onion, finely chopped
Salt to taste
Pepper to taste

½ cup vegetable oil
⅓ cup cider vinegar
½ cup ice water

Rinse and remove shell fragments from crab. Spread half the chopped onion on bottom of a large bowl. Spread crabmeat over onion; add remaining onion, salt, and pepper. Mix oil, vinegar, and ice water. Pour over the crabmeat and onion. Cover and marinate in the refrigerator for 6 to 8 hours or overnight.

Helen Neighbors   Yield: 2 to 4 servings

Shrimp Fettucini

2 onions, chopped
2 ribs celery, chopped
1 large bell pepper, chopped
2 cloves garlic, minced
1 cup butter or margarine
4 tablespoons flour
1 pint half and half
3 tablespoons dry parsley

⅔ pound pasteurized processed
   cheese, divided
2 jalapeño peppers, finely chopped
3 pounds raw shrimp, peeled
1 (10-ounce) package fettucini
   noodles or 1 (12-ounce) package
   egg noodles
Romano cheese

Sauté onions, celery, bell pepper, and garlic in butter for 15 minutes. Stir in flour and slowly add cream to make sauce. Add parsley, ½ cheese, and jalapeño peppers. Cook over low heat for five minutes. Add shrimp and continue cooking about 15 minutes. Stir occasionally. Boil noodles, drain, and add noodles to mixture. Pour into a greased 9x13-inch casserole, sprinkle with Romano cheese, and cut-up remaining cheese on top. Bake at 350 degrees for 15 to 20 minutes.

Ruthie Carr   Yield: 12 servings

Barbecued Shrimp

5 pounds shrimp
1 (16-ounce) bottle Italian salad
   dressing
1/2 cup lemon juice

2 cups butter
Worcestershire to taste
Tabasco to taste
Garlic salt to taste

Place shrimp unpeeled in 9x13-inch pan. Pour salad dressing and lemon juice over shrimp. Cut butter into small pieces and scatter over shrimp. Sprinkle with seasonings. When melted, liquid should cover shrimp. Bake at 300 degrees for 1 hour.

Sara Crum Blackwell

Yield: 10 to 12 servings

New Orleans Style Shrimp

1 cup butter, DO NOT
   SUBSTITUTE
2 tablespoons soy sauce
1 tablespoon lemon juice
Garlic powder to taste

Tabasco to taste
2 teaspoons gumbo filé powder
2 pounds raw shrimp, medium to
   large

Preheat oven to 450 degrees. Combine butter, soy sauce, lemon juice, garlic powder, and Tabasco in saucepan and cook. Remove from heat and add filé powder. Coat unpeeled shrimp with sauce and bake 20 to 30 minutes. Do not overcook.

Milly Noah

Yield: 4 servings

Shrimp Casserole

1 pound shrimp, cooked, peeled,
   and deveined
1 (14-ounce) can artichoke hearts
1 (10¾-ounce) can cream of
   mushroom soup
2 tablespoons sherry

1 tablespoon minced onion
1/8 teaspoon pepper
1/8 teaspoon garlic salt
1 teaspoon salt
1 cup grated Cheddar cheese

Place shrimp and artichokes in a 2-quart casserole dish. Combine soup, sherry, onion, pepper, garlic salt, and salt. Pour over shrimp and artichokes. Sprinkle with grated cheese. Bake at 400 degrees for 20 minutes.

Teri Beck

Yield: 4 servings

Shrimp Creole

1 pound shrimp, fresh or frozen
1/2 cup chopped onion
1/2 cup chopped celery
1/2 teaspoon garlic
3 tablespoons vegetable oil
1 (16-ounce) can tomatoes,
   drained and chopped
1 (8-ounce) can tomato sauce
1 tablespoon Worcestershire sauce

1 teaspoon salt
1 teaspoon sugar
1 teaspoon chili powder
1/2 teaspoon Tabasco
1/2 to 1 cup cut okra
1/2 cup chopped green pepper
1 tablespoon gumbo filé, optional
Rice

Clean or thaw shrimp. Sauté onion, celery, and garlic in oil until tender. Add tomatoes, tomato sauce, Worcestershire, salt, sugar, chili powder, Tabasco, and okra. Simmer uncovered for 45 minutes. Add shrimp and green pepper. Cover and simmer 5 minutes. Add filé and stir just before serving over rice.

Ron Pugh   Yield: 6 to 8 servings

Shrimp Fried Rice

2 cups chopped shrimp
1/4 cup vegetable oil
2 eggs, slightly beaten
1 (4-ounce) can mushrooms
1 teaspoon salt

Freshly ground black pepper to
   taste
4 cups cooked rice
2 tablespoons soy sauce
1/2 cup chopped green onions

Fry shrimp in oil in deep frying pan for 1 minute, stirring constantly. Add eggs, mushrooms, salt, pepper and fry over medium heat for 5 minutes, stirring constantly. Add rice and soy sauce and fry for 5 minutes, stirring frequently. Mix with chopped green onions.

Stephanie Sewell Piper   Yield: 6 servings
  Class of 1975

Shrimp and Eggplant Casserole

1 medium eggplant
1 egg, beaten
1/2 pound New York State cheese, grated
Ritz cracker crumbs, about 1 cup
1 medium onion, finely chopped
3 ribs celery, finely chopped
1 small bell pepper, finely chopped

2 tablespoons margarine
1/2 (16-ounce) can tomatoes and juice
Salt to taste
Pepper to taste
1 pound shrimp, cooked, peeled, and deveined

Peel and slice eggplant and cook until tender in enough water to keep from sticking. Mash. Add the beaten egg, the cheese and crackers to the eggplant, reserving enough cheese and crackers to cover top. Make sauce by browning chopped onion, celery, and bell pepper in margarine. Add tomatoes and juice. Season to taste and simmer until tender. Add cooked shrimp to sauce and pour into eggplant mixture. Pour into baking dish and cover with crumbs and cheese. Bake at 350 degrees for 20 to 30 minutes.

Leika Collins

Yield: 8 servings

Seafood Stuffed Eggplant

6 medium eggplants
4 bell peppers, chopped
4 medium onions, chopped
1/2 cup chopped celery
3 cloves garlic
3 tablespoons margarine
Salt to taste

Pepper to taste
1 pound small shrimp
1 pound white lump crabmeat
1/2 cup chopped parsley
Breadcrumbs
Paprika
Margarine

Boil eggplants until soft; dig out meat. Save eggplant shells. Sauté bell peppers, onions, celery, and garlic in 3 tablespoons margarine until limp; add eggplant meat, salt, and pepper. Let smother on medium heat until most water is cooked out; add shrimp. Cook for another 20 minutes, put all of this in another bowl and fold in crabmeat and parsley. Let cook briefly; add enough breadcrumbs to be firm enough to stuff shells. Sprinkle a few breadcrumbs and paprika on top. Dot a little margarine on top. Bake at 350 degrees for 25 minutes or until brown.

Peggy Striplin

Yield: 12 servings

Shrimp and Deviled Egg Casserole

6 hard cooked eggs
1 cup cooked shrimp

1 (4-ounce) can mushrooms

Devil the eggs with mayonnaise, mustard, horseradish, salt and pepper to taste. Place eggs in individual greased ramekins. Add shrimp and mushrooms and cover with cheese sauce.

Cheese Sauce:
2 tablespoons butter
2 tablespoons flour
1 1/2 cups milk
1/2 cup grated New York State
   sharp cheese

1 tablespoon Worcestershire sauce
Salt to taste
Pepper to taste

Melt butter and blend in flour; add milk and cook stirring constantly until thick. Add cheese and seasonings. Bake at 350 degrees until heated thoroughly.

Sarah James   Yield: 6 servings

Seafood Thermidor

1/4 cup chopped onion
1/3 cup chopped green pepper
2 tablespoons butter
1 (10¾-ounce) can cream of
   potato soup

1/2 cup milk
1/2 cup shredded cheese
2 (4½-ounce) cans peeled shrimp
1 tablespoon sherry
Hot cooked rice

Sauté onion and pepper in butter until tender. Add soup, milk, and stir until well blended. Add cheese; stir until melted. Fold in seafood and sherry and heat thoroughly. Serve on rice.

Note: Crabmeat or lobster may be used.

Geri Craig   Yield: 4 to 6 servings

Seafood Casserole

½ pound frozen shrimp or
   2 (4½-ounce) cans shrimp
½ pound crabmeat or
   1 (6½-ounce) can crabmeat
1 pint half and half
2 cups mayonnaise

2 cups plus 2 slices soft bread,
   crumbled
1 teaspoon seasoned salt
4 hard cooked eggs, grated
1 tablespoon dried parsley
1 tablespoon instant onion

Preheat oven to 350 degrees. Wash and drain shrimp. Mix all ingredients together and pour into a greased 2-quart casserole. Bake for 30 to 45 minutes.

Note: This can be made 1 to 2 days ahead and refrigerated.

Helen Shivers

Yield: 6 to 8 servings

Seafood Delight

1 (6½-ounce) can white lump
   crabmeat, drained
1 (4½-ounce) can shrimp, drained
1 (8-ounce) can oysters, drained

1 (11-ounce) can cheese soup
½ cup mayonnaise
1 small onion, chopped
Potato chips, crushed

Combine all ingredients, except chips, in a greased 2-quart casserole. Top with chips. Bake at 350 degrees for 15 minutes.

Senator Earl Goodwin

Yield: 4 to 6 servings

Oysters on Toast

½ cup butter, melted
3 green onions, finely chopped
1 large clove garlic
½ teaspoon Tabasco

1 pint small to medium oysters,
   drained
Toasted bread
Parsley

Simmer butter, onion, garlic, and Tabasco for 10 minutes. Add oysters and heat until edges curl. Serve oysters on toasted bread that has been buttered and quartered. Garnish with chopped parsley.

Terry Hunter

Yield: 6 to 8 servings

Baked Oysters Alabama

¼ cup butter
1 large onion, minced
¼ bunch parsley, minced
1 rib celery, minced
2 dozen oysters, well drained

Dash Worcestershire sauce
1 large egg, well beaten
2 cups finely crumbled saltine
   crackers, divided
Salt to taste

Melt butter in skillet. Add minced vegetables and sauté. Add oysters and Worcestershire sauce. Large oysters may be cut in half. Remove skillet from heat and add egg. Return to heat, stirring lightly until egg is cooked. Add 1 cup cracker crumbs and salt mixing well. Place mixture on half-shells or in a greased shallow 2-quart casserole. Sprinkle with remaining cracker crumbs and dot with additional butter. Bake at 400 degrees for 10 minutes.

Louise Nolen   Yield: 4 to 6 servings

Oysters and Wild Rice

2 (5-ounce) boxes brown and wild
   rice mix
¼ cup butter
1 quart oysters, drained
Salt to taste
Pepper to taste
Dash of Tabasco
1½ tablespoons curry powder

¼ cup hot water
1 (10¾-ounce) can cream of
   mushroom soup
1 cup light cream
1½ teaspoons onion powder
¾ teaspoon thyme
½ cup minced parsley, optional

Cook rice according to package directions and add butter. Pour ½ rice in 2-quart casserole; cover with oysters and season with salt, pepper, and Tabasco. Pour remaining rice on oysters. Dissolve curry powder in hot water. In a saucepan combine soup, cream, onion powder, thyme, and curry powder. Cook over low heat, stirring constantly, until mixture is blended. Pour over rice and oyster mixture. Bake at 325 degrees for 45 minutes. Sprinkle with parsley.

Patty Sexton   Yield: 4 to 6 servings

Baked Oysters

2 tablespoons butter
¼ cup chopped green onions
¼ cup chopped white onion
½ cup sliced fresh mushrooms
1 tablespoon diced peeled
  tomatoes
2 cups milk
½ cup flour
1 cup fish stock, court bouillon
  may be used
1 cup white wine
1 teaspoon Worcestershire sauce
2 bay leaves

1 clove garlic, minced
Salt to taste
White pepper to taste
2 egg yolks
½ cup cream
36 oysters on the half shell or 1
  pint oysters
Hollandaise sauce, may use
  packaged sauce
Parmesan cheese
Breadcrumbs
Lemon wedges

Melt butter in a 3-quart casserole dish and sauté onions and mushrooms for about 3 minutes. Add tomatoes and mix well. In a saucepan heat milk and stir in flour. Add heated milk, fish stock, and white wine. Bring to a boil. Stir until thick and creamy. Add Worcestershire sauce, bay leaves, garlic salt, and pepper. Mix egg yolks and cream together; stir into sauce, bringing to another boil. Remove from heat and cool. Place sauce into shells or ramekins, and place the oysters on top. Bake at 350 degrees for 3 to 4 minutes. Remove from oven; cover with Hollandaise sauce, sprinkle with Parmesan cheese and breadcrumbs. Broil until brown. Serve with lemon wedges.

Sonia Martin   Yield: 6 to 8 servings

Baked Tuna

2 (7-ounce) cans tuna
⅔ cup chopped onion
¼ cup chopped green pepper
¼ cup chopped pimento

⅔ cup mayonnaise
¼ cup fine dry breadcrumbs
¼ cup Parmesan cheese

Combine tuna, onion, pepper, pimento, and mayonnaise in a shallow 1½-quart baking dish. Sprinkle with breadcrumbs and cheese. Bake at 350 degrees for 20 minutes or until thoroughly heated.

Margaret Wilson   Yield: 4 servings

Salmon Mousse

2 (1-ounce) envelopes
　unflavored gelatin
½ cup cold water
1 cup boiling water
1 tablespoon vinegar
3 tablespoons lemon juice
1 (15½-ounce) can pink salmon

1 cup mayonnaise
1 cup whipping cream
½ teaspoon salt
1 tablespoon Worcestershire sauce
1 medium onion, grated
2 cups celery or cucumber diced

Soak gelatin in cold water. Then dissolve in hot water. Add vinegar and lemon juice. Place in refrigerator to thicken. Flake salmon very finely and combine with mayonnaise and whipped cream. Add remaining ingredients and fold into the thickened gelatin. Pour into a 2-quart mold or individual molds. Garnish with thin sliced cucumbers.

Note: Best made a day ahead.

Virginia Moseley   Yield: 8 to 12 servings

Salmon Pie

3 hard cooked eggs
1 (9-inch) pie shell, unbaked
1 (15½-ounce) can pink salmon
2 eggs, beaten

¼ cup butter, melted
2 teaspoons chopped parsley
¼ teaspoon salt

Slice eggs into bottom of pie shell. Set aside. Flake salmon in mixing bowl; add eggs, butter, parsley, and salt. Pour salmon mixture over sliced eggs. Bake at 425 degrees for 20 to 25 minutes.

Sauce:
1 medium cucumber
1 teaspoon onion
½ cup mayonnaise
2 teaspoons vinegar

½ cup sour cream
2 teaspoons parsley flakes
Salt to taste
Pepper to taste

Grate cucumber and onion together. Press into strainer to remove juice. Keep pulp; add remaining ingredients and mix well. Serve sauce over slice of salmon pie.

Elsie Randall   Yield: 4 to 6 servings

Salmon Loaf

1 (15½-ounce) can salmon
½ cup self-rising corn meal
¼ cup crushed cracker crumbs
2 eggs, beaten

2 tablespoons butter, melted
1 cup buttermilk
Salt to taste
Pepper to taste

Drain salmon, flake, and remove bones. Mix all ingredients thoroughly. Pour into a greased 1½-quart casserole dish. Bake at 400 degrees for 30 minutes or until set and light brown on top.

Millie Thomas

Yield: 4 servings

"Poor Man's" Lobster

1 (3-ounce) bag crab boil
1 lemon, halved and squeezed
1 large onion, quartered
1 bay leaf

1 teaspoon salt
½ cup vinegar
Lemon pepper to taste
2 to 3 pounds fish fillets

Fill Dutch oven ¾ full with water and bring to a boil. Add crab boil, lemon, onion, bay leaf, salt, vinegar, and lemon pepper; boil until liquid is reduced by half. Remove bag of crab boil. Add fillets and boil 8 to 10 minutes. Let fish stand in water about 10 more minutes. Drain. Serve fish with lemon butter or cocktail sauce.

Patty Sexton

Yield: 4 servings

Flounder Meuniere

4 (4-ounce) fish fillets
½ cup milk or cream
½ cup flour
Salt to taste
Pepper to taste

½ cup butter, DO
    NOT SUBSTITUTE
Juice of ½ lemon
1 tablespoon chopped parsley

Dry fish with a paper towel. Dip the fillets into milk. Mix flour, salt, pepper, and roll fillets gently into flour mixture. Melt butter in skillet and brown fillets very rapidly. Place fillets on a serving platter. Pour remaining butter and lemon juice over fillets and sprinkle with chopped parsley.

Sonia Martin

Yield: 4 servings

Fish Florentine

1 large onion, thinly sliced
1 tablespoon margarine
12 to 16 ounces frozen or fresh
   flounder or grouper fillets
1/8 teaspoon pepper
1 tablespoon lemon juice
1 (10-ounce) package frozen
   chopped spinach, thawed

1 (3-ounce) package cream cheese,
   softened
2 tablespoons milk
1 cup shredded Cheddar, Swiss, or
   Muenster cheese

Preheat oven to 350 degrees. Sauté onion rings in margarine and arrange slices on bottom of greased 6x10-inch baking dish. Pat fish dry with paper towel. Sprinkle with pepper and lemon juice. Place fish on onion slices. Mix together the spinach, cream cheese, and milk. Spread over fish and sprinkle with cheese. Bake 35 minutes.

Terry Hunter   Yield: 4 to 6 servings

Delicious Shrimp Batter

1 cup flour
1 1/2 teaspoons baking powder
1 teaspoon salt
2/3 cup water

2 tablespoons lemon juice
2 tablespoons vegetable oil
1 egg, beaten

Mix all ingredients together in a half gallon container with a cover. Add raw, peeled, and deveined shrimp and soak for at least 1 hour before cooking.

Ginger Wilson   Yield: 6 to 8 servings

Catfish in Beer Batter

1 cup beer	Salt to taste
2 cups flour	2 egg whites, beaten until stiff
1 to 2 tablespoons vegetable oil	12 catfish fillets

Let beer stand open for 2 hours. Mix all ingredients folding in egg whites last. Coat fillets and fry.

Note: Very light batter.

Fran Pearce   Yield: 6 to 8 servings

Pineapple Glaze for Ham

½ cup crushed pineapple, drained	1 teaspoon flour
¾ cup brown sugar	

Mix all ingredients and spoon over ham the last 30 minutes of baking time.

Gloria Sims Crump   Yield: 1¼ cups

Jamie's Mustard Sauce

1 cup vinegar	3 eggs
1 cup dry mustard	1 cup sugar

Mix vinegar and mustard together and allow to soak. Add remaining ingredients. Cook in double boiler until thick. Refrigerate.

Gloria Sims Crump   Yield: 2 cups

Pineapple Sauce

²/₃ cup sugar
1 tablespoon flour
½ teaspoon dry mustard

1 cup pineapple juice
1 egg, lightly beaten

Moisten dry ingredients with a small amount of pineapple juice. To this mixture, add egg and remaining juice. Cook until thickened, about 10 minutes. Serve over mixture of fresh or canned fruit.

Peggy Williamson   Yield: 1½ cups

Mama vonSeeberg's Sauce

1 (16-ounce) can tomatoes
1 medium onion, chopped
¾ cup sugar
½ cup vinegar

1 medium bell pepper, chopped
8 to 10 whole cloves
Salt to taste

Mix ingredients together and cook until tender. Refrigerate. Serve on vegetables.

Note: This is especially good on black-eyed peas and can be served either hot or cold.

Lois Sanford   Yield: 2½ cups

Beef Teriyaki Marinade

1 cup soy sauce
¼ cup sugar
1 tablespoon chopped onion
1¼ teaspoons ginger

4 bay leaves, crushed
4 cloves garlic, crushed
1 (6-ounce) can pineapple juice

Combine all ingredients. Marinate meat 4 to 6 hours or overnight.

Note: Juice drained from a can of pineapple slices or chunks may be used instead of can of pineapple juice.

Vickie Baldwin   Yield: 2 cups

Southern Flavor Marinade and Seasoning

Southern Flavor can be used on the following meats. It will enhance the taste of any meat. The more you use the better the taste. Tenderness of the meat will be increased. For a delicious charcoal flavor, use generously!

Beef or Venison:
4 pounds beef or venison roast
4 tablespoons Southern Flavor
   Seasoning

Baste roast with seasoning and cook in usual manner or for best results cook in crockpot overnight. Roast will have a delicious flavor and will be extremely tender.

Yield: 8 to 10 servings

Ground Beef:
2 pounds ground beef
2 tablespoons Southern Flavor
   Seasoning

Sprinkle 2 tablespoons of seasoning into beef and work into meat. Allow to marinate for 10 minutes. Form into 4 to 6 patties and cook on a grill, in oven, or skillet.

Yield: 4 to 6 servings

Pork Chops:
8 pork chops
2 tablespoons Southern Flavor
   Seasoning

Cover each chop on both sides with Southern Flavor and allow to marinate for 10 minutes. Cook on grill or stove to preferred doneness.

Note: Southern Flavor may be ordered with form in back of cookbook.

Leonard Ingram
Fred McCormick

Yield: 4 to 6 servings

Meat Marinade Sauce

1 teaspoon garlic powder
1 cup vegetable oil
½ cup vinegar
1 teaspoon salt
½ teaspoon pepper

2 teaspoons dry mustard
2 teaspoons Worcestershire sauce
Tabasco to taste
1 (14-ounce) can pineapple
    chunks with juice

Combine ingredients. Cover meat with marinade. Marinate for at least 4 hours, turning occasionally. Good for venison and beef kabobs.

Cheryl Watts   Yield: 2 cups

Marinade for Chicken or Beef

1 cup vegetable oil
⅓ cup lemon juice
2 tablespoons soy sauce
½ teaspoon garlic powder
2 tablespoons Worcestershire
    sauce

1 teaspoon oregano
1 teaspoon monosodium
    glutamate
½ teaspoon salt
½ teaspoon pepper

Mix all ingredients together. Cover meat with marinade and bake.

Gloria Sims Crump   Yield: 1½ cups

Barbecue Sauce

1 cup butter
1 cup vinegar
2 cups catsup
4 tablespoons Worcestershire
    sauce

1 tablespoon Tabasco
1 tablespoon salt
3 tablespoons mustard
Dash red pepper
Juice of 1 lemon

Melt butter and add vinegar. Add remaining ingredients. Stir well. Bring to a boil and let simmer a few minutes.

Juanita Brown   Yield: 3½ to 4 cups

Steak Sauce Alano

½ cup margarine
Juice of 2 lemons
Salt to taste

Granulated garlic to taste
Dash of Worcestershire sauce

Melt margarine. Add other ingredients.

Alan Hicks
  Class of 1972

Yield: 1 cup

Johnnie's Barbecue Sauce

1 large onion, chopped
½ cup vegetable oil
1 cup catsup
¾ cup water
⅓ cup lemon juice
3 tablespoons Worcestershire
  sauce

1 tablespoon mustard
2 teaspoons black pepper
⅓ cup vinegar
3 tablespoons brown sugar
2 teaspoons salt

Cook onion in oil until transparent. Add remaining ingredients. Simmer for 15 minutes.

Johnnie Newsome

Yield: 1 quart

Original "Twix and Tween" Barbecue Sauce

2 cups catsup
1 cup dill pickle juice
¾ cup mustard
3 tablespoons sugar
Pinch of garlic salt

1 teaspoon salt
1 teaspoon lemon juice
3 tablespoons Louisiana hot sauce
1 teaspoon paprika
2 teaspoons Worcestershire sauce

Mix all ingredients well in saucepan, and let come to a boil. Remove from heat and cool. Use with barbecued pork or beef.

Tim Wood

Yield: 3 cups

Gourmet Hamburger Sauce

1½ tablespoons mayonnaise
1 tablespoon catsup
1 tablespoon mustard
1 tablespoon horseradish

1 teaspoon gin
1 teaspoon vermouth
1 tablespoon light corn syrup
1 tablespoon sweet pickle relish

Mix all ingredients and spread on hamburgers.

Kitty Mueller   Yield: sauce for 4 hamburgers

Bill's Barbecued Catfish Sauce

2 pounds margarine
1 pint lemon juice
1 (6½-ounce) jar Durkees sauce
2 tablespoons salt

1 tablespoon Worcestershire
  sauce
1 tablespoon horseradish
Tabasco to taste

Simmer above ingredients for 10 minutes. Dip the catfish in oil, then salt the cavity of the fish. Spray two grills with a non-stick spray so the fish will not stick. Place the catfish between the grills and clamp together so it will be easy to turn. Cook over charcoal for about 1 hour until catfish are golden brown and crispy. Baste with sauce while cooking.

Bill Kyser   Yield: 1½ quarts

Crab Cocktail Sauce

2 cups mayonnaise
1 cup chili sauce
1 tablespoon Worcestershire sauce

1 teaspoon steak sauce
½ teaspoon anchovy sauce
3 dashes Tabasco

Mix all ingredients together and pour over crab meat. Serve very cold!

Note: This recipe is from the Old Pickwick Cafe, Montgomery, Alabama.

Sarah James   Yield: 3 cups

Fresh Tartar Sauce

½ cup mayonnaise or salad
   dressing

¼ cup chopped sweet pickles
Few drops red-pepper seasonings

Combine all ingredients in a small bowl. Cover and chill at least 1 hour to blend flavors.

Gloria Sims Crump   Yield: ¾ cup

White Sauce

2 tablespoons butter
½ teaspoon salt

2 tablespoons flour
1 cup milk

Melt butter in a saucepan. Add salt and flour; mix well making a smooth paste. Add milk slowly stirring constantly. Cook until thick, stirring to prevent lumping.

Note: To increase thickness, increase amounts of butter and flour by 1 tablespoon each.

Smyly Kirkpatrick   Yield: 1 cup

Hollandaise Sauce

4 egg yolks
2 tablespoons lemon juice

1 cup butter, melted
¼ teaspoon salt

In top of double boiler, beat egg yolks and stir in lemon juice. Cook very slowly over low heat, never allowing water in bottom pan to come to a boil. Add butter, a little at a time. Stir constantly with a wooden spoon. Add salt. Continue cooking slowly until thickened.

Cookbook Committee   Yield: 1 cup

Béarnaise Sauce

1 cup Hollandaise sauce   **¹⁄₂ teaspoon parsley**
¹⁄₈ teaspoon chives   **¹⁄₈ teaspoon dry tarragon leaves**

Combine all ingredients and blend well. Refrigerate.

Note: Recipe for Hollandaise sauce fround in Sauce section.

Cookbook Committee   Yield: 1 cup

Vegetables
And Fruits

Artichoke Rice

1 (8-ounce) package chicken
   flavored Rice-a-Roni
2 (6-ounce) jars marinated
   artichoke hearts
4 green onions, chopped

½ bell pepper, chopped
12 small stuffed olives, sliced
¾ teaspoon curry powder
⅓ cup mayonnaise

Cook rice as directed; cool. Drain artichokes, reserve liquid from one jar, and slice. Combine artichoke liquid with onions, pepper, olives, curry powder, and mayonnaise; mix lightly with rice. Serve at room temperature.

Note: Good with any meat, especially roast.

Mary McDavid
Yield: 4 to 6 servings

Asparagus Casserole

1 (10¾-ounce) can cream of
   mushroom soup
2 (15-ounce) cans asparagus
3 hard cooked eggs

1 (4-ounce) jar diced pimento
1 cup grated cheese
1 cup breadcrumbs
½ cup butter or margarine, melted

Pour mushroom soup into 2-quart casserole. Layer asparagus, eggs, pimento, and cheese. Top with breadcrumbs and pour butter on top. Bake at 300 degrees for 45 to 50 minutes.

Variation: 1 (17-ounce) can English peas, drained, and 1 (4-ounce) can sliced mushrooms, drained may be added.

Sara Adams
Cullie Smith
  Class of 1981
Yield: 6 to 8 servings

Broccoli and Rice Casserole

1 cup uncooked rice
¾ cup chopped onion
¾ cup chopped pepper
1 cup chopped celery
4 tablespoons butter or margarine
2 (10-ounce) packages frozen
   chopped broccoli
1 (8-ounce) jar pasteurized cheese
   spread

1 (10¾-ounce) can cream of
   mushroom soup
1 (10½-ounce) can cream of
   chicken soup
1 (4-ounce) can chopped
   mushrooms

Cook rice according to package directions. Sauté onion, pepper, and celery in butter. Cook broccoli; drain and combine with cheese spread, sautéed vegetables, undiluted soups, and mushrooms. Fold in cooked rice and pour into a greased 3-quart casserole. Bake at 350 degrees for 30 minutes or until bubbly.

Anna Speir
Cullie Smith
   Class of 1981

Yield: 10 servings

Broccoli-Corn Casserole

2 (10-ounce) packages frozen
   chopped broccoli, thawed,
   drained
2 (17-ounce) cans cream style corn

1 egg, beaten
1 cup breadcrumbs or cracker
   crumbs
1 cup grated Cheddar cheese

Combine broccoli, corn, and egg. Place in a 3-quart casserole dish. Top with breadcrumbs. Bake uncovered at 350 degrees for 45 minutes. Sprinkle cheese on top. Bake 15 minutes longer or until cheese melts.

Julie McCormick Yelverton
   Class of 1974

Yield: 6 to 8 servings

Broccoli Casserole

2 (10-ounce) packages broccoli
spears
1 (8-ounce) can sliced water
chestnuts

1 (1³⁄₈-ounce) envelope dry onion
soup mix
½ cup butter, melted
½ cup chopped pecans

Cook broccoli according to package directions. Cut into bite-size pieces. Place broccoli in a 1½-quart casserole. Top with water chestnuts and onion soup mix. Pour butter over and sprinkle with chopped pecans. Bake at 325 degrees for 20 minutes or until heated thoroughly.

Martha Jackson   Yield: 4 to 6 servings

Red Beans and Rice

1 cup chopped onion
½ cup chopped bell pepper
½ cup thinly sliced celery
2 cloves garlic
2 tablespoons butter
2 (16-ounce) cans red kidney
beans

Salt to taste
Pepper to taste
Thyme to taste
2 bay leaves
1 link sausage, sliced
Ham, cut in chunks, optional
Cooked rice

Brown onion, pepper, celery, and garlic in butter. Add beans, seasonings, and meat. Simmer for 1 hour. Serve over hot rice.

Alston Noah   Yield: 4 servings
  Class of 1979

Baked Beans

1 pound ground beef
1 medium onion, chopped
1 (28-ounce) can pork and beans
1 tablespoon brown sugar

1 (8-ounce) can tomato sauce
1 teaspoon dry mustard
3 slices bacon, cut in thirds

Brown beef and onion together. Drain. Combine with beans, sugar, tomato sauce, mustard, and bacon. Pour into a slow cooker. Cook on low for 6 to 8 hours or on high for 3 to 4 hours.

Barbara Rosser   Yield: 4 to 6 servings

Three Bean Casserole

1 (16-ounce) can butterbeans
1 (16-ounce) can French style
  green beans
1 (16-ounce) can English peas

1 teaspoon salt
¼ teaspoon pepper
4 tablespoons oil

Combine all ingredients in a large saucepan and cook a few minutes to season. Drain.

Sauce:

1 cup mayonnaise
2 hard cooked eggs, chopped
1 tablespoon mustard
1 tablespoon Worcestershire sauce
1 medium onion, grated

1 tablespoon salad dressing
Dash of Tabasco sauce
Cracker crumbs
1 (3-ounce) can French fried
  onion rings

Mix all ingredients together except cracker crumbs and onion rings. In 9x13-inch casserole alternate layers of vegetables and sauce, ending with sauce. Bake at 350 degrees for 30 minutes until sauce bubbles. Cover with cracker crumbs and bake until brown. Top with onion rings.

Faye Carter   Yield: 8 to 10 servings

Green Bean Casserole

3 (16-ounce) cans French style
  green beans, drained
1 (8-ounce) can sliced water
  chestnuts, drained
1 (16-ounce) can bean sprouts,
  drained
1 medium onion, chopped

2 (10¾-ounce) cans cream of
  mushroom soup
2 cups grated sharp American
  cheese
Salt to taste
1 (3-ounce) can fried onion rings

In a 3-quart casserole, layer half the green beans, water chestnuts, bean sprouts, and onion. Cover with half the mushroom soup. Sprinkle half the cheese and salt to taste. Repeat layering. Bake at 350 degrees for about 30 minutes or until bubbly hot. Top with onion rings 5 minutes before removing from oven.

Mae Bruner Morgan   Yield: 10 to 12 servings

Brussels Sprouts Oriental

2 pounds brussels sprouts
Salt to taste
1 teaspoon soy sauce
½ teaspoon seasoned salt

1 tablespoon butter
1 (5-ounce) can water chestnuts, sliced

Combine all ingredients in small amount of water in saucepan. Simmer until sprouts are tender.

Joy Beers

Yield: 6 servings

Corn Oysters

2 eggs, separated
1 (16-ounce) can whole kernel corn, drained
½ teaspoon Worcestershire sauce

½ teaspoon salt
¼ teaspoon pepper
¼ cup flour
¼ teaspoon baking powder

Beat egg whites until stiff. Set aside. Beat yolks slightly; add corn, Worcestershire sauce, salt, and pepper. Stir in flour and baking powder. Fold in egg whites. Drop by teaspoon into hot oil until golden brown. Drain on paper towel.

Katherine Sandifer

Yield: 1 dozen

Spicy Corn-On-The-Cob

¼ cup butter or margarine, melted
1 teaspoon chili powder
¼ teaspoon garlic salt

1 to 2 quarts water
1 teaspoon sugar
4 ears fresh corn

Combine butter, chili powder, and garlic salt. Mix well and set aside. Combine water and sugar in Dutch oven and bring to a boil. Add corn, cover, reduce heat, and simmer 8 to 10 minutes. Drain and brush with butter mixture.

Nicky Stinson
  Class of 1976

Yield: 4 servings

Baked Corn with Sour Cream

6 strips bacon
2 tablespoons chopped onion
2 tablespoons butter
2 tablespoons flour
2 teaspoons salt

1 cup sour cream
2 (12-ounce) cans shoe peg corn
1 tablespoon chopped parsley,
  optional

Cook and crumble bacon or substitute bacon bits. Cook onion in butter; blend in flour and salt. Add sour cream gradually, stirring to keep smooth. Bring to a boil and add corn. Cook until heated thoroughly. Fold in half of bacon and pour into a 9x13-inch greased baking dish. Garnish with parsley and remaining bacon. Bake at 350 degrees for 30 minutes or until bubbly.

Meg Smith   Yield: 8 servings

Corn Custard Casserole

2 cups cream corn
2 eggs, well beaten
½ cup cracker crumbs
¼ cup shredded carrots
¼ cup milk
¼ cup chopped green pepper
1 tablespoon chopped celery

1 tablespoon finely chopped onion
4 drops Tabasco
¼ teaspoon pepper
½ teaspoon salt
1 teaspoon sugar
½ cup grated cheese
Paprika, optional

Preheat oven to 350 degrees. Combine all ingredients except cheese. Pour into a well greased 2-quart casserole. Bake uncovered for 30 minutes. Add cheese and return to oven for 5 minutes. Sprinkle with paprika.

Smyly Kirkpatrick   Yield: 4 to 6 servings

Shoe Peg Corn Casserole

1 cup sour cream
1 (10¾-ounce) can cream of
  celery soup
1 (15½-ounce) can French style
  green beans, drained
1 (12-ounce) can shoe peg corn,
  drained

½ cup chopped onion
¼ cup chopped green pepper
½ cup chopped celery
½ cup grated sharp cheese
1 sleeve Ritz crackers
¼ cup margarine, melted

Combine all ingredients, except crackers and butter. Pour into a 9x13-inch greased casserole dish. Crush crackers and mix with butter. Pour over casserole. Bake at 350 degrees for 45 minutes.

Note: Can be made in advance and refrigerated until ready to bake and serve.

Betty Schroeder   Yield: 6 to 8 servings

Golden Corn Casserole

2 (16-ounce) cans whole kernel
  corn or 6 ears fresh corn
⅓ cup butter or margarine
¼ cup sugar
1 tablespoon flour

½ teaspoon salt
½ cup evaporated milk
2 eggs, well beaten
2 tablespoons chopped parsley
1½ teaspoons baking powder

With a sharp knife, cut corn from ears or drain canned corn. Set aside. Melt butter in medium size saucepan. Add sugar, mix well. Stir in flour and salt until well blended. Remove from heat. Gradually add milk and stir in eggs, blending well. Add parsley and baking powder, mixing quickly. Fold in corn. Pour into a lightly buttered 1-quart casserole. Bake at 350 degrees for 35 to 40 minutes.

Gayle Willis   Yield: 6 to 8 servings

Creamy Shoe Peg Corn

3 tablespoons margarine
3 tablespoons flour
1 cup whipping cream

2 (12-ounce) cans shoe peg corn,
DO NOT DRAIN

Mix margarine and flour in saucepan, melting and blending completely. Add cream slowly until mixture is bubbly. Stir constantly to prevent sticking. Add corn. Pour into a greased 2-quart casserole. Bake at 350 degrees for 45 minutes.

Ada Callen Keys

Yield: 6 to 8 servings

Barbecue Corn

2 (16-ounce) cans whole kernel
  corn
1 cup barbecue sauce
⅓ cup catsup

½ cup water
1 (⅜-ounce) envelope dry onion
  soup mix
2 strips bacon

Mix all ingredients together, except bacon. Pour into a 2-quart casserole and place bacon on top. Bake at 350 degrees for 1 hour.

Carol Walton
  Class of 1981

Yield: 4 to 6 servings

Cornbread Casserole

1 egg
¼ cup self-rising flour
2 tablespoons sugar
1 (16-ounce) can cream-style corn
1 (12-ounce) can whole kernel
  corn

Salt to taste
Pepper to taste
1 (8½-ounce) box cornbread mix

Preheat oven to 350 degrees. Mix egg, flour, sugar, corn, salt, and pepper until smooth. Pour into an 8-inch greased casserole dish. Prepare cornbread mix according to the directions on the box. Spread over top of corn mixture and bake 30 minutes or until cornbread is done.

Terri Till
  Class of 1981

Yield: 6 to 8 servings

Eggplant Creole

1 large eggplant
1 onion, sliced
1 bell pepper, sliced
3 ribs celery, chopped
1 (16-ounce) can tomatoes
1 teaspoon salt

$1/4$ teaspoon black pepper
$1/4$ teaspoon red pepper
3 tablespoons olive oil
2 tablespoons vinegar
$2/3$ cup grated cheese

Rinse eggplant, peel, and slice almost all the way through (accordian style). Place eggplant in a 2-quart saucepan. Place onion and bell pepper slices between eggplant slices. Combine celery, tomatoes, salt, peppers, oil, and vinegar. Pour over eggplant and cook covered over medium heat until eggplant is tender (about 20 minutes). Place in serving dish and sprinkle with cheese.

Cheryl Watts   Yield: 6 to 8 servings

Fire and Ice Tomatoes

6 large tomatoes, sliced
1 large bell pepper, sliced
1 large onion, sliced
$3/4$ cup vinegar

2 teaspoons salt
$4^1/2$ teaspoons sugar
$1/4$ cup water
$1/4$ to $1/2$ teaspoon red pepper

Combine vegetables in a bowl. Boil vinegar, salt, sugar, water, and red pepper for 1 minute. Pour over vegetables and chill 24 hours.

Anna Speir   Yield: 6 to 8 servings

Scalloped Cheese Tomatoes

1 (16-ounce) can whole tomatoes
1 tablespoon butter
1 tablespoon bacon grease
$1/2$ teaspoon seasoned salt
$1/4$ teaspoon garlic salt

2 teaspoons sugar
1 cup finely chopped onion
$3/4$ cup grated cheese
$1/4$ teaspoon oregano
$1/2$ cup herb stuffing

Slice tomatoes. Add butter, grease, salts, and sugar. Layer tomatoes in a dish, cover with onions, then a layer of cheese. Repeat layers; ending with cheese. Sprinkle with oregano. Top with stuffing mix. Bake at 350 degrees for 30 minutes.

Ruth Moore   Yield: 4 to 6 servings

Squash Patties

1 cup flour
1 teaspoon sugar
½ teaspoon salt
¾ cup milk
1 egg

¼ cup vegetable oil
3 cups grated yellow squash
1 medium onion, chopped
2 to 3 teaspoons red pepper

Combine flour, sugar, salt, milk, egg, and oil. Beat with a mixer. Fold in squash, onion, and pepper. Drop by tablespoon into hot grease and fry. Turn once. Drain on paper towel.

Ellen Traylor   Yield: 2 to 2½ dozen

Baked Cheese Squash

2½ cups cooked squash
2 tablespoons butter, melted
2 eggs, beaten
Salt to taste

Pepper to taste
1 cup buttered breadcrumbs
½ cup grated cheese

Combine squash with butter, eggs, salt, and pepper. In a greased 2-quart casserole arrange alternate layers of squash mixture with breadcrumbs and cheese. Bake at 350 degrees for 20 minutes. Sprinkle top with grated cheese before serving.

Helen Neighbors   Yield: 4 to 6 servings

Squash Casserole

1 pound yellow squash, sliced
1 medium onion, chopped
½ teaspoon salt
1 teaspoon sugar
14 crackers, crushed

1 cup grated cheese
2 eggs, beaten
1 cup milk
½ cup butter

Cook squash and onion with salt. Drain. Add remaining ingredients, reserving enough cracker crumbs for top. Pour into a well greased 1½-quart casserole and set in a pan of water. Bake at 400 degrees for 1 hour or until set.

Peggy Striplin   Yield: 8 servings

179

Microwave Stuffed Zucchini

2 medium zucchini	½ teaspoon salt
½ cup cooked rice	¼ teaspoon basil
¼ cup chopped onion	1 small tomato, peeled, seeded,
¼ cup chopped green pepper	and chopped

Cut zucchini in half lengthwise, scrape out pulp leaving a ¼-inch shell. Chop pulp. Combine with rice, onion, green pepper, salt, and basil. Place zucchini shells into 8x8-inch baking dish. Mound ¼ of vegetable mixture into each shell. Top with tomato. Cover with waxed paper. Microwave on HIGH 5 to 7 minutes or until shells are tender; rotating dish half a turn after 3 minutes.

Faye W. Bailey   Yield: 4 servings

Baked Vidalia Onions

4 Vidalia onions	Salt to taste
Butter, cut into pieces	Pepper to taste

Peel onions and slightly hollow out top of each. Place in baking dish; cover with plastic wrap. Microwave on HIGH about 3 minutes. Place pat of butter on top of each onion; season with salt and pepper. Microwave on HIGH until tender. Timing will depend on number and size of onions.

Variation: Top each onion with 1 slice pasteurized processed cheese and garlic powder. Microwave on HIGH 1 to 3 minutes or until melted.

Faye W. Bailey   Yield: 4 servings

French Fried Onion Rings

1½ cups flour	3 large yellow onions
1½ cups beer	

Thoroughly blend flour and beer. Cover and allow to sit at room temperature approximately 3 hours. Slice onions and separate into rings. Coat with beer batter and deep fat fry until golden brown. Drain on brown paper bag on cookie sheet and place in a 200 degree oven. This will "hold" until all rings are fried.

Millie Thomas   Yield: 6 to 8 servings

Turnip Greens

1 bunch fresh turnip greens
4 cups water
1 thick slice bacon

1½ teaspoons salt
½ teaspoon sugar, optional

Wash and clean greens at least twice to remove stems and grit. In a large pot boil water with bacon and salt. Add greens, reduce heat, cover and cook slowly at least 1 hour. Stir occasionally and add more water if necessary to make good pot likker. Serve with hot cornbread.

Cheryl Watts   Yield: 4 servings

English Pea Casserole

1 onion, chopped
1 bell pepper, chopped
½ cup melted margarine
1 (17-ounce) can English peas,
  drained

1 (10¾-ounce) can cream of
  mushroom soup
1 sleeve Ritz crackers, crushed

Sauté onion and bell pepper in ¼ cup margarine until tender. Mix peas, soup, pepper, and onion; pour into a 2-quart casserole. Cover with cracker crumbs. Pour remaining ¼ cup margarine on top. Bake at 350 degrees for 30 minutes or until bubbly.

Connie Pugh   Yield: 4 to 6 servings

Fresh or Frozen Black-Eyed Peas

2 cups black-eyed peas
2 cups water
½ slice bacon

1 teaspoon salt
½ cup chopped onion, optional

Wash and clean peas. In a 2-quart saucepan, boil water with bacon and salt. Add peas. Bring to a second boil. Reduce heat to medium, cover and cook 45 to 60 minutes. Stir occasionally and add more water if needed to keep peas from burning.

Cheryl Watts   Yield: 6 servings

Carrot Casserole

2 pounds carrots, sliced ¼-inch
thick
1 small onion, minced
¼ cup margarine
¼ cup flour
¼ teaspoon dry mustard
1 teaspoon salt

Pepper to taste
¼ teaspoon celery salt
1½ cups milk
¼ to ½ pound sharp Cheddar
cheese, grated
1½ cups buttered breadcrumbs

Cook carrots in salty water until almost tender; drain. Sauté onion in margarine. Mix flour, mustard, salt, pepper, celery salt, and milk; blend into onion mixture. Layer cooked carrots and cheese in a greased 2½ to 3-quart casserole dish. Pour sauce over carrots. Top with buttered breadcrumbs. Bake at 350 degrees for 35 to 45 minutes.

Note: Freezes beautifully. Take out of freezer the day before and refrigerate to thaw.

Sherie Sherrer   Yield: 8 servings

Baked Creamed Cabbage

1 medium head cabbage
½ cup boiling salted water
3 tablespoons butter
3 tablespoons flour

½ teaspoon salt
1½ cups milk
¼ cup breadcrumbs

Shred cabbage and cook 9 minutes in boiling salted water. Remove cabbage, drain well, and place in a buttered 1½-quart casserole. Melt butter in pan, stir in flour and salt until smooth. Add milk gradually. Continue stirring until thick. Pour sauce over cabbage and sprinkle breadcrumbs over top. Bake at 325 degrees for 15 minutes or until crumbs are browned.

Joy Beers   Yield: 4 to 6 servings

Sautéed Mushrooms

1½ cartons fresh mushrooms
¼ cup butter

3 tablespoons lemon juice
2½ tablespoons white wine

Sauté mushrooms in butter. As they begin to brown add lemon juice. Continue to sauté until lightly browned. Add white wine. Remove from heat and serve.

Vickie Baldwin

Yield: 4 to 6 servings

Sloppy Potato Skins

1 (16-ounce) package frozen
  potato wedges
Salt to taste
1 small onion, sliced, optional
1 (³⁄₈-ounce) package ranch
  dressing mix

1 cup Hellmann's Mayonnaise
1 cup buttermilk
1 (8-ounce) package pasteurized
  processed cheese, grated

Deep fry wedges until done; drain on paper towels and add salt. Stir fry onion, if desired; set aside. Place potatoes in a 8x10-inch baking dish. Combine dressing mix, mayonnaise, and buttermilk; pour over potatoes. Bake at 350 degrees for 4 to 6 minutes. Remove from oven; top with cheese and onion, if desired. Return to oven to melt cheese. Serve immediately.

Faye W. Bailey

Yield: 4 servings

Spinach Casserole

3 (10-ounce) packages frozen
chopped spinach
1 cup sour cream

1 (³/₈-ounce) envelope onion
soup mix

Cook spinach according to the package directions and drain. Add sour cream and onion soup mix. Bake at 350 degrees for 30 minutes.

Meg Smith   Yield: 8 servings

Parmesan Hominy

2 slices bacon
2 tablespoons chopped onion
2 tablespoons chopped green
pepper

1 (20-ounce) can hominy, drained
Seasoned salt to taste
Parmesan cheese

Dice bacon and fry until transparent. Add onion and pepper. Fry until tender. Add drained hominy and season to taste with seasoned salt. Heat thoroughly. Serve topped with Parmesan cheese.

Margaret Anne Beers   Yield: 3 to 4 servings

Golden Parmesan Potatoes

¼ cup flour
¼ cup grated Parmesan cheese
¾ teaspoon salt
⅛ teaspoon pepper
6 large potatoes, peeled and cut
into eighths

⅓ cup butter, melted
2 tablespoons chopped parsley,
optional

Combine flour, cheese, salt, and pepper in a bag. Moisten potatoes with water, shaking off excess. Shake a few potatoes at a time in bag, coating well. Pour butter into a 9x13-inch casserole dish. Place potatoes in dish in a single layer. Bake at 375 degrees for 1 hour. Turn once during baking. Sprinkle with parsley.

Carolyn Weissinger   Yield: 6 to 8 servings

Potato Casserole

1 (2-pound) bag frozen hash
  browns
1 (10½-ounce) can cream of
  chicken soup
½ cup chopped onion
2 (8-ounce) cartons sour cream

1 teaspoon salt
½ teaspoon pepper
½ cup margarine, melted
1 (8-ounce) package sharp cheese,
  grated
Crushed corn flakes

Mix all ingredients together except corn flakes. Pour into a 9x13-inch casserole and top with crushed corn flakes. Bake uncovered at 300 degrees for 1 hour.

Kathy Jones
Ada Callen Keys

Yield: 12 servings

Sow's Ears and Silver Purses

6 large baking potatoes
½ cup margarine or butter
Milk
1 (8-ounce) package shredded
  Cheddar cheese

½ pound fried and crumbled
  bacon, divided

Wrap potatoes in heavy aluminum foil and bake until done. Cool slightly. Split in half and scrape insides into medium size bowl. Leave potato shells in their "silver purses". Fold in cheese and bacon, reserving enough bacon to sprinkle on top. Spoon into shells and bake at 350 degrees for 20 to 25 minutes or until heated thoroughly.

Note: The stuffed potatoes may be wrapped in foil and frozen for up to 3 months.

Terry Hunter

Yield: 12 servings

Microwave Scalloped Potatoes

4 medium potatoes, peeled	¼ cup chopped onion
1 tablespoon flour	1½ cups milk
1 teaspoon salt	¼ cup margarine

Slice potatoes. Arrange in a 3-quart casserole dish. Sprinkle with flour, salt, and onion. Pour milk over and dot with margarine. Cover with plastic wrap. Microwave on HIGH for 10 minutes. Stir, recover, and continue cooking for 10 minutes more or until fork tender. Let stand a few minutes before serving.

Jo Ann Medders   Yield: 6 to 8 servings

Refrigerator Mashed Potatoes

5 pounds potatoes	2 teaspoons onion salt
2 (3-ounce) packages cream cheese, softened	¼ teaspoon pepper
1 cup sour cream	2 tablespoons butter

Cook peeled and diced potatoes in salted water until tender; drain and mash smooth. Add cream cheese, sour cream, salt, pepper, and butter; beat until light and fluffy. Cool. Cover and place in refrigerator. May be used anytime within 2 weeks. To use, place desired amount in a greased casserole, dot with butter, and bake at 350 degrees about 30 minutes. Freezes well.

Carolyn Weissinger   Yield: 12 servings

Sweet Potato Pecan Balls

2 to 3 pounds sweet potatoes
1 (8-ounce) can sliced pineapple
4 tablespoons margarine
¼ cup brown sugar

2 tablespoons honey
2 tablespoons pineapple juice
½ cup chopped pecans

Cook, skin, and mash potatoes or use canned. Drain pineapple and reserve juice. Melt margarine in saucepan, stir in brown sugar, honey, and pineapple juice. Cook until sugar is dissolved. Pour into a 9x13-inch casserole dish. Place pineapple slices in the syrup, turning once. Mix ¼ cup pecans with mashed potatoes and form into balls. Place on pineapple slices and sprinkle remaining nuts on top. Bake at 350 degrees for 20 minutes or until thoroughly heated.

Terry Hunter 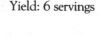 Yield: 6 servings

Senator Russell's Sweet Potatoes

3 cups cooked mashed sweet
   potatoes
1 cup sugar
2 eggs, beaten

1 teaspoon vanilla
½ cup milk
½ cup butter

Mix potatoes, sugar, eggs, vanilla, milk, and butter together and pour into a greased 9x13-inch casserole.

Topping Mix:
⅓ cup butter
1 cup brown sugar

⅓ cup flour
1 cup chopped nuts

Cream butter, sugar, and flour; add nuts. Sprinkle on top of sweet potatoes. Bake at 350 degrees for 30 minutes.

Debbie Gresham
Patricia Murray

Yield: 6 to 8 servings

Vegetable Casserole

1 pound grated pasteurized
  processed cheese
2 hard cooked eggs, chopped
1 cup mayonnaise
2 (16-ounce) cans mixed
  vegetables, drained

1 (16-ounce) can English peas,
  drained
1 cup chopped celery
1 cup finely chopped onion
1 (8-ounce) package cornbread
  dressing with herbs

Freeze cheese before grating. In large mixing bowl combine cheese, eggs, and mayonnaise together. Add mixed vegetables, peas, celery, and onion; blend well. Pour into a 3-quart casserole and top with cornbread dressing. Bake at 325 degrees for 30 to 40 minutes or until bubbly.

Gigi Campbell   Yield: 10 to 12 servings

David's Vegetable Surprise

1 (10-ounce) package frozen
  chopped broccoli
1 (10-ounce) package frozen lima
  beans
1 (10¾-ounce) can cream of
  mushroom soup
1 (1⅜-ounce) envelope dried
  onion soup mix

1 cup sour cream
1 (8-ounce) can sliced water
  chestnuts, drained
½ cup butter, melted
3 cups crispy rice cereal, crushed

Cook vegetables according to directions. Drain. Combine vegetables, soups, sour cream, and chestnuts. Place in a greased 9x13-inch casserole dish. Combine butter and cereal and spoon over casserole. Bake at 350 degrees for 30 minutes.

David Massey, Jr.   Yield: 8 servings

Microwave Vegetable-Rice

1 cup sliced green onions
1 cup shredded carrots
¼ cup margarine

2½ cups chicken broth
1 cup rice
1 teaspoon salt

Cook onions, carrots, and margarine in the chicken broth at 6 minutes on HIGH or until it boils. Add rice and salt to broth and cook 15 to 17 minutes on 50% power or until done. Reheat later on HIGH for 2 minutes.

Note: Delicious with Chicken Cordon Bleu.

Ann Till   Yield: 6 to 8 servings

French Fried Okra

1 pound okra
½ teaspoon salt
1½ cups buttermilk

2 cups self-rising flour
Vegetable oil

Wash okra, and drain well. Remove tip and stem end; cut okra into 1-inch slices. Sprinkle okra with salt; add buttermilk, stirring until well coated. Let stand 15 minutes; drain okra well, and dredge in flour. Deep fry okra in hot oil (375 degrees) until golden brown. Drain on paper towel.

Helen S. Stewart   Yield: 6 servings

Southern Beets

3 tablespoons vinegar
2½ cups cooked sliced beets
¼ teaspoon ground cloves
½ teaspoon salt

¼ cup sugar
1 sliced onion
2 tablespoons butter

Place vinegar, ½ cup beets, cloves, salt, sugar, onion, and butter in blender; cover and blend until smooth. Pour over remaining beets in saucepan. Simmer, stirring frequently, about 20 minutes.

Sherie Sherrer   Yield: 6 servings

Baked Cranberry Casserole

2 cups raw cranberries, washed	¼ cup uncooked oatmeal
3 cups peeled and sliced apples	⅓ cup flour
1 (8¼-ounce) can crushed	1 cup brown sugar
pineapple	1 cup chopped pecans
¾ cup sugar	½ cup margarine, melted

Place cranberries in a 9x13-inch casserole. Top with sliced apples and pineapple. Mix sugar, oatmeal, flour, brown sugar, and pecans; spread over fruit. Pour melted margarine over all. Bake at 350 degrees until brown, about 30 minutes.

Joanne Dillingham   Yield: 10 to 12 servings

Savory Cucumbers

2 cucumbers, unpeeled	⅛ teaspoon pepper
1 teaspoon garlic salt	½ teaspoon celery salt
1 cup sour cream	½ teaspoon onion salt

Slice cucumbers paper thin. Soak for at least one hour in ice water to which garlic salt has been added. Drain cucumbers until thoroughly dry. Combine and mix well the sour cream, pepper, celery salt, and onion salt. Add to cucumbers, toss lightly, and serve.

Gale Bedgood   Yield: 4 servings

Baked Apricots

3 (16-ounce) cans apricot halves	1 cup margarine
1 (16-ounce) box brown sugar	
1½ sleeves round butter crackers, broken	

Drain apricots. Layer a 9x13-inch pan with apricots, brown sugar, crackers, and margarine (cut not melted); then repeat layers. Bake at 300 degrees for 1 hour.

Linda Thompson   Yield: 8 to 10 servings

Curried Fruit

1 (20-ounce) can sliced pineapple
1 (16-ounce) can peach halves
1 (17-ounce) can apricots
1 (16-ounce) can pears

1 teaspoon curry powder
1 cup brown sugar
½ cup cream sherry
½ cup margarine

Drain fruits and layer in a 9x13-inch glass casserole. Mix together curry powder, sugar, and sherry and pour over fruit. Dot with margarine. Bake at 350 degrees for 30 minutes or until bubbly. Serve hot.

Gigi Campbell   Yield: 6 to 8 servings

Hot Fruit Casserole

20 (2½-inch) coconut macaroons
2 bananas
3 (17-ounce) cans mixed fruit, drained
1 (6-ounce) jar cherries, stemless
½ cup butter

1 cup brown sugar
½ cup sherry, NOT COOKING sherry
1 (2-ounce) package slivered almonds

Crumble cookies in bottom of a 9x13-inch baking dish. Slice bananas and place on top of cookies. Layer with mixed fruit and cherries. Melt butter and add sugar; remove from heat, pour in sherry, and stir for one minute. Pour over fruit mixture. Top with almonds. Bake at 350 degrees for 30 to 35 minutes.

Vickie Baldwin   Yield: 8 to 10 servings

Pineapple Casserole

¾ cup margarine
1½ cups sugar
3 eggs, beaten

1 (12-ounce) can chunk pineapple, drained
4 hamburger buns, cubed

Melt margarine; add sugar, eggs, pineapple. Grease a 2-quart casserole; add cubed buns and pour pineapple mixture over buns. Bake at 350 degrees for 45 minutes to 1 hour.

Helen Shivers   Yield: 4 to 6 servings

Hot Pineapple Casserole

2 (15¼-ounce) cans chunk
   pineapple and juice
5 tablespoons flour
1 cup sugar

1 cup grated sharp cheese
¾ sleeve round butter crackers,
   crumbled
½ cup margarine, melted

Lightly grease a 9x13-inch casserole; pour in pineapple and juice. Add flour and sugar. Blend ½ cup cheese, crackers, and melted margarine. Mix together. Add remaining cheese on top. Bake at 350 degrees for 30 minutes.

Christine Moore　　　　　　　　　　　　　　　　　　　　Yield: 8 servings

Spiced Apple Rings

2 large apples, pared, cored, and
   sliced in ½-inch rings
¼ cup red cinnamon candies
¾ cup water

½ cup light corn syrup
2 teaspoons vinegar
¼ teaspoon cinnamon

Place large size 14x20-inch cooking bag in 8x12-inch glass baking dish. Arrange apple rings in single layer in bag. Mix candies, water, corn syrup, vinegar, and cinnamon; pour over apple rings. Close bag with string, make 6 half-inch slits in top near closure. Microwave at HIGH power 12 minutes, turning dish periodically.

Kay Foster　　　　　　　　　　　　　　　　　　　　　Yield: 4 servings

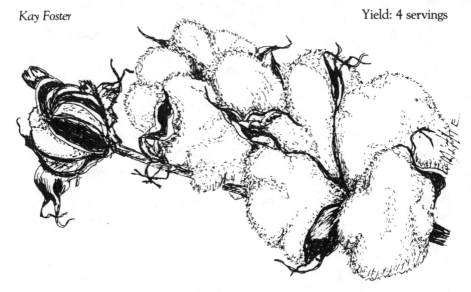

Breads

Specialty of the House Cornbread

1 cup shortening
1 cup self-rising cornmeal
1 tablespoon sugar

1 egg
1 cup buttermilk

Preheat oven to 425 degrees. Melt shortening in a 7-inch iron skillet. In a small mixing bowl add other ingredients. After shortening melts, pour half into cornbread mixture and stir well. Pour cornbread mixture into hot skillet with remaining shortening. Bake for 20 to 25 minutes.

Note: Also makes 1 dozen muffins.

Cheryl Watts   Yield: 6 servings

Mexican Cornbread I

3 cups self-rising cornmeal
3 eggs, beaten
2½ cups milk
½ cup vegetable oil
1 cup cream style corn

¼ cup diced pimento
1 large onion, chopped
½ cup minced jalapeño peppers
1 bell pepper, chopped, optional
1 cup grated Cheddar cheese

Mix all ingredients together and pour into an 11x16-inch greased pan. Bake at 350 to 400 degrees for 45 to 60 minutes.

Note: May be frozen in aluminum foil and reheated.

Jerry Goodwin   Yield: 15 to 18 servings

Mexican Cornbread II

1 cup self-rising flour
1 cup self-rising cornmeal
1 cup grated cheese
½ cup chopped onion
½ cup chopped bell pepper

1 (7½-ounce) jar baby food
   creamed corn
3 eggs
½ cup vegetable oil

Preheat oven to 350 degrees. Mix all ingredients together. Bake for 45 minutes in a 10-inch iron skillet.

Joanne Dillingham   Yield: 8 servings

Cracklin' Bread

2 cups self-rising cornmeal
2 tablespoons flour
2 eggs

1½ cups buttermilk
4 tablespoons bacon drippings
1 cup cracklin's

Preheat oven to 450 degrees. In a mixing bowl, mix cornmeal, flour, eggs, and buttermilk and beat by hand. Melt bacon drippings in a 9-inch square pan, pour into cornmeal mixture, and beat well. Fold in cracklin's, pour mixture into pan, and bake for 30 minutes.

Note: When buying cracklin's be sure and get them with skin trimmed off. This will keep cracklin's from being tough.

Annie Lee Lewis   Yield: 9 servings

Tasty Italian Bread Strips

1 loaf sliced French bread
Softened margarine or butter to
   taste
1 (¼-ounce) can herbal Italian
   seasoning

1 (1½-ounce) can grated Italian
   blend cheese

Lightly toast bread slices. Spread entire top with margarine. Sprinkle with seasoning and cheese. Run under broiler until cheese melts. Remove from oven and cut bread slices into strips.

Adrienne DeRamus   Yield: 5 dozen

Spoon Bread

2⅔ cups milk
⅔ cup cornmeal
1¾ tablespoons butter

¾ teaspoon salt
3 eggs, separated

Warm milk. Slowly pour cornmeal into milk, stirring constantly. Cook and stir until thick. Add butter and salt. Beat and cool. Beat in egg yolks, one at a time. Beat egg whites until stiff and fold into mixture. Pour into a greased 1½-quart casserole. Bake at 375 degrees for 35 to 40 minutes. Serve at once with butter or gravy.

Note: A souffle-like bread served in place of potatoes. Good with ham and green beans or peas.

Cookbook Committee   Yield: 6 servings

Cornbread Dressing

Pan of cornbread	**2 eggs, well beaten**
1 large onion, chopped	**Chicken stock**
6 green onions with tops, chopped	**Salt to taste**
4 ribs celery, chopped	**Pepper to taste**
1 bell pepper, chopped	

Preheat oven to 350 degrees. Bake and cool cornbread. Crumble into very fine mixture. Add onions, celery, bell pepper, and eggs. Mix well. Pour chicken stock over mixture until mixture is thin. Add salt and pepper. Pour into a 9x13-inch casserole dish and bake for 30 to 45 minutes. Do not let dressing get too brown.

Note: The secret of good dressing is to taste and add as you go. One can of chicken broth may be added to stock if needed for a thin bread mixture.

Jerry Goodwin   Yield: 8 to 10 servings

Hush Puppies

3 cups cornmeal	**2 cups buttermilk**
1 cup chopped onions	**2 eggs, well beaten**
½ teaspoon baking soda	**2 teaspoons salt**

Mix all of the above ingredients until well blended. Heat vegetable or peanut oil in a deep fat fryer to 375 degrees. Drop heaping teaspoons of batter into hot grease. Turn hush puppies after one side browns for even browning. Total cooking time between 3 and 4 minutes. Drain on absorbent paper before serving.

Note: Amount of oil will vary according to size of cooker. Use enough oil for hush puppies to float freely.

Fran Pearce   Yield: 6 servings

French Toast

3 eggs
¼ cup milk
Salt to taste
½ teaspoon cinnamon
⅛ teaspoon nutmeg
8 slices French bread, or firm
  textured bread

2 tablespoons butter
1 tablespoon vegetable oil
4 tablespoons powdered sugar
Maple syrup

Combine eggs with milk, salt, cinnamon, and nutmeg. Cut each slice of bread in half. Dip bread slices in egg mixture. Divide oil and butter between two heavy skillets so that toast may be prepared more quickly and served piping hot. Fry bread three or four minutes on each side until golden brown. Sprinkle bread with sifted powdered sugar and serve with hot maple syrup.

Gale Bedgood

Yield: 4 servings

Rodney's Rapjacks for a Crowd

2 dozen eggs
1 pound sugar
6½ pounds self-rising flour

1 gallon milk
1½ pounds margarine, melted
Vanilla to taste

In a mixing bowl large enough to handle the quantity desired, beat eggs. Add sugar and mix well. Stir in flour and milk. Using either a mixer or whisk, beat until smooth. Add melted margarine and stir thoroughly. Add vanilla. Pour onto preheated skillet or electric griddle. Be sure to turn pancakes over when bubbles appear.

Note: If pancakes do not brown sufficiently, add more sugar to batter. For thinner batter, add additional milk.

Variation: For variety, sprinkle chopped pecans on pancakes as soon as they are poured on griddle or skillet.

Carolyn Harris

Yield: 75 servings

Paw Paw's Pancakes

2 eggs
1½ tablespoons sugar
1½ cups self-rising flour
1 cup milk

3 to 4 tablespoons margarine,
   melted
Vanilla to taste

In a mixing bowl beat eggs; add sugar and mix well. Stir in flour and milk. Using either a mixer or whisk, beat until smooth. Add melted margarine and stir thoroughly. Add vanilla. Pour onto preheated skillet or electric griddle. Be sure to turn pancakes over when bubbles appear.

Note: If pancakes do not brown sufficiently, add more sugar to batter. For thinner batter, add additional milk.

Variation: For variety, sprinkle chopped pecans on pancakes as soon as they are poured on griddle.

Carolyn Harris   Yield: 5 servings

Parmesan Croutons

2 to 3 (1-inch thick) slices French
   bread, cut in half
¼ cup margarine, melted

¼ cup grated Parmesan cheese

Preheat oven to 350 degrees. Brush bread with margarine. Sprinkle with cheese. Bake for 20 minutes. Cut into croutons.

Carolyn Weissinger   Yield: 3 to 4 dozen

Lemonade Biscuits

12 tablespoons frozen lemonade
   concentrate, thawed
12 tablespoons brown sugar
1 recipe biscuits

6 tablespoons frozen lemonade
   concentrate, thawed
6 tablespoons brown sugar
¼ cup chopped pecans

Preheat oven to 350 degrees. Combine 12 tablespoons of lemonade and 12 tablespoons of brown sugar. Place 1 tablespoon of this mixture in bottom of 12 muffin cups. Prepare favorite biscuit recipe. Roll dough to ¼-inch. Combine 6 tablespoons of lemonade, sugar and pecans. Spread on dough and roll like jelly roll. Slice 1-inch thick and place in muffin cups. Bake for 15 to 20 minutes.

Mae Bruner Morgan   Yield: 1 dozen

Biscuits

²/₃ cup shortening   1¼ cups buttermilk
2½ cups self-rising flour

Preheat oven to 450 degrees. Cut shortening into flour. Gradually add buttermilk until mixture is sticky. Pour onto floured surface and knead flour into biscuit mixture. Flatten dough with fingers and fold over once. Roll dough out to ¾-inch thick. Cut with 2-inch biscuit cutter. Place on a greased pan and bake for 20 minutes.

Cheryl Watts   Yield: 1 dozen
Katherine Sandifer

Beer Biscuits

4 cups biscuit mix   4 tablespoons sugar
1 (12-ounce) can beer

Preheat oven to 425 degrees. Combine all ingredients and put in greased muffin tins. Bake until golden brown.

Note: The bread may be baked in a 5x9-inch loaf pan at 350 degrees for 50 minutes.

Dorann Frazer   Yield: 3 dozen

Mayonnaise Biscuits

2 cups self-rising flour   1 cup milk
¼ cup mayonnaise

Preheat oven to 425 degrees. Blend flour and mayonnaise with fork until mixture resembles coarse meal. Add milk and blend all ingredients. Fill greased muffin tins ½ full and bake for 10 minutes.

Variation: All purpose flour may be used by adding 1 teaspoon baking powder and ½ teaspoon salt to each cup of flour.

Vickie Baldwin   Yield: 1 dozen
Pat Labbe

Angel Biscuits

1 envelope yeast
1/4 cup warm water
2 1/2 cups flour
1/2 teaspoon baking powder

1 teaspoon salt
2 tablespoons sugar
1/2 cup shortening
1 cup buttermilk

Preheat oven to 400 degrees. Dissolve yeast in water. Mix all dry ingredients together; cut in shortening. Stir in yeast and buttermilk. Knead on floured surface; roll out and cut. Let rise slightly before baking. Bake for 12 to 15 minutes.

Ginger Wilson   Yield: 3 dozen

Spoon Rolls

1 envelope yeast
2 cups warm water
3/4 cup butter or margarine

1/4 cup sugar
1 egg
4 cups self-rising flour

Preheat oven to 425 degrees. Dissolve yeast in water. Add butter, sugar, and egg. Stir in flour. Place in a greased bowl in refrigerator for 1 hour. Bake in greased muffin tins for 20 minutes. Dough may be kept in refrigerator for several days.

Faye Carter   Yield: 2 dozen

Refrigerator Rolls

2 cups water
1 cup sugar
1 cup shortening or butter
1 1/2 teaspoons salt

2 envelopes yeast
2 eggs, beaten
6 cups unbleached flour, sifted

Boil water; pour over sugar, shortening, and salt. Stir to dissolve; cool. Add yeast and dissolve; add beaten eggs. Stir in flour gradually and mix well. Cover and refrigerate overnight. Roll out dough on floured board and make into desired shape. Place on buttered pan and let rise for one hour. Bake at 350 degrees for 20 to 30 minutes or until top is slightly brown.

Note: Rolls should be removed after 15 minutes if they are going to be frozen.

Fran Pearce   Yield: 5 to 6 dozen

60 Minute Hamburger Buns

2 envelopes yeast	1 teaspoon salt
¼ cup water	2 tablespoons margarine
1¼ cups milk	4 cups flour
3 tablespoons sugar	

Preheat oven to 425 degrees. Dissolve yeast in warm water. In large saucepan heat milk, sugar, salt, and margarine until dissolved and lukewarm. Add dissolved yeast and flour to the saucepan. Mix well and let rise in a warm place for 15 minutes. Turn onto floured surface and pat to ½ inch thickness. Cut with coffee can edge and place on greased cookie sheet. Let rise in a warm place for 15 minutes. Bake for 10 minutes or until brown.

Dorann Frazer   Yield: 1 dozen

Judy's Honey and Cracked Wheat Bread

4 cups whole wheat flour	2 tablespoons vegetable oil
1 tablespoon salt	1 egg, lightly beaten
2 envelopes yeast	4½ to 5 cups flour
3 cups milk	2 tablespoons cracked wheat
½ cup honey	

Combine 3 cups of whole wheat flour, salt, and yeast in a large bowl. In a saucepan over low heat combine milk, honey, and oil. Heat until warm. Pour over flour mixture and blend well. Add egg and beat well. Add remaining flours and cracked wheat. Knead dough for 5 minutes and place in a greased bowl. Cover with a damp cloth and let rise for 45 to 60 minutes or until doubled in bulk. Punch down dough and divide into thirds. Place into greased 5x9-inch loaf pans; cover with damp cloth and let rise 45 to 60 minutes or until doubled. Put in cold oven and bake at 350 degrees for 30 minutes or until golden brown.

Variation: May brush tops of bread with egg yolk and sprinkle with extra cracked wheat before baking.

Judy Oxford   Yield: 3 loaves

Old Fashioned Honey Wheat Bread

1½ cups water
1 cup creamed cottage cheese
½ cup honey
¼ cup margarine or butter
5 cups sifted all-purpose or
    unbleached flour

2 cups sifted whole wheat flour
2 tablespoons sugar
3 teaspoons salt
2 envelopes yeast
2 eggs

Heat water, cottage cheese, honey, and margarine in medium saucepan until very warm (120 to 130 degrees). Combine warm liquid, 2 cups all-purpose flour, and remaining ingredients in large bowl; beat about 2 minutes at medium speed. By hand stir in remaining flour to make stiff dough. Knead dough on well floured surface until smooth and elastic, about 2 minutes. Place in greased bowl. Cover; let rise in warm place until light and doubled in bulk (about 45 to 60 minutes). Grease (not oil) two 5x9-inch or 4x8-inch loaf pans. Punch down dough; divide and shape into 2 loaves. Place in greased pans. Cover; let rise in warm place until light and doubled in bulk, about 45 to 60 minutes. Bake at 350 degrees for 40 to 50 minutes until deep golden brown and loaves sound hollow when lightly tapped. Immediately remove from pans. If desired brush loaves with margarine.

Helen S. Stewart   Yield: 2 loaves

Potato Bread

1 cup mashed potatoes
1½ cups potato water
1 envelope yeast
½ cup warm water
2 eggs

¾ cup shortening
¾ cup sugar
1 tablespoon salt
7 cups flour

Boil potatoes and let water cool. Dissolve yeast in ½ cup warm water. Beat eggs and set aside. Cream shortening, sugar, and salt; add potatoes, eggs, yeast, and potato water. Add flour 2 cups at a time and mix well. Knead on floured surface. Refrigerate covered for several hours (preferably overnight). Knead before making up. Bake at 350 degrees for loaf bread and 325 degrees for dinner rolls for 20 to 25 minutes.

Faye Kelly   Yield: 3 loaves

Graham Nut Bread

2⅓ cups graham cracker crumbs
½ cup sugar
2½ teaspoons baking powder
½ teaspoon salt
1 cup chopped walnuts

3 eggs
½ cup milk
½ cup shortening, melted
2 tablespoons grated orange rind

Mix crumbs, sugar, baking powder, salt, and nuts. Set aside. Beat eggs; add milk, shortening, and rind. Blend into crumb mixture. Pour into a greased 5x9-inch loaf pan. Bake at 350 degrees for about 45 minutes or until brown. Remove from pan and cool on rack.

Cookbook Committee   Yield: 1 loaf

Whole Wheat Banana Bread

½ cup butter or margarine
½ cup firmly packed brown sugar
2 eggs, lightly beaten
1 cup mashed bananas
1 teaspoon vanilla
1½ cups whole wheat flour

½ teaspoon baking soda
½ teaspoon nutmeg
½ teaspoon salt
½ cup half and half
½ cup chopped pecans

Preheat oven to 350 degrees. Cream butter and sugar until light and fluffy. Add eggs, bananas, and vanilla, blending well. Combine dry ingredients. Stir into banana mixture. Add half and half and pecans. Spoon into a greased 5x9-inch loaf pan. Bake for 60 to 75 minutes. If glaze is desired, combine all ingredients and spoon over cooled bread.

Glaze:
3 tablespoons butter, melted
1 cup powdered sugar
¼ teaspoon almond extract

¼ teaspoon vanilla
1 tablespoon milk

Judy Oxford   Yield: 8 servings

Banana Nut Bread

½ cup shortening
1½ cups sugar
2 eggs
1 cup ripe bananas, mashed
2 cups flour
½ teaspoon baking powder

¾ teaspoon soda
½ teaspoon salt
¼ cup buttermilk
1 teaspoon vanilla
½ to 1 cup chopped nuts

Preheat oven to 300 degrees. Cream shortening and sugar; add eggs, one at a time beating well after each addition. Add bananas. Sift flour, baking powder, soda, and salt together. Add flour mixture alternately with buttermilk. Add vanilla and nuts. Bake in a greased 5x9-inch loaf pan for 1 hour and 15 minutes. Cool; wrap in plastic wrap. Will keep for about 2 weeks.

Helen S. Stewart   Yield: 1 loaf

Blu-Bana Bread

1 cup butter
2 cups sugar
4 eggs
2 teaspoons vanilla
5 medium bananas, mashed
4 cups flour

3 teaspoons allspice
2 teaspoons soda
1 teaspoon baking powder
½ teaspoon salt
2 cups fresh or frozen blueberries

Preheat oven to 350 degrees. Grease and flour two 5x9-inch loaf pans. Cream together butter and sugar. Beat in eggs and add vanilla. Fold in bananas and 2 cups flour. Reserve 2 tablespoons of flour to coat blueberries. Sift together the remaining flour, allspice, soda, baking powder, and salt; fold into banana mixture. Sprinkle the 2 tablespoons of flour onto blueberries; coat well and fold into batter. Divide the batter into loaf pans. Bake for approximately 50 minutes. Test with toothpick to determine when done.

Betty Ford   Yield: 2 loaves
  First Lady, 1974-1977

Cranberry-Cheese Bread

2 cups flour	2 tablespoons shortening
1 cup sugar	Juice from 1 orange
1½ teaspoons baking powder	1½ cups shredded Cheddar cheese
½ teaspoon soda	1 egg, beaten
½ teaspoon salt	1 cup cranberries, halved
2 teaspoons grated orange peel	½ cup finely chopped walnuts

Preheat oven to 350 degrees. Grease a 5x9-inch loaf pan. Measure flour, sugar, baking powder, soda, salt, and orange peel into a bowl. Cut in shortening. Add water to orange juice to measure ¾ cup. Add juice, cheese, and egg to flour mixture. Stir in cranberries and nuts. Pour into pan and bake 60 to 70 minutes or until wooden pick inserted in center comes out clean. Remove from pan; let loaf stand at least 8 hours before serving.

Janice Stapp   Yield: 1 loaf

Dilly Casserole Bread

1 envelope yeast	2 tablespoons butter, melted
½ cup warm water	2 teaspoons dill seed
1 cup creamed cottage cheese	¼ teaspoon soda
2 tablespoons sugar	1 egg
1 tablespoon minced onion	2¼ to 2½ cups flour

Preheat oven to 350 degrees. Dissolve yeast in water. Combine cottage cheese, sugar, onion, butter, dill seed, soda, and egg. Add dissolved yeast. Add flour to form a stiff dough. Let rise in a warm place until double in size (approximately 50 to 60 minutes). Stir down and pour into a greased 2-quart round casserole. Let rise 30 to 40 minutes. Bake for 40 to 50 minutes. Brush with butter and sprinkle with salt.

Faye Carter   Yield: 8 to 10 servings

Poppy Seed Bread

3 cups flour
2¼ cups sugar
1½ teaspoons baking powder
1½ teaspoons salt
3 eggs
1½ cups milk

1⅛ cups vegetable oil
1 tablespoon poppy seed
1½ teaspoons vanilla
1½ teaspoons almond flavoring
1½ teaspoons butter flavoring

Preheat oven to 350 degrees. Mix all ingredients and beat for 2 minutes. Grease and flour 5x9-inch loaf pans. Bake for 1 hour or until loaves test done.

Phyllis McCaughan   Yield: 2 loaves

Spicy Italian Bread

1 cup butter
1 (⅝-ounce) package dry Italian
    dressing mix

1 (25-ounce) package frozen roll
    dough

Melt butter and add seasoning mix. Roll frozen dough balls in butter mixture. Drop into a well greased bundt pan. Bake at 350 degrees for 30 minutes or until done.

Kay Oakes   Yield: 12 to 15 servings

Onion-Cheese Supper Bread

½ cup chopped onion
1 tablespoon butter
1½ cups flour
1½ teaspoons baking powder
½ teaspoon soda
1 teaspoon salt

1 cup grated Cheddar cheese
1 egg, beaten
⅓ cup milk
1 tablespoon poppy seed
2 tablespoons butter, melted

Preheat oven to 400 degrees. Sauté onion in butter until tender and light brown. Combine flour, baking powder, soda, and salt. Add onion and half of cheese to flour mixture. Combine egg and milk; add to flour mixture and stir until dry ingredients are moistened. Spread dough in a greased 8-inch round baking dish. Sprinkle top with remaining cheese and poppy seed. Drizzle melted butter over all. Bake about 20 minutes or until golden brown. Serve hot.

Pat Labbe   Yield: 6 to 8 servings

Sourdough Starter

1 envelope yeast
2½ cups warm water

2 cups sifted flour
1 tablespoon sugar

Dissolve yeast in ½ cup of the water; stir in remaining water, flour and sugar. Beat until smooth. Cover with cheesecloth. Let stand at room temperature for 5 to 10 days, stirring 2 and 3 times a day. The warmer the room the less time it takes. Cover and refrigerate until ready to use.

Note: To keep Starter going add: ¾ cup water, ¾ cup sifted flour, and 1 teaspoon sugar to remaining starter after some is used. Let stand at room temperature until bubbly and well fermented, at least one day. Cover and refrigerate until used again. If not used within 10 days, add 1 teaspoon sugar. Repeat sugar every 10 days.

Edie Delp   Yield: 4 cups

Monkey Bread

2 envelopes yeast
1 cup lukewarm water
1 cup shortening
¾ cup sugar
1½ teaspoons salt

1 cup boiling water
2 eggs, beaten
6 cups flour
1 cup margarine, melted

Preheat oven to 350 degrees. In one bowl, dissolve yeast in lukewarm water. In another bowl, mix shortening, sugar, and salt; add boiling water and mix well. Add eggs and stir. Add yeast mixture and flour alternately to shortening mixture. Let dough rise until it doubles in size. Punch down. Roll out dough ½ inch thick on floured board. Cut into various shapes (squares, triangles, rounds, etc.). Dip into melted margarine and lay pieces in layers in a tube pan until pan is half full. Let rise to top of pan. Bake for 45 minutes or until brown.

Note: This recipe makes 2 tube pans or if you have a large boiler it can be used rather than tube pan.

Laura Wallace   Yield: 2 dozen

Quick Monkey Bread

½ cup chopped pecans
½ cup sugar
1 teaspoon cinnamon
3 (10-ounce) cans refrigerated
   buttermilk biscuits

1 cup firmly packed brown sugar
½ cup margarine, melted

Preheat oven to 350 degrees. Sprinkle chopped pecans evenly in the bottom of a well greased 10-inch bundt pan and set aside. Combine sugar and cinnamon. Cut biscuits into quarters. Roll each piece in the sugar mixture and layer in pan. Combine brown sugar and margarine and pour over biscuits. Bake for 30 minutes. Invert onto serving dish.

Rosemary Harris
Jean Sullivan

Yield: 12 servings

Orange Cream Cheese Coffee Cake

3 (10-ounce) cans refrigerated
   biscuits
½ cup sugar
1 tablespoon cinnamon
¾ cup butter or margarine

½ cup sugar
½ cup brown sugar
1 tablespoon cinnamon
1 cup chopped nuts

Cut each biscuit into fourths. Combine ½ cup sugar and cinnamon in a plastic bag and shake biscuit pieces to coat. Place biscuits in a well greased bundt pan. Melt butter and mix with sugars and cinnamon. Add nuts and pour over top of biscuits. Bake at 350 degrees for 30 minutes or until done. Turn coffee cake out and top with glaze.

Glaze:
1 (8-ounce) package cream cheese,
   softened

3 cups powdered sugar
1 medium orange

Cream the cheese and sugar. Grate orange rind into creamed mixture. Add the juice from the orange and mix well. Spread over warm coffee cake. As glaze hardens, add more.

Kay Oakes

Yield: 12 to 15 servings

Blow Your Diet Cinnamon Rolls

2/3 cup shortening
1/2 cup milk
1/2 cup sugar
1 teaspoon salt

2 envelopes yeast
1/2 cup very warm water
4 eggs, beaten
4 1/2 cups sifted flour

Combine shortening, milk, sugar, and salt in saucepan. Heat just until shortening is melted; cool to lukewarm. Sprinkle yeast into warm water in a large bowl. Add lukewarm milk mixture, eggs, and 2 cups of flour; beat until smooth. Add just enough of remaining flour to make soft dough. Turn out onto lightly floured surface. Knead until smooth and elastic, about 5 minutes, using only enough flour to keep dough from sticking, or knead for 5 minutes in mixer with dough hook. Place dough in a large greased bowl; turn to coat all over with shortening. Cover. Let rise in warm place 1 hour or until double in bulk. Punch dough down, knead a few times, and let rest 5 minutes. Roll dough into a rectangle 1/2 inch thick.

Filling:
1/2 cup butter, melted
3/4 cup dark brown sugar
1 1/2 tablespoons cinnamon

1 cup raisins, softened in warm
   water and then drained
1/2 cup butter, melted

Preheat oven to 375 degrees. Brush melted butter on dough rectangle. Combine sugar and cinnamon, sift over butter. Sprinkle dough with raisins. Tightly roll up jelly roll fashion, beginning at long side. Pinch edge and ends to seal. Cut roll into 1-inch slices. Place slices in a greased 9x13-inch pan (fit will be tight). May have some extra for smaller pan. Cover; let rise in warm place for 1 hour or until doubled in bulk. Melt 1/2 cup butter and pour over rolls. Bake for 10 minutes, turn down to 350 degrees for 20 minutes or until golden brown. Ice with confectioners sugar icing.

Note: Store rolls in airtight container.

Judy Oxford   Yield: 1 1/2 to 2 dozen

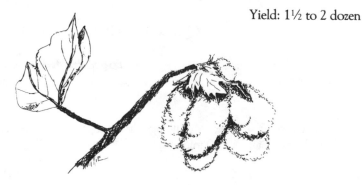

Blueberry Sweet Rolls

3¼ to 3½ cups flour
1 envelope yeast
2 (5-ounce) cans evaporated milk
6 tablespoons butter

¼ teaspoon salt
¼ cup sugar
1 egg
6 tablespoons butter, melted

In large mixing bowl combine 1½ cups flour and yeast. In a saucepan, heat milk, 6 tablespoons butter, salt, and sugar to 115 to 120 degrees, stirring until butter melts. Add to flour mixture. Add egg. Beat at low speed for 30 seconds, scraping the sides of bowl constantly. By hand, stir in enough of remaining flour to make a moderately stiff dough. Place in a greased bowl, turning once to coat surface. Cover. Let rise until double in bulk, about 1½ hours. Punch dough down and divide in half. Cover. Let rise 10 minutes. On floured surface, roll each half into an 8x14-inch rectangle. Brush dough with the melted butter.

Filling:
½ cup sugar
2 teaspoons cinnamon

1 teaspoon lemon peel, grated
2 cups fresh or frozen blueberries

Combine the sugar, cinnamon, and lemon peel and sprinkle on top of dough. Top with blueberries and press berries lightly into dough. Roll up jelly roll fashion, starting with long side. Seal edges. Cut into 12 slices. Place in two greased 9-inch round pans. Cover. Let rise until double, about 30 minutes. Bake at 375 degrees for 20 to 25 minutes.

Glaze:
1 cup powdered sugar
½ teaspoon vanilla

1 or 2 tablespoons milk

Mix together and top with glaze while rolls are warm.

Brenda Maske   Yield: 2 dozen

Quick Muffins

2 cups biscuit mix
1 cup sour cream
½ cup butter, softened

½ cup shredded cheese, optional
1 tablespoon chives, optional

Preheat oven to 350 degrees. Mix all ingredients together. Fill well greased muffin tins ½ to ⅔ full. Bake for 30 minutes.

Lula Wood   Yield: 1 dozen

Six Week Bran Muffins

1 (15-ounce) box Raisin Bran
5 cups flour
3 cups sugar
5 teaspoons soda

1 teaspoon salt
4 eggs
1 quart buttermilk
1 cup vegetable oil

Mix all ingredients and store in refrigerator in a covered container. Fill greased muffin tins ½ full. Bake at 400 degrees for 15 to 20 minutes. Will keep for 6 weeks.

Vickie Baldwin   Yield: 4 to 5 dozen

Onion Cheese Muffins

3 cups biscuit mix
1 teaspoon salt
¾ cup shredded Cheddar cheese
1 (3½-ounce) can French fried
   onions, crumbled

1 egg
1 cup milk

Combine all ingredients in a large bowl. Beat one minute. Fill muffin tins ⅔ full. Bake 400 degrees for about 15 minutes.

Note: These are wonderful with soups.

Cookbook Committee   Yield: 1 to 1½ dozen

Easy Wheat Muffins

2 cups wheat flour
2 teaspoons baking powder
1 teaspoon salt
1 egg, beaten

1 cup milk
¼ cup vegetable oil
¼ cup honey or sugar

Preheat oven to 400 degrees. Combine flour, baking powder, and salt. Combine egg, milk, oil, and honey or sugar mixing well. Pour flour mixture into egg mixture and stir until flour is moistened. Batter should be lumpy. Fill greased muffin tins ⅔ full. Bake for 20 to 25 minutes or until golden brown.

Linda Hill   Yield: 1 dozen

Sour Cream Muffins

1 cup margarine or butter   1 (8-ounce) carton sour cream
2 cups self-rising flour

Preheat oven to 350 degrees. Melt margarine; add flour and beat until well mixed. Add sour cream and beat until mixed. Pour into ungreased miniature muffin tins and bake for 20 minutes or until golden brown.

Variation: Add ¾ cup grated sharp Cheddar cheese and stir in with a spoon.

Nancy Cammack Littleford   Yield: 3 dozen
    Class of 1972

Pecan Muffins

2 eggs, beaten   ½ cup self-rising flour
1 cup brown sugar   1 teaspoon vanilla
⅓ cup butter, melted   1 cup chopped pecans

Combine all ingredients, mixing well. Spoon into a lightly greased or paper-lined muffin tin. Bake at 350 degrees for 25 minutes.

Edie Delp   Yield: 1 dozen

Banana Muffins

¾ cup butter or margarine   ½ teaspoon baking powder
1½ cups sugar   Pinch of salt
2 eggs   1¼ cups banana, mashed
2½ cups sifted flour   ¼ cup buttermilk
1 teaspoon soda   1 teaspoon vanilla

Cream butter and sugar. Add eggs, one at a time, and beat well. Sift together flour, soda, baking powder, and salt. Combine bananas and buttermilk. Add banana mixture alternately with flour mixture to creamed mixture. Add vanilla. Bake in paper-lined muffin tins at 350 degrees for 20 to 25 minutes.

Cheryl Watts   Yield: 2 dozen

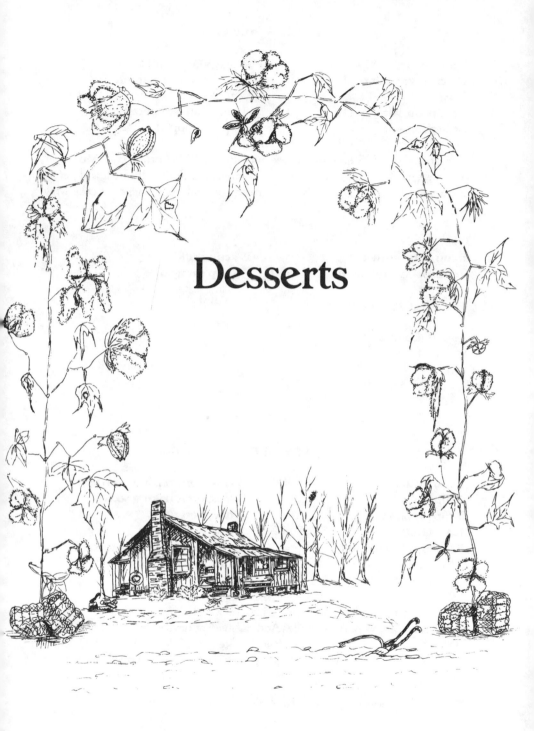

Desserts

Fresh Apple Cake

2 cups sugar
1¼ cups vegetable oil
3 eggs
1 teaspoon salt
1 teaspoon soda

1 teaspoon vanilla
½ teaspoon cinnamon
3 cups flour
1 cup chopped pecans
3 cups chopped apples

Preheat oven to 325 degrees. Grease and flour a 10-inch tube pan. Mix sugar, oil, and eggs. Add salt, soda, vanilla, cinnamon, and flour. Mix well; add pecans and apples. Bake for 1 hour. Remove from pan and pour glaze over cake while still warm.

Glaze:
1 cup light brown sugar
¼ teaspoon cinnamon

¼ cup milk
½ cup margarine

Mix well and pour over cake.

Anne Williamson
Sparkie Hobson

Mother's Applesauce Cake

1 cup butter
2 cups sugar
2 cups applesauce
4 cups flour
1 tablespoon cinnamon
2 teaspoons allspice
1 teaspoon cloves

2 teaspoons baking powder
2 teaspoons baking soda
1 teaspoon salt
1 teaspoon vanilla
1 (15-ounce) package seeded
   raisins, chopped

Cream butter and sugar; add applesauce. Gradually stir in flour and other dry ingredients. Mix well. Add vanilla. Add raisins that have been coated with a little of the flour. Grease and flour two 8-inch cake pans. Bake at 325 to 350 degrees for 20 to 25 minutes. Invert and leave pans over cake until perfectly cold before handling.

Note: This is delicious frosted with Mother's White Icing.

Carolyn Weissinger

Apricot Nectar Cake

1 (18½-ounce) box lemon cake
   mix
½ cup sugar

¾ cup vegetable oil
1 cup apricot nectar
4 eggs

Combine cake mix, sugar, oil, and apricot nectar together. Blend well. Add eggs one at a time. Beat well after each addition. Bake 1 hour in a greased 10-inch tube pan at 325 degrees.

Glaze:
1 cup powdered sugar

Juice from 1 lemon

Mix well and spread on top of hot cake.

Patricia Redd

Carrot Cake

2 cups sugar
1½ cups vegetable oil
4 eggs
2 cups flour

2 teaspoons baking soda
2 teaspoons cinnamon
3 cups grated raw carrots

Cream sugar and oil together; add eggs, one at a time. Sift dry ingredients together and add alternately with carrots to mixture. Bake in three greased and floured 9-inch cake pans at 350 degrees for about 25 minutes.

Icing:
½ cup butter and margarine,
   softened
1 (8-ounce) package cream cheese,
   softened

1 (16-ounce) box powdered sugar
2 teaspoons vanilla
1 cup chopped pecans

Cream margarine and cream cheese together; add the remaining ingredients and mix until smooth. Spread on all layers and on top of cake.

Smyly Kirkpatrick

Fig Cake

2 cups flour
1 teaspoon salt
1 teaspoon soda
1 teaspoon cloves
1 teaspoon cinnamon
1 teaspoon nutmeg
1 teaspoon allspice

1 cup vegetable oil
3 eggs
1 cup buttermilk
1 cup fig preserves
1 cup chopped nuts
1 teaspoon vanilla

Preheat oven to 325 degrees. Grease and flour a 10-inch tube pan. Sift dry ingredients; add oil and beat well. Add eggs one at a time; add buttermilk gradually. Fold in figs, nuts, and vanilla. Bake for 1 hour and 5 minutes.

Joy Davis

Fruit Cocktail Cake

2 cups flour
1½ cups sugar
2 teaspoons baking soda

1 (17-ounce) can fruit cocktail
2 eggs, beaten

Sift together dry ingredients. Add fruit cocktail (do not drain), and beaten eggs; mix well. Bake in a 9x13-inch pan for 35 minutes at 350 degrees. Do not remove from pan.

Icing:
¾ cup sugar
½ cup margarine
½ cup evaporated milk

½ cup chopped nuts
1 teaspoon vanilla
1 (3½-ounce) can coconut

Boil sugar, margarine, and milk together in a heavy saucepan for 2 minutes. Remove from heat. Add nuts, vanilla, and coconut. Pour over hot cake. Return to hot oven until coconut is brown. Cool cake and cut into squares.

Terry Hunter
Jane Singley

Autumn Fruitcake

1 cup margarine
2 cups sugar
5 eggs
1 (16-ounce) box honey graham
    crackers

1 cup chopped pecans
1 cup coconut
1 cup crushed pineapple, reserve
    juice
1 teaspoon baking powder

Cream margarine and sugar. Add eggs, one at a time, beating until creamy. Add crushed crackers, pecans, coconut, pineapple, and baking powder. Bake at 325 degrees in greased and floured 9x5x3-inch loaf pan for 1 hour and 10 minutes.

Icing:
½ cup margarine
1 (16-ounce) box powdered sugar

Juice from drained pineapple

Cream margarine and sugar. Add juice as needed to make mixture of spreading consistency.

Carolyn Weissinger

Bev's Fruitcake

2 eggs
2 cups water
2 (15½-ounce) packages of date
    or nut quick bread mix

2 cups pecans
1 cup raisins
4 cups mixed fruitcake mix

Grease and flour pans. In a large bowl, combine eggs and water. Add remaining ingredients and stir by hand until blended. Bake as directed below at 350 degrees. Cool for 15 minutes, loosen edges, and remove from pan. Cool completely. To store; wrap tightly and store in refrigerator. If desired, glaze with warm corn syrup.

Baking Directions:
8x4-inch loaf pans: 70 to 80 minutes (recipe will make 2)
9x5-inch loaf pans: 60 to 70 minutes (recipe will make 2)
10-inch tube or bundt pan: 65 to 75 minutes (recipe will make 1)
Ring mold: 40 to 50 minutes (recipe will make 1)
Soup cans: fill ¾ full; 35 to 45 minutes (recipe will make 10)
Muffin cups: use paper liners and fill ⅔ full; 20 to 25 minutes.

Lynnie Kopp

White Fruitcake

2 cups butter
1 cup sugar
5 large eggs, well beaten
¾ pound glazed cherries
1 pound glazed pineapple

4 cups pecans
1¾ cups flour
½ teaspoon baking powder
1 teaspoon vanilla
1 teaspoon almond flavoring

Cream butter and sugar; add eggs, blend thoroughly. Chop fruits and nuts; coat with part of the flour. Sift remaining flour and baking powder into egg and butter mixture. Add flavorings, fruits, and nuts. Pour into a greased paper-lined 10-inch tube pan. Place in cold oven and bake at 250 degrees for 3 hours. This cake can be eaten the day after it is baked or it can be kept for 2 months. Makes a 5 pound cake.

Louise Nolen

Hummingbird Cake

3 cups flour
2 cups sugar
1 teaspoon salt
1 teaspoon baking soda
1 teaspoon cinnamon
3 eggs, beaten

1½ cups vegetable oil
1½ teaspoons vanilla
1 (8-ounce) can crushed
   pineapple, undrained
2 cups chopped nuts
2 cups chopped bananas

Combine dry ingredients in a large mixing bowl. Add eggs and oil; stir until dry ingredients are moistened. Do not beat. Stir in vanilla, pineapple, nuts, and bananas. Spoon into 3 greased and floured 9-inch cake pans. Bake at 350 degrees for 25 to 30 minutes. Cool. Frost with cream cheese icing. Sprinkle chopped nuts on top.

Cream Cheese Icing:
1 (8-ounce) package cream cheese,
   softened
½ cup margarine, softened
2 (16-ounce) boxes powdered
   sugar

Milk
2 teaspoons vanilla

Combine cream cheese and butter until smooth. Add powdered sugar and enough milk to make fluffy. Add vanilla and mix.

Pat Labbe

Pecan Cake

3 cups sugar
1 cup shortening
1/2 cup butter
5 eggs
3 cups flour

1/8 teaspoon salt
1 cup milk
1 teaspoon vanilla
2 cups pecans, chopped

Preheat oven to 300 degrees. Cream sugar, shortening, and butter together; add eggs one at a time. Sift flour and salt together and add alternately with milk to the creamed mixture. Add vanilla and pecans. Bake in greased and floured 10-inch tube pan for 2 hours and 15 minutes.

Cheryl Watts

Plum Cake

2 cups self-rising flour
1 teaspoon cinnamon
1 teaspoon cloves
2 cups sugar

1 cup vegetable oil
3 eggs
2 (4½-ounce) jars baby plum
    tapioca

Sift flour before measuring. Add spices to flour. Mix sugar and oil; add eggs and plum tapioca. Pour into a greased and floured 10-inch tube pan and bake at 325 degrees for 1 hour. Let cool 15 minutes before turning out of pan.

Virginia Moseley

Strawberry Cake

4 eggs
3/4 cup vegetable oil
1 (18½-ounce) box white cake
    mix
1 (3-ounce) box strawberry gelatin

1 (10-ounce) package frozen
    strawberries, thawed and
    reserve 1/3 cup
1 pint whipping cream

Preheat oven to 325 degrees. In large mixing bowl, beat eggs and oil. Add cake mix, gelatin, and strawberries. Mix at medium speed for 3 minutes. Pour into 2 greased and floured 8-inch round cake pans. Bake for 20 to 25 minutes. Cool. Whip cream and gradually add remaining strawberries. Spread whipped cream between layers and on top. Keep refrigerated.

Cheryl Watts

Mandarin Orange Cake

1 (18½-ounce) box butter cake
  mix
1 (11-ounce) can mandarin
  oranges, drained
1 (7-ounce) can coconut

1 tablespoon margarine
⅓ cup margarine
4 ounces cream cheese
1 (16-ounce) box powdered sugar
1 to 2 teaspoons milk

Mix cake according to package directions and add oranges. Bake according to directions on package, using two 9-inch round cake pans. Brown 1 cup coconut in 1 tablespoon margarine and set aside. Soften the ⅓ cup margarine and cream cheese and mix well with sugar, milk, and remaining coconut. After cake has cooled, frost, and sprinkle top and sides of cake with browned coconut.

Variation: This cake may also be frosted with whipped topping and garnished with additional orange slices.

Betty Schroeder

Caramel Cake

1 (18½-ounce) package Duncan
  Hines Butter Golden Cake Mix
1 (8-ounce) container sour
  cream

⅓ cup vegetable oil
¼ cup sugar
¼ cup water
4 eggs

In a large bowl, mix all ingredients together with an electric mixer for 2 minutes, using the high speed. Pour into three greased and floured 9-inch cake pans and bake in a preheated oven at 350 degrees for 25 to 30 minutes. Cool and frost with Caramel Icing.

Caramel Icing:
3 cups sugar
2 sticks butter (no substitute)

¾ cup evaporated milk
2 teaspoons vanilla flavoring

Combine 2½ cups sugar, the milk and the butter in a non-stick boiler and bring to a boil. Brown ½ cup sugar in a small non-stick skillet. Watch this closely; it will burn easily. When this sugar has melted and turned to light brown, add it to the milk mixture, constantly stirring. When mixture reaches the soft ball stage (230 degrees on a candy thermometer), remove from the heat, and beat until the mixture reaches spreading consistency. Spread quickly over the layers.

Juanita Hayes Cammack

Creole Cake

2 eggs
2 cups sugar
½ cup vegetable oil
2 tablespoons cocoa
½ cup buttermilk

1 teaspoon soda
½ teaspoon vanilla
2 cups flour
1 cup boiling water

Mix ingredients in order given. Be sure to add boiling water last. Bake in 11x16-inch greased pan for 30 minutes at 350 degrees. Spread topping on hot cake.

Topping:
½ cup butter, melted
1 (16-ounce) box brown sugar
1 (7-ounce) can coconut

½ cup chopped nuts
1 (5-ounce) can evaporated milk
1 teaspoon vanilla

Mix well and pour over hot cake and place under broiler until bubbling. Cool and cut in squares.

Laura Wallace

Red Velvet Cake

2½ cups flour
1½ cups sugar
1 teaspoon soda
1 teaspoon salt
2 tablespoons cocoa
1 cup buttermilk

1½ cups vegetable oil
1 teaspoon vinegar
2 eggs
1 (1-ounce) bottle red food
   coloring
1 teaspoon vanilla

Sift together dry ingredients. Add other ingredients in order and mix thoroughly. Bake in 2 greased and floured 8-inch cake pans. Bake at 350 degrees for 25 minutes.

Icing:
½ cup margarine
1 (8-ounce) package cream cheese
1 (16-ounce) box powdered sugar

½ teaspoon vanilla
1 cup chopped nuts

Let margarine and cream cheese soften at room temperature. Cream well; add sugar and continue beating until smooth. Add vanilla and nuts. Spread on cake.

Barbara Rosser
Annie Lee Lewis

Chocolate Mound Cake

1 cup shortening	1 cup all-purpose flour
2 cups sugar	1 cup self-rising flour
5 large eggs	1 cup milk

Cream shortening; gradually add sugar and beat until light and fluffy. Add eggs, one at a time, beating until smooth after each addition. Combine flours; add to creamed mixture alternately with milk, beginning and ending with flour. Pour batter into three greased and floured 9-inch round cake pans. Bake at 325 degrees for 25 minutes or until wooden pick inserted in center comes out clean. Cool in pans 5 minutes; remove from pans and cool completely.

Filling:

1 cup sugar	1 (12-ounce) package coconut
1 cup milk	12 large marshmallows
1 teaspoon vanilla	

Combine sugar and milk in a saucepan and bring to a boil. Add vanilla, coconut, and marshmallows. Boil over medium heat 5 minutes. Spread between cake layers.

Frosting:

½ cup butter or margarine	1 (6-ounce) package semi-sweet
⅔ cup evaporated milk	chocolate morsels
2 cups sugar	

Combine all ingredients in saucepan. Boil 2 to 3 minutes, stirring constantly. Remove from heat; cool. Frost cake.

Variation: 1 (18½-ounce) box dark chocolate cake mix can be substituted for cake.

Peggy Raybon
Lula Wood

Easy Chocolate Cake

½ cup margarine
1 cup sugar
4 eggs, beaten

1 (16-ounce) can chocolate syrup
1 teaspoon vanilla
1 cup self-rising flour

Cream margarine and sugar. Add remaining ingredients. Bake in 9x13-inch pan for 30 minutes at 325 degrees.

Icing:
4 tablespoons cocoa
½ cup butter
7 tablespoons evaporated milk

1 (16-ounce) box powdered sugar
1 cup chopped nuts

Mix ingredients in medium saucepan and bring to boil. Pour over hot cake.

Kaye Plummer

White Chocolate Cake

½ cup water
4 ounces white chocolate
1 cup butter
2 cups sugar
4 eggs, separated

1 teaspoon vanilla
2½ cups cake flour, sifted
½ teaspoon salt
1 teaspoon soda
1 cup buttermilk

Preheat oven to 350 degrees. Bring water to boil, then add chocolate and stir until melted. Cool. Cream butter and sugar. Add egg yolks, one at a time. Add chocolate and vanilla. Mix dry ingredients. Add dry ingredients alternately with buttermilk, beating after each addition. Beat egg whites until stiff and fold into batter. Pour into three 9-inch cake pans or 9x13-inch cake pan, which have been greased and floured. Bake at 350 degrees for 30 to 35 minutes. Cool, then frost.

White Chocolate Frosting:
3 egg yolks
1 cup condensed milk
1 cup sugar
½ cup butter, melted

4 ounces white chocolate, grated
  or shaved
1 cup pecans, chopped

Mix egg yolks with milk. Add sugar and butter and cook in double boiler until "pudding thickness". Add shaved or grated chocolate and stir until smooth. Add pecans. Spread on cake.

Sherry Taylor

Vanilla Wafer Cake

1 cup margarine
2 cups sugar
6 eggs
1 (12-ounce) package vanilla
  wafers, crumbled

½ cup milk
1 (7-ounce) package coconut
1 cup chopped pecans

Cream margarine and sugar. Add eggs one at a time, beating after each one. Add crumbled vanilla wafers and milk alternately. Add coconut and pecans. Bake at 350 degrees in a well greased and floured 10-inch tube pan for 1 hour and 10 minutes.

Lynnie Kopp

Seven Up Cake

1 (18½-ounce) box lemon
  supreme cake mix
¾ cup vegetable oil
1 (10-ounce) bottle "Regular
  Seven Up"

1 (3-ounce) package lemon instant
  pudding
4 eggs

Mix all ingredients together 3 minutes with electric mixer on medium speed. Pour into three 8-inch greased and floured cake pans. Bake at 350 degrees for 25 to 30 minutes or until tested done.

Icing:
1½ cups sugar
½ cup butter
1 tablespoon flour
2 eggs

1 cup crushed pineapple, drained
1 cup coconut
1 cup chopped pecans

In saucepan combine sugar, butter, flour, and eggs. Cook until thickened. Add pineapple, coconut, and pecans to cooked mixture. Spread between layers and on top of cooled cake.

Laura Wallace

Happy Birthday Cake

1 (18½-ounce) box white cake
    mix
4 eggs
1 cup cold water
1 package powdered whipped
    topping

2 tablespoons vanilla butter & nut
    flavoring
½ cup sugar

Preheat oven to 350 degrees. Mix all ingredients in large bowl. Beat at medium speed for 5 minutes. Pour into greased and floured 9x13-inch pan or two 9-inch layer pans. Bake 30 to 40 minutes, or until tested done.

Icing:
½ cup margarine
1 cup shortening
1 (16-ounce) box powdered sugar

1 teaspoon vanilla
¼ cup milk

Cream together with mixer and spread on cool cake.

Edie Delp

Coconut Sour Cream Dream Cake

1 (18½-ounce) box butter
    flavored cake mix
2 cups sugar
1 cup sour cream
1 (12-ounce) package frozen
    coconut, thawed

1½ cups whipping cream or 1
    (12-ounce) carton whipped
    topping

Prepare the cake according to package directions, making two 8-inch layers. Split both layers horizontally after they have cooled. Blend together the sugar, sour cream, and coconut; chill. Spread all but 1 cup of sour cream mixture between the four layers. Blend the remaining cup of the mixture with the whipped cream and spread on the top and sides of the cake. Seal in an airtight container and refrigerate for three days before serving. Keep refrigerated after cutting.

Patricia H. Murray
Pat Labbe

Coffee Chiffon Cake

2 eggs
1½ cups sugar
½ cup milk
½ cup cold coffee
⅛ teaspoon baking soda

2½ cups cake flour, sifted
3 teaspoons baking powder
1 teaspoon salt
⅓ cup vegetable oil
2 teaspoons vanilla

Separate eggs. Beat egg whites until frothy. Gradually beat in ½ cup sugar. Continue beating until stiff and glossy; set aside. Combine milk, coffee, and baking soda; set aside. Sift remaining sugar, flour, baking powder, and salt in mixing bowl. Pour oil into flour mixture with ½ coffee mixture. Add vanilla. Beat one minute on medium speed of mixer. Scrape sides and bottom of bowl often. Add remaining coffee mixture and egg yolks. Beat one minute longer, scraping sides constantly. Fold in egg whites. Pour into 2 well greased and floured 8-inch cake pans. Bake at 350 degrees for 30 to 35 minutes. Remove from pans and cool. Split each layer and frost. Chill well.

Fluffy Coffee Icing:
1½ cups shortening
1 cup sugar
½ teaspoon salt

¼ cup cold coffee
1 teaspoon vanilla
2 eggs

Beat all ingredients at high speed until fluffy. Frost. Keep refrigerated.

Rosemary Harris

Triple Fudge Cake

1 (3-ounce) package chocolate
pudding
1 (18½-ounce) box devils food
cake mix

½ cup semisweet chocolate pieces
½ cup chopped nuts
Whipped cream

Preheat oven to 350 degrees. Grease and flour 9x13x2-inch pan. In large saucepan, cook pudding as directed on package. Stir cake mix into hot pudding. Beat 2 minutes on medium speed. Pour into pan. Sprinkle chocolate and nuts on batter. Bake for 35 to 40 minutes. Serve warm with whipped cream.

Connie Pugh

Almond Pound Cake

3½ cups flour
½ teaspoon baking powder
Pinch of salt
3 cups sugar
½ cup butter
1 cup vegetable oil

5 eggs
1 cup milk
1 teaspoon vanilla
1 teaspoon almond flavoring
1 teaspoon lemon juice

Sift together flour, baking powder, and salt. Set aside. Cream sugar, butter, and oil. Add eggs one at a time, beating well after each. Add flour mixture and milk alternately. Add flavorings. Mix well. Bake 1 hour and 30 minutes at 325 degrees in a greased and floured 10-inch tube pan.

Glaze:
1½ cups powdered sugar
1 tablespoon soft butter

2 to 3 tablespoons warm water
1 teaspoon almond flavoring

Blend ingredients until smooth and spread over pound cake while cake is still hot.

Cheryl Watts

Coconut Pound Cake

1 cup margarine
½ cup shortening
3 cups sugar
6 eggs
3 cups flour

1 cup milk
½ teaspoon coconut flavoring
½ teaspoon almond flavoring
1 (3½-ounce) can flaked coconut

Do not preheat oven. Cream margarine, shortening, and sugar. Add eggs one at a time, beating 2 minutes after each. Add flour alternately with milk. Blend in flavorings and coconut until well mixed. Bake at 350 degrees in a well greased 10-inch tube pan or bundt pan for 1 hour and 15 minutes.

Mary Jean Averyt
Barbara Rosser

Chocolate Pound Cake

1 cup butter
1/2 cup shortening
3 cups sugar
5 eggs
3 cups flour

1/2 teaspoon baking powder
1/2 teaspoon salt
4 tablespoons cocoa
1 cup milk
1 teaspoon vanilla

Cream together butter, shortening, and sugar. Add eggs, one at a time. Sift dry ingredients together. Add flour mixture and milk alternately to creamed mixture. Add vanilla and mix well. Bake in a greased and floured 10-inch tube pan at 325 degrees for 80 to 90 minutes.

Icing:
2 1/4 cups sugar
1/4 cup butter
16 large marshmallows
1/4 teaspoon salt

1 cup evaporated milk
1 teaspoon vanilla
1 (6-ounce) package semi-sweet
   morsels

Mix sugar, butter, marshmallows, salt, and milk together in a heavy saucepan. Cook and stir over medium heat until mixture boils; continue cooking for 10 minutes. Stir in vanilla and chocolate morsels. Beat until creamy and thick enough to spread on cake. Let it run down the sides.

Note: The icing recipe can be used to make fudge. Just add nuts and spread on platter and cool.

Peggy Striplin
Fran Pearce
Susan Brinkley

Cream Cheese Pound Cake

1 1/2 cups butter
1 (8-ounce) package cream cheese
3 cups sugar
6 eggs

2 cups flour
Pinch of salt
3 teaspoons vanilla

Combine butter and cheese. Add sugar and cream well. Add eggs one at a time beating well after each addition. Stir flour and salt; add vanilla. Bake in greased and floured 10-inch tube or bundt pan. Start in cold oven, and bake at 300 degrees for 2 hours.

Betty Jones
Margie Swift

Cinnamon Pound Cake

1 (18½-ounce) box butter cake
   mix
¾ cup vegetable oil

1 cup sour cream
½ cup sugar
4 eggs

Cinnamon Sugar Mix:
3 tablespoons sugar

½ teaspoon cinnamon

Combine cake mix, oil, sour cream, sugar, and eggs. Pour ½ the batter into a well greased floured bundt pan. Sprinkle ½ the cinnamon sugar mix on top. Add remaining batter and cover with remaining cinnamon sugar mix. Bake 1 hour at 325 degrees.

Eady McCormick

Million Dollar Pound Cake

3 cups sugar
2 cups butter, softened
6 eggs
4 cups flour

¾ cup milk
1 teaspoon vanilla
1 teaspoon almond flavoring

Cream sugar and butter; add eggs one at a time and beat well. Alternate flour and liquids. Bake in 10-inch tube pan at 325 degrees for 1 hour and 50 minutes.

Elizabeth Kish

Grandma's Buttermilk Pound Cake

1 cup shortening
3 cups sugar
6 eggs
3 cups flour

¼ teaspoon soda
½ teaspoon salt
1 cup buttermilk
1 teaspoon vanilla

Cream shortening and sugar. Add eggs one at a time, beating well after each. Sift flour with soda and salt. Add flour mixture and buttermilk alternately to cream mixture. Add vanilla and beat 3 to 4 minutes until smooth. Bake in greased and lightly floured 10-inch tube pan at 300 degrees for 1 hour and 30 minutes.

Note: Always add love to your cooking and it will be better.

Deen Clower

Whipping Cream Pound Cake

1 cup butter
3 cups sugar
6 eggs
3 cups cake flour

½ pint whipping cream
1½ teaspoons lemon extract
1½ teaspoons vanilla

Cream butter and sugar. Beat eggs and add to mixture, beating at high speed. Sift flour. Reduce to low speed and add alternately the flour and whipping cream; begin and end with flour. Add flavorings and mix well. Pour into a bundt pan that has been sprayed with a vegetable cooking spray. Put into a cold oven and bake at 325 degrees for 1 hour and 10 to 15 minutes.

Betty Hicks
Susan Brinkley
Ann Hendrix

Swedish Pound Cake

1 cup butter
2 cups sugar
5 eggs
1 teaspoon vanilla

2 cups flour
1 cup coconut
1 cup chopped nuts

Cream butter and sugar together. Add eggs; beating well after each. Add vanilla and flour. Fold in coconut and nuts. Bake at 325 degrees for 1 hour and 30 minutes in a greased and floured 10-inch tube pan. Remove cake from oven and punch holes in cake with ice pick. Do not remove from pan. Pour syrup over cake and let stand in pan until cool.

Syrup:
¾ cup sugar
¾ cup water

¼ cup margarine
1 teaspoon almond flavoring

Boil together for 5 minutes and pour over cake.

Eloise Anderson

Old Fashioned Sour Cream Pound Cake

1 ½ cups butter, NO SUBSTITUTE
3 cups sugar
6 large eggs, beaten

1 cup sour cream
3 cups flour, sifted
¼ teaspoon soda

Preheat oven to 325 degrees. Cream butter and sugar. Add beaten eggs and sour cream. Mix flour and soda together and add gradually to butter mixture. Beat until light and fluffy (about 2 minutes). Bake in greased and floured 10-inch tube pan for 1 hour and 10 minutes.

Note: Mixture will not fit in a bundt pan.

Linda Hill
Carol Cleveland

Caramel Cake Icing

2 ½ cups sugar
1 cup milk
Pinch of salt

¼ cup butter
1 teaspoon vanilla

Brown ½ cup sugar in an iron skillet. Cook remaining sugar and milk together slowly in heavy saucepan; add browned sugar and cook until at the soft stage (a drop forms a soft ball in cold water). Remove from heat and add butter and vanilla. Beat until creamy. Spread on cake.

Nellie Kate Tepper
Carolyn Weissinger
Margie Swift

Easy Never Fail Chocolate Icing

½ cup margarine
½ cup cocoa
1 (16-ounce) box powdered
   sugar, sifted

½ to ¼ cup milk
1 teaspoon vanilla

Using double boiler, melt margarine and add cocoa. Mix well and remove from heat. Stir in sugar; add milk as needed for consistency. Add vanilla.

Maggie P. Whitlow
Ginger Wilson

Mother's White Icing

2 egg whites
1/3 cup water
2 cups sugar

1/3 cup light corn syrup
3 teaspoons boiling water

Beat egg whites until stiff. Mix water, sugar, and syrup. Cook until a drop forms a ball in cold water (250 degrees on candy thermometer). Pour mixture gradually over the stiffly beaten egg whites and beat. When stiff add 3 teaspoons boiling water, one at a time, beating constantly. This should be the consistency of whipped cream.

Note: If icing looks like it isn't going to set up, put into top of double boiler and continue beating until it sets.

Carolyn Weissinger

Pie Crust

2 cups flour
1 1/2 teaspoons salt

1/2 cup vegetable oil
1/4 cup cold milk

Preheat oven to 475 degrees. Mix flour and salt together; add oil and milk to flour mixture. Mix until dough rounds up and leaves sides of bowl. Divide dough into 2 portions and roll each half into a circle between waxed paper. Lift top waxed paper off and turn dough into pie pan and peel off other paper. Bake for 8 to 10 minutes.

Katherine Sandifer   Yield: 2 crusts

Easy Miracle Pie

1 cup sugar
4 eggs
1/2 cup flour
1/4 cup butter

2 cups milk
1/2 teaspoon baking powder
1 teaspoon vanilla

Combine all ingredients in blender; blend well. Pour into a buttered 9-inch pie plate. Bake at 350 degrees for 60 minutes.

Arlene Deason-Johnson   Yield: 6 servings

Egg Pie

1 cup sugar
1 heaping tablespoon flour
¼ cup butter, melted
2 eggs
1 cup milk

1 teaspoon vanilla
1 (9-inch) deep dish pie shell, unbaked
Nutmeg

Combine all ingredients. Pour in pie shell and bake at 400 degrees for 30 to 45 minutes. Sprinkle with nutmeg.

Joy Davis   Yield: 6 servings

Chess Pie

4 eggs, beaten
1½ cups sugar
1 tablespoon self-rising cornmeal
1 tablespoon vinegar

1 teaspoon nutmeg
½ cup margarine, melted
1 (9-inch) deep dish pie shell, unbaked

Mix all ingredients. Pour into pie shell and bake at 350 degrees for 50 minutes.

Kaye Plummer   Yield: 6 servings

Granny's Buttermilk Pie

3 eggs
1 cup sugar
2 tablespoons flour
½ cup butter, melted
1 cup buttermilk

1 teaspoon vanilla or lemon flavoring
Dash nutmeg
1 (9-inch) deep dish pie shell

Preheat oven to 325 degrees. Beat eggs until fluffy; then add sugar and flour. Continue to beat for one minute. Add butter, buttermilk, flavoring and nutmeg; mix well. Pour mixture into pie shell and bake until set, approximately 40 minutes.

Note: Beat an egg white and brush over pie shell. Bake a few minutes before pouring mixture into shell to bake pie. This will help keep pie shell from being overly moist.

Toni A. Hughes   Yield: 6 servings
Annie Lee Lewis

Toffee Shortbread Pie

Crust:
1 cup butter
2½ cups flour

½ teaspoon salt
½ cup sugar

Cut butter into flour, salt, and sugar until it resembles cornmeal. Press into 2 (7-inch) quiche pans. Bake at 325 degrees for 15 to 20 minutes or until light brown. Cool.

Filling:
1½ cups butter
1 cup sugar
3 tablespoons light corn syrup

1 (14-ounce) can sweetened condensed milk
1 teaspoon vanilla

Combine all ingredients in a heavy saucepan and boil about 4 minutes until caramel colored. Cool and pour into shells.

Topping:
3 squares unsweetened chocolate
2 tablespoons butter

Buttermilk

Melt chocolate and butter over low heat. Add enough buttermilk for spreading consistency. Spread over filling. Freezes for up to one month.

Anne Williamson

Yield: 12 servings

Angel Pie

½ pint whipping cream
⅓ cup sugar
Juice of two lemons
1 (14-ounce) can sweetened condensed milk

1 (8-ounce) can crushed pineapple, drained
1 cup chopped pecans
2 (9-inch) pie shells, baked

Whip cream and add sugar; set aside. Stir lemon juice into condensed milk; add pineapple and nuts. Fold mixture into whipped cream. Pour into pie shells. Chill at least two hours before serving. May be made the day before.

Sherie Sherrer

Yield: 12 servings

Citrus Chiffon Pie

4 egg yolks
½ cup lemon juice
½ cup orange juice
¼ cup water
1 (1-ounce) envelope unflavored
  gelatin
½ cup sugar

Dash of salt
½ teaspoon grated lemon peel
½ teaspoon grated orange peel
4 egg whites
½ cup sugar
1 (9-inch) pie shell, baked

Beat egg yolks, fruit juices, and water. Place in saucepan and add gelatin, ½ cup sugar, and salt. Cook over medium heat until mixture comes to a boil. Remove from heat; stir in peelings. Chill, stirring occasionally until mixture mounds slightly when dropped from a spoon. Beat egg whites until soft peaks form. Gradually add ½ cup sugar beating until stiff. Fold in gelatin mixture. Spoon into pie shell. Chill until firm.

Note: Trim with whipped cream and garnish with orange slices and sprig of mint.

Linda Hollingsworth   Yield: 6 servings

Orange Chiffon Pie

1 (14-ounce) can sweetened
  condensed milk
1 medium orange
½ cup lemon juice

1 (8-ounce) carton whipped
  topping
1 (9-inch) graham cracker crust

Mix milk with juice of orange and grated rind. Add lemon juice and fold in whipped topping. Pour into graham cracker crust and chill before serving.

Kay Oakes   Yield: 6 to 8 servings

Mile High Pie

Almond Pie Shell:

¼ cup butter
¼ teaspoon salt
2 tablespoons sugar
1 egg yolk

¾ cup sifted flour
¼ cup finely chopped almonds
  or pecans

Cream butter, salt, and sugar. Add egg yolk; stir in flour and nuts. Press dough into a 9-inch pie plate. Refrigerate for 30 minutes. Bake at 350 degrees for 15 minutes. Chill before pouring in filling.

Filling:

1 (10-ounce) package frozen
  strawberries
1 cup sugar
2 egg whites, at room temperature

1 tablespoon lemon juice
Pinch of salt
1 cup whipping cream
½ teaspoon almond extract

Thaw strawberries and reserve a few for garnish. In mixing bowl, combine berries, sugar, egg whites, lemon juice, and salt. Beat for 15 minutes or until stiff. Whip cream with almond extract. Fold into berry mixture. Mound in almond pie shell and freeze until firm. Garnish with berries.

Edie Delp   Yield: 6 to 8 servings

Strawberry Pie

1 cup sugar
1 tablespoon cornstarch
1 (3-ounce) package strawberry
  gelatin
2 cups water

2 cups sliced fresh strawberries
1 (9-inch) graham cracker pie
  crust
Whipped topping, optional

Mix sugar, cornstarch, and gelatin in saucepan; add water and boil until clear (about 1 minute). Cool until mixture begins to thicken. Arrange strawberries in pie crust and pour mixture over strawberries. Cool in refrigerator until set. Garnish with whipped topping if desired.

Reyndy Wilkinson   Yield: 6 servings
  Class of 1975
Beth Hicks Baker
  Class of 1980
Eady McCormick

Sugarless Strawberry Pie

1 (3-ounce) package sugar-free
  strawberry gelatin
²/₃ cup boiling water
2 cups ice cubes, not crushed

1 pint fresh strawberries
1 (8-ounce) carton whipped cream
1 (9-inch) graham cracker crust

Dissolve gelatin in boiling water. Put in ice cubes and stir with a wire whip until it begins to thicken. Remove unmelted ice. Stir in fruit. Fold in whipped cream and stir gently. Place in refrigerator for 20 to 30 minutes. Remove from refrigerator and pour into pie crust. Refrigerate for 1 to 2 hours or longer. May top with additional whipped cream and garnish with fresh strawberries. Very light dessert!

Faye Bailey   Yield: 6 to 8 servings

Easy Peach Cobbler

½ cup flour
1 teaspoon baking powder
½ cup sugar
½ cup milk

2 cups fresh peaches, sweetened to
  taste
¼ cup butter, melted

Mix flour, baking powder, sugar, and milk. Place peaches in a 2-quart baking dish. Pour mixture over peaches; top with melted butter and bake for 30 to 45 minutes at 400 degrees. Makes its own crust.

Variation: May substitute fruit of your choice. If apples are used, add 1 teaspoon of cinnamon.

Lula Wood   Yield: 4 to 6 servings
Susan Whitlow Meadows
  Class of 1973

Coconut Pie I

2 eggs
1 cup sugar
½ cup margarine
1 (5-ounce) can evaporated milk

1 tablespoon vanilla
1 (3½-ounce) can coconut
1 (9-inch) pie shell, unbaked

Preheat oven to 350 degrees. Cream eggs and sugar together. Melt margarine and mix with creamed mixture. Add milk, vanilla, and ¾ can coconut. Pour into pie shell. Sprinkle with remaining coconut. Bake for 30 to 45 minutes.

Cynthia B. Tyus
Toni A. Hughes
Joy Davis

Yield: 6 servings

Coconut Pie II

½ cup margarine, melted
2½ cups sugar
5 beaten eggs
½ cup buttermilk

1 teaspoon vanilla
1 (3½-ounce) can coconut
2 (9-inch) pie shells, unbaked

In a mixing bowl cream margarine and sugar. Add eggs, buttermilk, and vanilla; mix well. Add coconut. Pour mixture into pie shells. Bake at 350 degrees for 45 minutes to 1 hour.

Carolyn Harris

Yield: 12 servings

Christmas Pies

2 cups sugar
1 cup butter or margarine
3 eggs, beaten
1 cup shredded coconut
1 cup chopped pecans
2 tablespoons sherry

½ teaspoon allspice
½ teaspoon cinnamon
½ teaspoon cloves
2 teaspoons vanilla
2 (9-inch) pie shells, unbaked

Cream together sugar and butter; add eggs and mix. Stir in the remaining ingredients. Pour mixture into pie shells and bake at 350 degrees for 35 to 40 minutes.

Peggy Christian

Yield: 12 servings

Raisin Pie

1 cup raisins
½ cup butter, melted
1 cup sugar
2 eggs

1 teaspoon vanilla
1 teaspoon vinegar
1 (9-inch) pie shell, unbaked

Mix all the ingredients and pour into pie shell. Bake for 45 minutes at 350 degrees.

Joy Davis   Yield: 6 servings

Japanese Fruitcake Pie

2 eggs, beaten
½ cup margarine, melted
1¼ cups sugar
½ teaspoon vanilla
½ teaspoon vinegar

½ cup raisins
½ cup coconut
½ cup chopped pecans
1 (9-inch) pie shell, unbaked

Mix all ingredients and pour into pie shell. Bake at 350 degrees for 45 minutes.

Janice Stapp   Yield: 6 servings

Sweet Potato Pie

5 large sweet potatoes
5 eggs, separated
2 cups sugar
1 teaspoon nutmeg

1 teaspoon allspice
1 teaspoon cinnamon
½ cup margarine, melted
1 (9-inch) pie shell, unbaked

Bake potatoes in a 400 degree oven for one hour. Cool and peel. Beat egg whites; set aside. Beat egg yolks and add to sweet potatoes. Beat with mixer. Add sugar, spices, and margarine. Continue beating until smooth. Fold in egg whites. Pour in pie shell and bake at 350 degrees for 30 minutes.

Doll Wilkinson Cowart   Yield: 6 servings
  Class of 1980
Toni A. Hughes

Pecan Pie I

3 eggs, beaten
1 cup light corn syrup
1 cup light brown sugar
½ cup margarine
½ teaspoon salt

1 teaspoon vanilla
1 cup chopped pecans
1 (9-inch) deep dish pie shell, unbaked

Mix eggs, syrup, sugar, margarine, salt, and vanilla. Add nuts. Pour into pie shell. Bake for 10 minutes at 450 degrees; reduce heat to 350 degrees and bake for 45 minutes. Never fails!

Helen Holmes
Sara Adams

Yield: 6 servings

Pecan Pie II

½ cup margarine
1 cup dark corn syrup
1 cup sugar
3 eggs, beaten

1 teaspoon vanilla
2½ cups chopped pecans
2 (9-inch) pie shells, unbaked

Cream together margarine, syrup, and sugar. Add eggs and vanilla; mix well. Fold in nuts. Pour into pie shells. Bake at 350 degrees for 45 minutes.

Helen S. Stewart
Patricia H. Murray

Yield: 12 servings

Teresa's Butter Pecan Pie

½ cup margarine
1 cup sugar
2 eggs, beaten

1 teaspoon vanilla
1 cup chopped pecans
1 (9-inch) pie shell, unbaked

Melt margarine and add sugar. Add eggs, vanilla, and pecans. Pour into pie shell. Bake for 10 minutes at 400 degrees; reduce oven to 350 degrees and bake until firm, about 45 minutes.

Becky Mott Sommerville

Yield: 6 servings

French Pecan Pie

22 Ritz crackers, crushed
1 cup sugar
1 cup chopped pecans
2 egg whites, stiffly beaten
1 teaspoon vanilla

Pinch of salt
1 cup whipping cream
1 (1-ounce) square semi-sweet
    chocolate, grated

Combine all ingredients except cream and chocolate. Bake in buttered pie pan at 350 degrees for 20 minutes. Chill. Cover with whipped cream and grated chocolate.

Sarah James   Yield: 8 servings

Pecan Pie with Cream Cheese Crust

2 (3-ounce) packages cream
cheese, softened

1 cup butter, softened
2 cups flour

Cream together and chill for 1 hour. Roll out on waxed paper. Place dough in a 9-inch pie pan.

Filling:
½ cup sugar
1½ cups dark corn syrup
3 tablespoons butter
3 eggs

1 tablespoon flour
1 teaspoon vanilla
1 cup pecans, chopped

With an electric mixer, blend all of the ingredients except pecans. Add pecans and stir. Pour into pie crust. Bake at 350 degrees for 45 minutes to 1 hour.

Note: Can be made in mini muffin tins but cooking time is shortened.

Ginger Wilson   Yield: 6 servings

Creamy Peanut Butter Pie

1 (8-ounce) package cream cheese
½ cup peanut butter
1 cup powdered sugar
¼ cup half and half
1 (12-ounce) carton whipped
   topping

1 (9-inch) pie shell, graham
   cracker or chocolate
Grated chocolate

Cream together cream cheese and peanut butter. Add sugar and beat well. Add half and half and fold in whipped topping. Pour into pie shell and sprinkle with chocolate.

Note: This pie may be refrigerated or frozen.

Sandy Greene
Janice Stapp
Carolyn Sikes

Yield: 6 servings

Walnut Pie

½ cup brown sugar
2 tablespoons flour
1¼ cups light corn syrup
3 tablespoons margarine
¼ teaspoon salt

3 eggs
1½ teaspoons vanilla
1 (9-inch) pie shell, unbaked
1 cup English walnuts, large pieces

Mix brown sugar and flour in saucepan. Add corn syrup, margarine, and salt. Heat on low until margarine is melted. Do not boil. Beat eggs lightly with vanilla. Stir into sugar mixture and pour into pie shell. Sprinkle walnuts on top. Bake below oven center at 375 degrees for 40 to 45 minutes or until filling is set in the center. Cool before cutting.

Betty Jones

Yield: 6 servings

Black Bottom Pie

Crust:

14 gingersnaps   5 tablespoons butter, melted

Crush gingersnaps and roll out fine. Add melted butter and pat into 9-inch pie pan. Bake at 400 degrees for 10 minutes and allow to cool.

Filling:

1 egg yolk, well beaten   1½ tablespoons cornstarch
2 cups scalded milk   1½ squares bitter chocolate
½ cup sugar   1 teaspoon vanilla

Add egg yolks slowly to hot milk. Combine sugar and cornstarch and stir into milk mixture. Cook in double boiler for 20 minutes, stirring occasionally, until it coats spoon. Remove one cup of custard mixture. Add chocolate to cup and beat well as it cools. Add vanilla to chocolate mixture and chill.

Second Mixture:

1 tablespoon unflavored gelatin   ½ teaspoon cream of tartar
2 tablespoons cold water   2 tablespoons rum or whiskey
4 egg whites   Whipped cream, optional
½ cup sugar   Bitter chocolate shavings, optional

Dissolve gelatin in cold water, and add remaining custard, and cool. Beat egg whites until foamy; add sugar and cream of tartar and beat until stiff. Add rum and fold into plain custard mixture. Layer on top of chocolate mixture in pie crust. Chill. Garnish pie with whipped cream and shavings of bitter chocolate.

Louise Nolen   Yield: 6 to 8 servings

Libbett's Black Bottom Ice Cream Pie

1 ½ cups gingersnap crumbs
¼ cup powdered sugar
⅓ cup butter, melted

1 cup chocolate ice cream, softened
Creamy chocolate sauce
1 quart vanilla ice cream, softened

In mixing bowl combine gingersnap crumbs, sugar, and butter; mixing well. Press firmly into bottom and sides of a 9-inch pie pan that has been sprayed with vegetable shortening. Chill. Spread chocolate ice cream in bottom of crust, freeze until firm. Spread half of cooled creamy chocolate sauce over ice cream and freeze until set. Spoon vanilla ice cream over chocolate sauce and freeze. Drizzle remaining chocolate sauce evenly over pie. Freeze.

Creamy Chocolate Sauce:
1 (6-ounce) package semi-sweet
   chocolate morsels

½ cup whipping cream
½ teaspoon vanilla

Combine chocolate morsels and cream in small saucepan. Place over low heat stirring constantly until melted. Remove from heat, stir in vanilla and cool completely.

Martha Keith   Yield: 6 to 8 servings

Calypso Pie

18 Nabisco Oreo cookies
¼ cup butter, melted
1 quart coffee ice cream
Chocolate syrup

1 (8-ounce) carton whipped
   topping
1 cup coarsely chopped pecans
Cherries

Crush Oreo cookies until very fine. Stir in butter and press into a 10-inch pie pan. Chill. Soften ice cream. Fill pie shell with ice cream, cover with plastic wrap, and freeze. When ready to serve, slice pie and top each serving with chocolate syrup, whipped topping, more chocolate syrup, chopped nuts, and a cherry.

Note: If you cannot get coffee ice cream, make your own by adding ½ cup coffee plus 2 tablespoons instant coffee to a softened gallon of vanilla ice cream.

The Crossing   Yield: 6 to 8 servings

Sweet Angel Chocolate Pie

Crust:

3 egg whites
⅛ teaspoon salt
⅛ teaspoon cream of tartar

½ cup sugar
½ cup finely chopped nuts
½ teaspoon vanilla

Combine egg whites, salt, and cream of tartar in mixing bowl. Beat until foamy. Add sugar, 2 tablespoons at a time, beating after each until sugar is blended. Beat until stiff peaks form. Fold in nuts and vanilla. Spoon into a greased 9-inch pie pan making a nest. Bake at 300 degrees for 50 minutes.

Filling:

1 (4-ounce) package German
   sweet chocolate
3 tablespoons water

1 teaspoon vanilla
½ pint whipping cream

Combine chocolate and water in saucepan over low heat. Stir until chocolate is melted. Cool. Add vanilla and fold in whipped cream. Spoon into meringue shell and chill 2 hours before serving.

Variation: You may add 2 tablespoons prepared coffee to filling for a different flavor.

Cheryl Watts   Yield: 6 servings

Hot Fudge Pie

1 cup sugar
½ cup flour
½ cup margarine, melted
2 tablespoons cocoa

1 teaspoon vanilla
2 eggs
1 (9-inch) pie shell, unbaked
Ice cream

Combine and mix sugar, flour, margarine, cocoa, vanilla, and eggs. Pour into pie shell. Bake at 350 degrees for 30 minutes. Cool. Top with ice cream. Can be served while pie is still warm.

Note: Quick and easy—perfect for emergencies!

Kathryn Hardy   Yield: 6 servings
Becky Mott Sommerville
Leah McLaughlin

Chocolate Meringue Pie

Pie Crust:

3 cups sifted flour
½ teaspoon salt
1 cup shortening

6 tablespoons ice water
1 egg, well beaten

Combine flour and salt in mixing bowl; cut in shortening until mixture resembles coarse meal. Add water and egg. Stir with a fork until all dry ingredients are moistened. Shape dough into a ball, roll out to fit a 9-inch pie pan. Bake at 400 degrees for 8 to 10 minutes. Shape leftover dough into a ball, wrap, and store in refrigerator. It can be stored for up to one week.

Filling:

2 cups milk
1 cup sugar
¼ cup plus 1 tablespoon flour
¼ cup plus 2 tablespoons cocoa

3 egg yolks, slightly beaten
1 tablespoon butter
1 teaspoon vanilla

Pour milk into a double boiler; combine dry ingredients and add to milk. Cook until thickened, stirring constantly. Stir a small amount of the hot mixture into egg yolks until well mixed. Add egg mixture to hot mixture and cook for 2 or 3 minutes. Remove from heat; add butter and vanilla and beat for 2 to 3 minutes. Cool. Pour filling into a cooled baked pastry shell. Top with meringue. Bake at 350 degrees for 12 minutes or until lightly browned.

Meringue:

3 egg whites
¼ teaspoon cream of tartar

¼ cup plus 2 tablespoons sugar

Combine egg whites and cream of tartar, beat together until foamy. Gradually add sugar, beating until stiff.

Nellie Kate Tepper
Joy Davis
Laura Wallace

Yield: 6 servings

Chocolate Chip Pie

2 eggs
½ cup flour
½ cup sugar
½ cup firmly packed brown sugar
1 cup margarine, melted and
   cooled
1 (6-ounce) package semi-sweet
   chocolate chips

1 cup chopped walnuts or pecans
1 (9-inch) deep dish pie shell,
   unbaked
Whipped topping or ice cream,
   optional

Preheat oven to 325 degrees. In bowl beat eggs until foamy. Add flour, sugar, and brown sugar; beat until well blended. Blend in melted margarine; add chocolate chips and nuts. Pour into pie shell. Bake for 1 hour. Serve with whipped topping or ice cream.

Betty Jones
Barbara Rosser

Yield: 6 servings

"Quickie" Chocolate Pie

1 (9-inch) pie shell
2 squares unsweetened chocolate
1 (14-ounce) can sweetened
   condensed milk

1 (16-ounce) carton whipped
   topping

Cook pie shell and allow to cool. Melt chocolate squares very slowly in double boiler. Add sweetened condensed milk. Blend mixture together while slowly cooking until smooth and thick. Cool slightly. Stir ½ to one carton of whipped topping into chocolate mixture. Increase or decrease whipped topping depending on chocolate thickness desired. Stir until blended and pour into pie shell. This will freeze indefinitely. Remove from freezer a few minutes before serving. Very simple and very rich!

Rosemary Turner

Yield: 6 servings

Granny Bobo's Trillby

½ gallon milk
1 (13-ounce) can evaporated milk
1 milk can water
1 teaspoon vanilla
⅔ cup flour

3½ cups sugar
10 egg yolks, beaten
10 egg whites, whipped
6 oranges, peeled and segmented

Mix all liquids; add flour and sugar. Cook on medium heat until mixture starts to thicken, stirring constantly. Add egg yolks and continue to cook. When slightly thickened, slowly add egg whites, mixing well. Continue cooking until thickened; strain if necessary. Cut up oranges and place in mixture.

Note: This recipe is well over 60 years old. We have this dish every Christmas.

Beverly Scott
    Class of 1972

Yield: 8 to 10 servings

Trifle

1 (10x12-inch) sponge cake
Raspberry jam
1 cup sherry or port
Bananas or peaches, sliced

½ pint soft custard
½ pint cream, whipped
Nuts
Cherries

Split sponge cake in half by slicing through the middle horizontally. Cover bottom layer with raspberry jam. Put layers together. Pour sherry over cake, and allow to soak. Top cake with bananas or peaches. Prepare soft custard, chill, and pour over the entire dessert. Refrigerate until cold, then frost with whipped cream and decorate with nuts and cherries.

Soft Custard:
2 eggs
⅛ cup sugar
Dash of salt

1 cup milk
½ teaspoon vanilla

Beat eggs lightly; add sugar and salt. Scald and stir in milk. Cook over hot water or very low heat until custard thickens (do not allow to boil). Add flavoring, and chill thoroughly.

Variation: Rum or sherry may be substituted for vanilla.

Edie Delp

Yield: 8 to 10 servings

Chocolate Trifle

1 (23½-ounce) box family size
   brownie mix
1 (12-ounce) carton whipped
   topping

1 (4-ounce) can chocolate syrup
½ to 1 cup chopped nuts
Red cherries, with stems

Make brownies according to directions on package, omitting pecans. Slice into at least 24 pieces. Using a trifle bowl, layer brownies, whipped topping, drizzled chocolate syrup, and chopped nuts. Repeat layers 2 to 3 more times. Garnish with pecans and red cherries.

Note: Men and chocolate lovers adore this.

Joy Beers
          Yield: 8 servings

Amaretto Trifle

6 miniature jelly rolls, each cut
   into 4 slices
¼ cup amaretto liqueur

1 recipe of soft custard
1 cup whipping cream

In a 2-quart casserole, layer ⅓ of the sliced jelly rolls. Sprinkle ⅓ of the liqueur over jelly rolls and cover with custard. Repeat layers two more times and top with whipped cream.

Custard:
1½ cups sugar
3 tablespoons flour
Dash of salt

4 large eggs
1 quart milk, scalded
2 teaspoons vanilla

Mix sugar, flour, salt, and eggs in top of double boiler. Make sure that boiling water does not touch the bottom of the top boiler. Add scalded milk very slowly into mixture. Stir constantly until custard coats spoon. Remove from heat and stir in vanilla. Chill custard but do not cover airtight.

Evelyn Sherrer
          Yield: 8 to 10 servings

French Strawberry Mousse

1 cup flour	1 cup chopped pecans
½ cup brown sugar	½ cup butter

Mix together and spread in a 9x13-inch pan and bake at 350 degrees for 20 minutes. Cool, then crumble mixture.

Mousse:

2 egg whites	2 (½-pint) cartons whipping
1 cup sugar	cream
2 teaspoons lemon juice	3 (3-ounce) packages lady fingers
1 (10-ounce) package frozen	
strawberries	

Beat egg whites, sugar, lemon juice, and frozen strawberries for 15 minutes. (Do not underbeat.) Whip one carton of whipping cream and fold into the berry mixture. Line and layer sides of a large trifle bowl with lady fingers. Pour ⅓ of the berry mixture over the bottom layer of lady fingers. Add ⅓ of the crumb mixture and continue layers. Top with the other carton of whipped cream, whipped and sweetened. Garnish with fresh unhulled strawberries.

Edie Delp   Yield: 12 servings

Punch Bowl Cake

1 (18½-ounce) box white or yellow cake mix	2 (21-ounce) cans apple, cherry or strawberry pie filling, chilled
1 (6-ounce) and 1 (3-ounce) box vanilla instant pudding	1 (12-ounce) carton whipped topping
2½ cups milk	Coconut, optional
2 (20-ounce) cans crushed pineapple, well drained and chilled	Nuts, optional

Bake cake according to directions and cool. Using large punch bowl crumble ½-inch layer of cooled cake in the bottom. Mix both packages of pudding with milk. Pour ½ pudding mix over cake. Spoon ½ can drained pineapple over pudding. Cover with 1 can pie filling and layer with ½ of the whipped topping, coconut, and nuts. Repeat layers. Chill and refrigerate.

Joanne Dillingham   Yield: 18 to 20 servings

Chocolate Eclair Dessert

2 (3-ounce) packages instant
   vanilla pudding
3 cups milk
1 (8-ounce) carton whipped
   topping

1 teaspoon vanilla
Honey graham crackers

Mix together instant pudding and milk. Fold in whipped topping and add vanilla. On bottom of 9x13-inch pan place a layer of graham crackers. Pour layer of pudding over crackers. Repeat layers ending with pudding.

Icing:
3 tablespoons butter
3 (1-ounce) squares semi-sweet
   chocolate

3 tablespoons milk
3 tablespoons white corn syrup
½ cup powdered sugar

Melt butter and chocolate over very low heat. Add remaining ingredients. Cool slightly before frosting. Refrigerate overnight or until well chilled. Cut into squares.

Ruthie Carr
Rosemary Harris

Yield: 10 to 12 servings

Charlotte

5 eggs, separated
1 cup sugar
2 (1-ounce) envelopes unflavored
   gelatin

½ cup water
½ cup cream sherry
1 pint whipping cream

Beat egg yolks until lemon color. Add sugar and beat until a light color. Dissolve gelatin in water over a double boiler (or over hot water). Add gelatin mixture and sherry to egg yolk mixture. Add whipped cream and fold in stiffly beaten egg whites. Cover and refrigerate until set.

Kate Himes

Yield: 4 servings

Jamie's Egg Custard

2 eggs
1/4 cup sugar
1/4 teaspoon salt

1 teaspoon vanilla
2 cups milk

Beat eggs and add sugar, salt, and vanilla. Scald milk and pour into egg mixture. Butter custard cups and pour custard into these. Bake in a pan of water at 350 degrees until set.

Gloria Sims Crump
Margie Swift

Yield: 4 servings

Delicious Boiled Custard

1 cup sugar
4 eggs
· 1 quart milk, warmed

5 or 6 large marshmallows, quartered
1 teaspoon vanilla

Combine sugar and eggs in the top of a double boiler, blending thoroughly. Gradually stir in milk. Place over hot water and stir constantly until mixture is hot. Add marshmallows and continue stirring until marshmallows are melted and mixture coats a metal spoon. Remove from heat and strain through a sieve. Stir in vanilla and chill well.

Jean Sullivan

Yield: 4 to 6 servings

Microwave Boiled Custard

1 tablespoon flour
1/2 cup sugar
5 eggs
1 quart milk

3 scoops vanilla ice cream
Whipped cream, optional
Scoop of vanilla ice cream, optional

In 2-quart covered casserole mix flour and sugar. Add eggs and milk; mix well. Cook in microwave on HIGH for 12 to 16 minutes, stirring every 2 minutes. After it is cooked, whip well; add ice cream and whip until ice cream has dissolved. Cool. Serve with whipped cream or a scoop of vanilla ice cream.

Kaye Plummer

Yield: 4 to 6 servings

Very Easy Banana Pudding

2 (3-ounce) packages instant
  vanilla pudding
3 cups milk
1 (14-ounce) can sweetened
  condensed milk

1 (8-ounce) carton whipped
  topping
Vanilla wafers
5 to 6 bananas

Mix the pudding, milk, and condensed milk. Fold in the whipped topping. Layer vanilla wafers, bananas, and pudding mixture. Repeat layers. Top with whipped topping or crushed vanilla wafers.

Note: If whipped topping is used for topping an extra carton is needed.

Lillian Riddle Gilley
  Class of 1972

Yield: 6 to 8 servings

Brandied Caramel Flan

Caramel:
³⁄₄ cup sugar

Place sugar in a large heavy skillet. Cook over medium heat until sugar melts and forms a light brown syrup, stir to blend. Immediately pour syrup into a heated 8-inch round shallow baking dish. Holding dish with pot holders, quickly rotate to cover bottom and sides completely. Set aside.

Custard:
2 cups milk
2 cups light cream
6 eggs
½ cup sugar

½ teaspoon salt
2 teaspoons vanilla
⅓ cup brandy
1 tablespoon brandy

In medium saucepan, heat milk and cream just until bubbles form around edge of pan. In large bowl, with rotary beater, beat eggs slightly. Add sugar, salt, and vanilla. Gradually stir in hot milk mixture and ⅓ cup brandy. Pour into prepared dish. Be sure to set dish in shallow pan before baking and pour boiling water to ½-inch level around dish. Bake at 325 degrees for 35 to 40 minutes or until silver knife inserted in center comes out clean. Let custard cool; refrigerate 4 hours or overnight. To serve, run a small spatula around edge of dish; shake gently to release. The caramel acts as a sauce. Warm 1 tablespoon brandy slightly; ignite quickly and pour over flan for a flaming dish that will impress your friends.

Cookbook Committee

Yield: 8 servings

Bread Pudding with Whiskey Sauce

3 tablespoons margarine, melted
1 loaf French bread
1 quart milk
3 eggs

2 cups sugar
2 tablespoons vanilla
1 cup raisins

Preheat oven to 350 degrees. Melt margarine in bottom of 3-quart baking dish. Remove from oven to cool. Soak bread in milk and crush with hands until mixed thoroughly. Add eggs, sugar, vanilla, and raisins; stir well. Pour mixture over melted margarine and bake 55 to 60 minutes or until very firm. Let cool; cube pudding and put into individual dessert dishes. When ready to serve, add Whiskey Sauce.

Whiskey Sauce:
1 cup sugar
½ cup butter or margarine

1 egg, well beaten
Whiskey to taste

In top of double boiler, heat sugar and butter until very hot and completely dissolved. Add egg, beating quickly so egg doesn't curdle. Let cool and add whiskey to taste.

Peggy Striplin   Yield: 6 to 8 servings

Royal Bread Pudding

2 tablespoons margarine or butter
2 cups hot milk
1 cup soft breadcrumbs
2 eggs, separated
⅓ cup sugar

¼ teaspoon salt
1 tablespoon cognac or
  1 teaspoon vanilla
Currant jelly
3 tablespoons sugar

Preheat oven to 350 degrees. Melt butter in milk and stir in the bread crumbs. Beat egg yolks; add and mix well ⅓ cup of sugar, salt, and egg yolks. Add this to the milk mixture. Stir in the cognac or vanilla and pour into a greased 2-quart baking dish. Place dish in a pan of hot water and bake 35 to 40 minutes or until set. Spread with currant jelly. Beat the egg whites until stiff and gradually beat in the remaining sugar. Spread meringue on top of the pudding and bake 10 minutes, or until meringue is browned.

Variation: Sometimes I add a few raisins to the pudding before baking.

Anne Minter   Yield: 6 to 8 servings

Hot Fudge Pudding

1 cup flour
2 teaspoons baking powder
¼ teaspoon salt
1 cup sugar
2 tablespoons cocoa
½ cup milk

2 tablespoons vegetable oil
½ cup chopped nuts
1 cup brown sugar
4 tablespoons cocoa
1¾ cups hot water

Sift together in a bowl flour, baking powder, salt, sugar, and 2 tablespoons cocoa. Stir in milk, oil, and nuts. Mix well. Spread in lightly greased 9-inch square pan. Mix brown sugar and 4 tablespoons cocoa in a small bowl; sprinkle on top of mixture. Pour hot water over entire batter. Bake at 350 degrees for 45 minutes. Serve hot with ice cream.

Joy Davis

Yield: 6 servings

Pugh's Ozark Pudding

1 egg
¾ cup sugar
1 tablespoon vanilla
3 heaping tablespoons flour
1¼ teaspoons baking powder

⅛ teaspoon salt
½ cup chopped apples
½ cup chopped nuts
1 cup whipped cream

Beat egg and add sugar and vanilla. Cream until light and creamy. Sift flour, baking powder, and salt. Add to creamed mixture. Fold in apples and nuts. Pour into greased, paper lined 2-quart dish. Bake at 350 degrees for 30 minutes. Serve with whipped cream.

Lois Sanford

Yield: 6 servings

Peach Crisp

5 cups fresh sliced peaches
½ cup sugar
¼ teaspoon nutmeg
½ teaspoon cinnamon

1 cup uncooked oats
½ cup brown sugar
⅓ cup flour, sifted
⅓ cup butter, melted

Place peaches in greased 8x8-inch baking dish. Combine sugar and spices and sprinkle over peaches. Mix oats, brown sugar, and flour; stir in butter and pour over peaches. Bake at 375 degrees for 30 minutes.

Jerry Goodwin

Yield: 6 to 8 servings

Swedish Pastry

Pastry:

1 cup butter
½ cup sugar
1 egg

1 teaspoon vanilla
2 cups sifted cake flour

Cream butter, sugar, and egg together until fluffy. Blend in vanilla. Add flour to form a ball. Place a piece of pastry the size of a marble into a small muffin tin. Use thumb to shape and line sides.

Filling:

2 eggs, beaten
1 cup sugar
2 tablespoons lemon juice
1 tablespoon lemon rind

½ teaspoon salt
1 cup moist coconut
1 cup chopped pecans
½ cup chopped dates

Combine all ingredients for the filling. Drop ½ to 1 teaspoon of filling into each pastry. Bake at 325 degrees for 25 minutes.

Frances Turner   Yield: 5 dozen

Tasty Finger Length Cake

4 eggs
2 cups biscuit mix
1 (16-ounce) box light brown
   sugar

2 teaspoons vanilla
2 cups chopped nuts

Beat eggs; add biscuit mix, sugar, vanilla, and chopped nuts. Pour into a lightly greased jelly roll pan. Bake at 350 degrees for 30 minutes. Cool; frost, and cut into tiny finger lengths.

Icing:

1 (8-ounce) package cream cheese,
   softened
½ cup margarine, softened

1 (16-ounce) box powdered sugar
Grated pecans

Mix ingredients together and frost cake. Sprinkle with pecans.

Christine Moore   Yield: 2 to 3 dozen

Nut Roll Extraordinaire

7 eggs, separated	1 teaspoon baking powder
¾ cup sugar	Powdered sugar
1½ cups ground pecans, walnuts or almonds	Whipped topping or whipped cream

Preheat oven to 350 degrees. Oil jellyroll pan; line pan with waxed paper and oil again. Beat 7 egg yolks with sugar until light in color and ribbon forms when dropped from spoon. Beat in ground nuts and baking powder. Fold in stiffly beaten egg whites. Spread in prepared pan and bake 15 to 20 minutes. Cool. Cover with damp towel and chill. Dust the top with powdered sugar and turn out onto waxed paper. It is now ready to fill and ice.

Note: Use one of the following fillings.

Filling #1:

1 (10-ounce) jar apricot preserves	¼ cup Grand Marnier

Blend ingredients in food processor or electric mixer. Spread over roll.

Filling #2:

1 (10-ounce) jar strawberry preserves	¼ cup Cointreau

Blend ingredients in food processor or electric mixer. Spread over roll.

TO ASSEMBLE: After spreading either filling over roll, start at long edge of roll and roll as for jellyroll. Cover with whipped cream or whipped topping and decorate with chocolate leaves or as desired.

Note: See Chocolate Leaves recipe.

Cookbook Committee   Yield: 10 to 12 servings

Angel Food Cakes

1 (18½-ounce) box angel food cake mix	1 tablespoon instant coffee granules
1 cup butter, NO SUBSTITUTE	1 tablespoon cool water
1 (16-ounce) box powdered sugar	Coarsely ground peanuts

Mix angel food cake according to directions on box and bake in 9x5x3-inch loaf pan. Cut cake with an electric knife into 5 lengthwise slices. Cut across 7 to 8 times to make about 40 pieces. Remove brown crust before icing. Cream butter until light and fluffy. Add sugar in small amounts and beat well after each addition until half of the sugar has been used. Mix coffee and water together and add in small amounts to mixture alternating with remaining sugar. Beat until fluffy. Ice cakes on four sides using 2 forks, and dipping in icing. Roll in coarsely ground peanuts. Press nuts into icing with fingers if necessary.

Note: Rectangular baked cake may be purchased.

Libba Riddle   Yield: 40 cakes

Banana Split Cake

2 cups graham cracker crumbs	Lemon juice
6 tablespoons butter, melted	1 (16-ounce) can crushed pineapple
6 tablespoons powdered sugar	
1 cup chopped pecans	1 (12-ounce) carton whipped topping
2 egg whites, beaten	
2 cups powdered sugar	2 pints fresh strawberries
½ cup butter, melted	Sugar
4 large bananas	

Mix graham cracker crumbs, 6 tablespoons melted butter, 6 tablespoons powdered sugar, and pecans. Press into bottom of greased 9x13-inch pyrex dish. Mix beaten egg whites, 2 cups powdered sugar, and ½ cup melted butter. Pour over first layer. Slice bananas and sprinkle with lemon juice to keep them from turning brown. Add to previous layers. Drain pineapple well and pour over bananas. Cover with whipped topping. Refrigerate. Slice strawberries, sprinkle with sugar, and refrigerate. Add to top of other layers just before serving.

Wyn Wadsworth Minor
  Class of 1972

Frozen Chocolate Crêpes with Custard Sauce

Crêpes:

2 eggs
½ cup biscuit mix
¾ cup milk
1 tablespoon shortening, melted

1 teaspoon vanilla
1 tablespoon sugar
2½ tablespoons cocoa

Combine eggs, biscuit mix, milk, shortening, vanilla, sugar, and cocoa in a blender until smooth. Batter will be thin and creamy. Chill in refrigerator for ½ hour. Grease lightly the bottom of a 6½-inch crêpe pan or iron skillet and place over medium-high heat. Using a 1-ounce measure, pour batter into hot pan. Tilt to cover bottom. Cook until crêpe looks almost dry on top, turn, and brown other side. Turn crêpe onto waxed paper. Grease pan with oil again, repeating each step. Layer crêpes between sheets of waxed paper.

Chocolate Filling:

1 (12-ounce) package semi-sweet
    chocolate chips
1½ teaspoons vanilla

⅛ teaspoon salt
1½ cups whipping cream, scalded
6 egg yolks

Combine chips, vanilla, and salt in blender. Add cream and mix for 30 seconds or until chips melt. Add eggs and mix for 5 seconds. Pour into a bowl and cool. Place a generous tablespoon of filling on each crêpe. Roll up and wrap well for freezer.

Custard:

4 large egg yolks
1½ tablespoons cornstarch
½ cup sugar

1½ cups half and half
½ teaspoon vanilla
Chocolate curls for garnish

Combine egg yolks, cornstarch, and sugar in a small bowl. Scald half and half; add slowly to egg mixture, whisking rapidly. Pour into top of a double boiler and cook slowly until thickened. When thickened, cool quickly by placing pan in cold water and stirring with whisk. Add vanilla. Strain to remove lumps if necessary. Remove crêpe from freezer 20 minutes before serving. Spoon warm custard over each crêpe and garnish with chocolate curls.

Cecile Youngblood   Yield: 10 to 12 crepes

Panic

1 (21-ounce) can pie filling
1 (18½-ounce) box cake mix

1 cup margarine, melted
½ cup chopped nuts

Preheat oven to 350 degrees. Pour pie filling into greased 9x13-inch pan. Sprinkle dry cake mix over filling. Pour melted margarine over cake mix and top with nuts. Bake for 30 to 40 minutes.

Variations: Use yellow cake mix with strawberry and cherry pie fillings; use white cake mix with peach filling; use spice cake with apple filling.

Connie Pugh
Fran Pearce

Yield: 8 to 10 servings

Pavlova Meringue

4 egg whites, at room temperature
1 cup sugar
1 tablespoon cornstarch

1 teaspoon vinegar
Fresh or canned fruit
Heavy cream

Preheat oven to 300 degrees. Beat egg whites as stiff as possible, adding sugar slowly until dissolved. Fold in cornstarch and vinegar. Pile on oiled heavy aluminum foil the sides of which have been built up to hold heat. (This is better than using a regular cookie sheet.) Bake slowly for 1 hour and 30 minutes. Turn onto flat platter and decorate with fruit and whipped cream or unwhipped cream.

Edie Delp

Yield: 6 servings

Heavenly Grapes

4 cups green seedless grapes
1 cup sour cream

Brown sugar

Wash grapes; drain well. Combine grapes and sour cream. Pour into a large bowl or individual dishes. Sprinkle top generously with brown sugar. Refrigerate. Stir before serving.

Joy Beers

Yield: 6 to 8 servings

Four Layer Lemon Dessert

¾ cup margarine
1¾ cups flour
¾ cup chopped pecans
1 (8-ounce) package cream cheese,
 softened
1 cup sugar
1 (12-ounce) carton whipped
 topping

4 large egg yolks
2 (14-ounce) cans sweetened
 condensed milk
½ cup lemon juice
2 teaspoons grated lemon rind

Melt margarine; add flour and nuts. Press into a 9x13-inch dish to make crust. Bake at 350 degrees for 25 minutes. Cool. Mix cream cheese, sugar, and ½ carton of whipped topping. Spread over crust. Beat egg yolks; add milk and mix well. Add lemon juice and rind. Spread over second layer. Refrigerate. When ready to serve add remaining whipped topping as fourth layer.

Variation: For third layer use favorite instant pudding mix or favorite canned pie filling.

Milly Noah
Cam Williams
 Class of 1985
Glady Stephens Elliott
 Class of 1972

Yield: 14 to 16 servings

Finger Gelatin

4 (1-ounce) packages unflavored
 gelatin
1 cup cold water
3 (3-ounce) packages gelatin,
 any flavor

½ cup sugar
4 cups boiling water
Powdered sugar, optional

Mix ingredients together in the order given. Stir until well mixed. Pour into 9x13-inch pan. Let set in refrigerator over night. Then cut into 1-inch cubes. Leave plain or roll in powdered sugar.

Note: Won't melt!!

Sue Lide

Yield: 10 to 12 servings

Baklava

4 cups walnuts
½ cup sugar
2 teaspoons cinnamon
1 teaspoon orange peel, grated
1 teaspoon lemon peel, grated

28 sheets phyllo pastry
1¼ cups butter or margarine,
   melted
Honey orange syrup

Grind, grate, or finely chop walnuts. Mix walnuts with sugar, cinnamon, orange and lemon peels. Set aside. Cut phyllo to fit 9x13-inch pan. Cover phyllo with plastic film while working to prevent drying. Brush bottom of pan with melted butter. Place one sheet of phyllo on pan and brush with butter. Cover with second sheet and brush with butter. Repeat making a layer of five sheets for bottom of pastry. Sprinkle with ¾ cup walnut mixture patting it to an even layer. Cover with 3 sheets of phyllo, brushing each with butter. Repeat layers until filling is used—should be about 7 layers of filling. Top with 5 layers of phyllo buttering each as before. With sharp knife, carefully cut lengthwise through top of phyllo layers making 5 strips. Make a second row of cuts, on the diagonal, forming diamonds. Bake at 350 degrees on rack above center of oven for 1 hour or until golden. Meanwhile, prepare and cool Honey orange syrup. Let Baklava stand 10 minutes, then spoon the cold syrup over the hot Baklava. Let stand overnight to absorb syrup before serving.

Honey Orange Syrup:
1 cup honey
¾ cup sugar
⅔ cup orange juice

1 stick cinnamon
1 tablespoon lemon juice

Combine honey, sugar, orange juice, and cinnamon. Heat to a full rolling boil, stirring until sugar dissolves. Remove from heat and stir in lemon juice. Cool thoroughly before spooning over the pastry. Remove cinnamon stick when cold.

Jack Vardaman
Headmaster
   1977-1983

Yield: 20 large diamond pieces or 80 medium squares

Bananas Foster

2 tablespoons brown sugar
1 tablespoon butter
1 ripe banana, peeled and sliced
   lengthwise

Dash of cinnamon
1 ounce light rum
1 large scoop vanilla ice cream

Melt brown sugar and butter in flat chafing dish. Add banana and sauté until tender. Sprinkle with cinnamon. Pour rum over banana and flame. Baste with warm liquid until flame burns out. Serve immediately over ice cream.

Faye W. Bailey   Yield: 1 serving

Coconut Cream Cheesecake

Crust:
²/₃ cup flour
1 tablespoon sugar

5 tablespoons well-chilled butter,
   cut into small pieces

Preheat oven to 325 degrees. Combine flour and sugar in large bowl. Using pastry blender or 2 knives cut in butter until mixture resembles coarse meal. Gather into ball, and wrap in plastic wrap. Refrigerate 15 minutes. Press dough into bottom of 10-inch springform pan. Bake until golden brown, 15 to 20 minutes. Cool slightly. Reduce oven temperature to 300 degrees.

Filling:
3 (8-ounce) packages cream cheese,
   softened
1½ cups sugar
4 eggs, room temperature
2 egg yolks, room temperature
2 cups flaked coconut

1 cup whipping cream
1 teaspoon fresh lemon juice
½ teaspoon vanilla
½ teaspoon almond extract
Toasted coconut, optional

In electric mixer, beat cream cheese and sugar until smooth. Beat in eggs and yolks one at a time. Mix in flaked coconut, whipping cream, fresh lemon juice, vanilla, and almond extract. Pour filling into crust. Bake in 300 degree oven until edges of filling are firm, about 70 minutes. Let cool completely. Remove from pan. Cover with plastic wrap and refrigerate 4 hours. Just before serving, may sprinkle with toasted coconut.

Edie Delp   Yield: 12 servings

Praline Cheesecake

Crust:

1¼ cups graham cracker crumbs
¼ cup sugar

¼ cup finely chopped pecans
¼ cup butter, melted

Combine all ingredients and press into a greased 10-inch springform pan. Bake at 300 degrees for 10 minutes.

Filling:

3 (8-ounce) packages cream cheese, softened
1 cup brown sugar
⅔ cup evaporated milk

2 tablespoons flour
1½ teaspoons vanilla
3 eggs

Combine all ingredients except eggs and blend well. Add eggs, one at a time, blending well after each. Pour into crust. Bake at 325 degrees for 50 minutes.

Note: Serve individual slices topped with prepared caramel topping, whipped cream, and nuts.

Kay Oakes   Yield: 12 to 15 servings

Mac's Cheesecake

Crust:

14 zwieback crackers, crumbled
½ cup butter, melted

½ cup sugar

Mix ingredients together. Press into bottom of a 9-inch springform cake pan.

Filling:

6 (8-ounce) packages cream cheese, softened
6 eggs
½ cup plus 2 tablespoons flour

2½ cups sugar
1½ cups heavy cream
1 teaspoon vanilla
Juice of one lemon

Mix all ingredients well and pour into crust-lined cake pan. Place a pan with an inch of water under cake while baking. Bake at 350 degrees for 1 hour or until cake begins to brown on top. Turn off oven and let cake remain for 30 minutes with oven door closed. Chill before unmolding. Best to refrigerate overnight.

John M. Oxford   Yield: 12 to 16 servings

Creamy Baked Cheesecake

2 (8-ounce) packages cream cheese, softened
1 (14-ounce) can sweetened condensed milk
3 eggs

1/4 teaspoon salt
1/4 cup lemon juice
1 (9-inch) graham cracker pie shell
1 (8-ounce) carton sour cream

In a large bowl, beat cream cheese until fluffy. Mix in milk, eggs, and salt until smooth. Add lemon juice and stir. Pour into pie shell and bake 50 to 55 minutes at 300 degrees. Turn oven off. Spread sour cream on cheesecake. Return to oven (not turned on) for 1 hour to minimize cracking. Chill. Garnish with fresh sliced strawberrries.

Carolyn Sikes   Yield: 8 to 10 servings

Cheesecake

Crust:
1 1/2 cups graham cracker crumbs
1/2 cup powdered sugar

1 teaspoon allspice
1/2 cup butter, melted

Make crust by combining all ingredients and spread into bottom of 9-inch springform pan, pressing up the sides about 1/2 to 3/4 inch.

Filling:
2 (8-ounce) packages cream cheese
1 teaspoon vanilla

2 eggs
2/3 cup sugar

Soften cream cheese. Beat with other ingredients until smooth and creamy. Pour into pan over crust. Bake at 350 degrees for 25 minutes or until set. Remove from oven. Leave oven on to maintain temperature. Cool 15 minutes. Pour topping over cake and return to oven for 15 to 20 minutes. Cool on rack for 2 hours. Cover, place in refrigerator for at least 24 hours.

Topping:
1 1/2 cups sour cream
1 teaspoon vanilla

1/4 cup sugar

Mix together and pour over baked cake.

Becky Bailey   Yield: 10 servings
Carolyn Weissinger

Easy Chocolate Cheesecake

1 cup graham cracker crumbs
3 tablespoons sugar
3 tablespoons margarine, melted
3 (8-ounce) packages cream cheese, softened

¾ cup sugar
3 eggs
1 teaspoon vanilla
1 cup semi-sweet chocolate chips

Combine cracker crumbs, 3 tablespoons sugar and margarine to make crust. Press into bottom of springform pan. Combine remaining ingredients and blend with electric mixer. Bake at 450 degrees for 10 minutes. Reduce temperature to 250 degrees and bake for 25 minutes. Cool. Loosen cake from rim before attempting to remove band. Chill before serving.

Terry Hunter   Yield: 10 to 12 servings

Milky Way No Bake Cheesecake

1½ cups chocolate wafer crumbs
4 tablespoons butter or margarine, melted
1 (1-ounce) envelope unflavored gelatin
1 cup milk
4 (2.23-ounce) Milky Way Bars, sliced

2 (8-ounce) packages cream cheese, softened
2 tablespoons sugar
1 teaspoon vanilla
1 cup heavy or whipping cream

Combine chocolate crumbs and butter; press into bottom and 2 inches up the side of an 8-inch springform pan; chill. Sprinkle gelatin over milk in a medium saucepan. Stir over low heat until mixture is smooth. Beat in candy bars, cream cheese, sugar, and vanilla. Add cream and beat at high speed for 4 minutes. Pour mixture into prepared crust. Chill until firm, about 4 hours. If desired, garnish with additional whipping cream and sliced candy bars.

Variation: This cheesecake is also good when served with a Fresh Strawberry Sauce: purée 2 cups strawberries with 1 tablespoon sugar in a blender.

Note: Milky Way is a registered trademark of Mars, Incorporated.

Edie Delp   Yield: 12 servings

Hot Fudge Sauce

3 tablespoons cocoa
1 cup sugar
1 (5-ounce) can evaporated milk

1 tablespoon butter
1 teaspoon vanilla

Combine cocoa and sugar in a saucepan and place over medium heat. Add milk; bring to a boil and stir constantly. Remove from heat and add butter and vanilla. Stir until butter melts.

Note: Delicious over ice cream or cake.

Kathryn Hardy   Yield: 1 cup

Chocolate Leaves

4 ounces semi-sweet chocolate
   pieces

Non-poisonous leaves
½-inch artist brush

Melt chocolate. Wash leaves. Brush melted chocolate on backs of leaves. Put in freezer for 2 to 3 minutes or until hard enough to peel leaf from chocolate. Put chocolate leaves in plastic bag which has air in it to cushion the leaves. Keep in refrigerator until needed.

Variation: To keep leaves for a longer time, use 6 ounces melted semi-sweet chocolate combined with a block of melted paraffin and follow preceding directions.

Note: A camellia leaf is good choice because of its size.

Cookbook Committee

Pineapple Cookies

1 cup shortening
1½ cups sugar
2 eggs
1 teaspoon lemon juice
3½ cups flour

1 teaspoon baking soda
1 teaspoon salt
1 (8-ounce) can crushed pineapple,
   undrained

Cream shortening and sugar. Add remaining ingredients. Drop by teaspoon onto cookie sheet and bake at 350 degrees for 10 to 12 minutes or until brown.

Martha Campbell   Yield: 3 dozen

Glazed Apple Cookies

½ cup shortening
1½ cups brown sugar
2 cups flour
½ teaspoon salt
¼ cup milk
1 cup finely chopped apples
1 teaspoon baking soda

1 egg
1 teaspoon cinnamon
1 teaspoon cloves
½ teaspoon nutmeg
1 cup raisins
1 cup chopped nuts

Mix all ingredients together and drop by teaspoon onto a greased cookie sheet.
Bake at 375 degrees for 10 to 12 minutes. Glaze cookies while still warm.

Glaze:
1½ cups powdered sugar
⅛ teaspoon salt
½ teaspoon vanilla

1 tablespoon butter
Half and half

Mix sugar, salt, vanilla, and butter. Add enough cream for spreading consistency.

Rosemary Harris   Yield: 3 dozen
Pat Labbe

Jewish Prune Cookies

2 cups flour
½ cup sugar
1½ teaspoons baking powder
¼ teaspoon salt
2 eggs

½ cup vegetable oil
1 teaspoon vanilla
1 (12-ounce) can Solo prune
   filling

Combine flour, sugar, baking powder, and salt. Mix together eggs, oil, and vanilla.
Mix all together and knead 8 to 10 minutes. Roll out on floured board. Cut
with a round cookie cutter and fill with ½ teaspoon filling. Fold up three sides
to form a pocket to hold filling in center. Bake at 350 degrees for 10 minutes or
until brown.

Variation: Any Solo filling may be used.

Rosemary Harris   Yield: 3 dozen

Fruitcake Cookies

½ pound red pineapple, chopped
½ pound green pineapple, chopped
1 (15-ounce) box white raisins
2 (8-ounce) boxes dates, chopped
3 cups flour, divided
1 cup brown sugar
½ cup margarine
4 egg yolks

3 tablespoons milk
3 teaspoons baking soda
6 ounces orange juice
1 teaspoon cloves
1 teaspoon allspice
1 teaspoon nutmeg
1 teaspoon cinnamon
5 cups pecans, chopped
4 egg whites, stiffly beaten

Dredge fruit in 1 cup flour. Add remaining ingredients and mix well. Drop by teaspoon onto a greased cookie sheet and bake at 300 degrees for 15 minutes.

Mary Elizabeth Whidby
Carolyn Weissinger
Carolyn Harris

Yield: 6 dozen

Best Gingerbread Cookie

1 cup margarine
1 cup brown sugar
1 egg
⅓ cup light molasses
2 tablespoons orange juice
3 cups all-purpose flour

1 cup whole wheat flour
3 teaspoons cinnamon
2 teaspoons ginger
1 teaspoon cloves
½ teaspoon baking soda
½ teaspoon salt

Cream margarine and brown sugar. Add egg and beat until fluffy. Blend in molasses and orange juice; mixing well. Sift together flours, cinnamon, ginger, cloves, soda, and salt. Stir in creamed mixture and chill. Roll on lightly floured surface and cut cookies. Place on ungreased cookie sheet. Bake at 375 degrees for 8 minutes.

Note: May be used for gingerbread men.

Gigi Campbell

Yield: 4 dozen

Butter Pecan Cookies

1 cup butter or margarine
¾ cup brown sugar
¾ cup sugar
2 eggs
1 teaspoon vanilla

2¼ cups flour
1 teaspoon baking soda
½ teaspoon salt
1 cup chopped pecans

Cream butter and sugars until fluffy. Beat in eggs and vanilla. Combine dry ingredients, add to creamed mixture, and mix well. Fold in pecans. Drop by teaspoon onto greased cookie sheet. Bake at 375 degrees for 10 minutes or until lightly browned.

Pat Labbe   Yield: 4 dozen

Peanut Blossoms

½ cup shortening
½ cup sugar
½ cup brown sugar
½ cup peanut butter
1 egg
2 tablespoons milk

1 teaspoon vanilla
1¾ cups flour
1 teaspoon baking soda
½ teaspoon salt
Powdered sugar
48 chocolate candy kisses

Cream shortening, sugars, and peanut butter. Stir in egg, milk, and vanilla; beat well. Combine flour, baking soda, and salt; add to creamed mixture. The dough will be very stiff. Shape dough into balls, using a rounded teaspoon for each. Roll balls in powdered sugar and placed on a lightly greased cookie sheet. Bake at 375 degrees for 10 to 12 minutes. After removing from oven, top each cookie with a candy kiss, and press down firmly.

Janine Harris   Yield: 4 dozen

Cinnamon Cookies

1 cup butter	2 cups flour
1 cup sugar	2 teaspoons cinnamon
2 eggs, separated	¾ cup chopped nuts
1 teaspoon vanilla	

Cream butter and sugar; add egg yolks and vanilla. Fold in flour and cinnamon. Press dough on large cookie sheet, cover with nuts and press down. Beat egg whites until frothy and brush top of dough. Bake at 350 degrees for 30 minutes. Cut into strips while hot and remove from cookie sheet at once.

Jerry Goodwin   Yield: 2 to 3 dozen

Brown Sugar Cookies

1 cup butter	1 teaspoon baking soda
½ cup dark brown sugar	1 teaspoon baking powder
1 cup sugar	1 teaspoon vanilla
2 eggs	1 cup chopped nuts or coconut,
3 cups flour	optional

Cream butter and sugars. Add eggs and mix well. Sift together flour, soda, and baking powder; add to creamed mixture. Blend in vanilla and nuts. Drop by ½ teaspoon onto greased cookie sheet. Bake at 350 degrees for 8 to 10 minutes.

Vickie Baldwin   Yield: 3 dozen

Peanut Butter Drop Cookies

1 cup peanut butter	½ cup sugar
½ cup butter	2 eggs
2 teaspoons vanilla	2½ cups flour
1 cup honey	½ teaspoon baking soda

Cream peanut butter, butter, and vanilla. Add honey and sugar; beating well after each addition. Add well beaten eggs. Sift together flour and soda and add to creamed mixture. Drop by teaspoon onto cookie sheet and bake at 375 degrees for 10 to 12 minutes. Check to make sure cookies do not brown too much. Keeps well.

Terry Hunter   Yield: 4 dozen

Snickerdoodles

¼ cup shortening	1 teaspoon cream of tartar
¼ cup butter	½ teaspoon baking soda
¾ cup sugar	⅛ teaspoon salt
1 egg	1 tablespoon sugar
1⅓ cups flour	1 teaspoon cinnamon

Cream shortening, butter, sugar, and egg thoroughly. Sift together flour, cream of tartar, soda, and salt. Add to the creamed mixture. Roll into balls the size of a small walnut. Mix sugar and cinnamon together and roll balls in mixture. Place 2 inches apart on ungreased cooking sheet. Bake at 400 degrees for 8 to 10 minutes until light brown but soft. Will be crisp when cool.

Ellen Traylor   Yield: 2 dozen

Ice Box Cookies

1 cup butter	1 teaspoon vanilla
1 cup brown sugar	3 eggs
1 cup sugar	1 teaspoon baking soda
4 cups flour	½ teaspoon salt
1 teaspoon cinnamon	2 cups nuts

Mix all ingredients and add nuts. Divide mixture into 5 or 6 portions and form into long rolls. Wrap rolls in waxed paper and refrigerate for 2 hours. Slice and bake on a greased cookie sheet at 375 degrees for 8 to 10 minutes.

Note: Rolls may be frozen for slicing and baked later as needed.

Carolyn Weissinger   Yield: 6 dozen

Ice Water Cookies

¾ cup butter	1 tablespoon ice water
4 tablespoons powdered sugar	1½ tablespoons vanilla
2 cups flour	1 cup finely chopped nuts

Cream butter and sugar. Sift in flour. Add ice water, vanilla, and nuts. Mix. Mold into finger shaped cookies. Bake at 300 degrees for 10 to 12 minutes or until lightly browned.

Jane Denton   Yield: 3 dozen
  Wife of former Alabama U.S. Senator Jeremiah Denton

Eugenia's Sugar Cookies

1 cup butter	2 eggs
1 cup vegetable oil	1 teaspoon cream of tartar
1 cup powdered sugar	1 teaspoon baking soda
1 cup sugar	1 teaspoon salt
1 teaspoon vanilla	4 cups flour

Cream butter, oil, and sugars. Add vanilla and eggs to creamed mixture. Sift dry ingredients and stir into creamed mixture. Drop by teaspoon onto greased cookie sheet. Bake at 375 degrees about 12 minutes or until lightly browned.

Icing:

½ cup margarine, melted	1 teaspoon almond flavoring
1 (16-ounce) box powdered sugar	

Mix together and ice cookies.

Jackie Hines   Yield: 5 dozen

Toffee Cookies

½ cup butter	1 teaspoon vanilla
½ cup shortening	½ teaspoon salt
1 cup brown sugar	2 cups flour
1 egg yolk	

Mix butter, shortening, and sugar together. Add in order listed: egg yolk, vanilla, salt, and flour. Grease and flour cookie sheet. Dough is very stiff. Pat out with dampened hands. Bake at 350 degrees for 20 minutes. Do not brown too much.

Icing:

3 tablespoons margarine	1 egg white
3 tablespoons cocoa	1½ cups powdered sugar

Mix all ingredients together. Spread on cookies and cut while still warm. Let cool and remove from pan.

Anna Speir   Yield: 3 dozen

"First Prize" Tea Cakes

1 cup sugar
1 cup margarine
1 cup vegetable oil
2 eggs
2 teaspoons vanilla

1 teaspoon baking soda
1 teaspoon cream of tartar
4½ cups flour
1 teaspoon baking powder
1 cup powdered sugar, optional

Cream sugar, margarine, oil, and eggs together. Add all other ingredients except powdered sugar and mix well. Drop dough by teaspoon onto cookie sheet and bake at 325 degrees for 15 minutes.

Note: These cookies are great rolled in powdered sugar while still warm.

Kay Traylor   Yield: 3 dozen

Graham Cracker Crisps

1 (16-ounce) box graham
   crackers
½ cup butter

½ cup margarine
½ cup sugar
Pecan halves for each cracker

Separate and align crackers so they are touching on jelly roll pan. Melt butter, margarine, and sugar. Boil 1 minute and pour over crackers. Place pecan half on top of each cracker. Bake 350 degrees for 9 to 10 minutes. Remove immediately and place on waxed paper to cool.

Steve Todd   Yield: 2 dozen
   Class of 1983
Sis Wood

Sand Tarts

1 cup butter
½ cup sugar
2 cups flour
½ teaspoon salt

2 teaspoons vanilla
2 cups chopped nuts
Powdered sugar

Cream butter and sugar; add flour, salt, and vanilla. Fold in nuts. Drop by teaspoon onto greased cookie sheet. Bake at 325 degrees for about 30 minutes. Sift powdered sugar over tarts while still hot.

Sallie Swindle   Yield: 5 dozen

Oatmeal Cookies

1 cup margarine
1 cup light brown sugar
1 cup sugar
2 eggs
1 teaspoon vanilla
2 cups flour
1 teaspoon baking soda

½ teaspoon salt
1 cup raisins, soaked in hot water
   for 1 minute and drained
3 cups quick cooking oats
1 cup chopped nuts
1 cup coconut

Cream margarine and sugars; add eggs and vanilla. Mix in sifted dry ingredients. Fold in raisins, oats, nuts, and coconut. Drop by teaspoon onto greased cookie sheet. Bake at 375 degrees for 12 to 15 minutes.

Variation: Add 1 cup pear, peach, or fig preserves or 1 cup apple butter and decrease sugar to ½ cup for delicious cookies.

Katherine Sandifer
Jane Singley

Yield: 6 dozen

Oatmeal Crispies

2 cups shortening
2 cups brown sugar
2 cups sugar
4 eggs, well beaten
2 teaspoons vanilla

3 cups flour
2 teaspoons salt
2 teaspoons baking soda
6 cups quick cooking oats
1 cup chopped pecans

Thoroughly cream shortening and sugars. Add eggs and vanilla, beating until smooth. Sift flour, salt, and baking soda; mix well with creamed mixture. Blend in oats and nuts. Shape into rolls, wrap in waxed paper, and freeze overnight. Slice ¼-inch thick with electric or very sharp knife. Bake on ungreased cookie sheet at 350 degrees for 8 to 10 minutes or until lightly browned. Cool before removing from cookie sheet.

Betty Jones

Yield: 6 dozen

Oatmeal Cookie Crisp

1 cup shortening	1 teaspoon allspice
1 cup brown sugar	1½ cups flour
1 cup sugar	1 teaspoon salt
2 eggs	1 teaspoon baking soda
1 teaspoon vanilla	3 cups quick cooking oats
1 teaspoon cinnamon	1 cup chopped nuts

Cream shortening, sugars, eggs, and vanilla. Add dry ingredients. Stir well before adding oats and nuts. Drop by teaspoon onto baking sheet and cook in slow oven at 250 to 300 degrees for 10 to 12 minutes or until brown.

Sis Traylor   Yield: 3 dozen

Granny's Chocolate Cookies

¾ cup vegetable oil	2 teaspoons vanilla
2 cups sugar	½ teaspoon salt
¾ cup cocoa	½ teaspoon baking powder
4 eggs	Powdered sugar
2 cups flour	

Combine oil, sugar, and cocoa. Add eggs, beating after each. Stir in flour, vanilla, salt, and baking powder. Chill at least 2 hours. Drop dough by teaspoon into a bowl of powdered sugar to coat all sides. Place on a greased cookie sheet and bake at 350 degrees for 10 to 12 minutes. Cookies will not look done but they are.

Note: Extra dough may be frozen. Make into long rolls, wrap, and freeze. To make cookies, slice dough, sprinkle with powdered sugar, and bake.

Ginger Wilson   Yield: 3 dozen

Famous Chocolate Chip Cookies

1 cup butter	¹/₂ teaspoon salt
1 cup sugar	1 teaspoon baking powder
1 cup brown sugar	1 teaspoon soda
2 eggs	1 (12-ounce) package semi-sweet
1 teaspoon vanilla	chocolate chips
2¹/₂ cups quick cooking oats,	1 (4-ounce) bar milk chocolate,
ground to fine texture	grated
2 cups flour	1¹/₂ to 2 cups chopped nuts

Cream together butter and sugars. Add eggs and vanilla; mix well. Oats may be ground in food processor or blender. Combine ground oats, flour, salt, baking powder, and soda; add to creamed mixture. Blend in chocolate chips, grated chocolate, and nuts. For large cookies, measure batter out with ¹/₄ cup measure. Bake on a greased cookie sheet at 375 degrees for 6 to 8 minutes. Do not remove from cookie sheet until cool. These continue cooking after removing from oven.

Cookbook Committee   Yield: 4 dozen

Date Tarts

¹/₂ pound extra sharp Cheddar	1³/₄ cups flour
cheese	¹/₄ teaspoon salt
¹/₂ cup margarine	1 (8-ounce) package dates

Grate cheese; cream with margarine. Work in flour and salt. Divide and roll small amounts between 2 sheets of waxed paper which have been sprinkled with flour. Cut in small squares. Cut dates in halves and place half a date on each square. Fold over with a knife. Place on ungreased cookie sheet. Bake at 450 degrees for 8 minutes. Reduce to 350 degrees and continue cooking for 3 to 5 minutes. Do not brown as they will be bitter.

Note: Chill dough for easier handling.

Elaine Walton   Yield: 2 dozen

Ritz Cracker Cookies

1 (16-ounce) package of white
   chocolate

1 cup peanut butter
1 (16-ounce) box Ritz crackers

Melt chocolate in top of double boiler. Spread peanut butter between two Ritz crackers and then dip in melted chocolate. Place on waxed paper until chocolate hardens.

Variation: Chocolate may be tinted for parties.

Meg Smith

Yield: 3 dozen

Potato Chip Cookies

2 cups margarine
1 cup sugar
3½ cups flour

1 tablespoon vanilla
2 cups crushed potato chips

Mix ingredients; drop by teaspoon onto cookie sheet. Bake at 350 degrees for 15 minutes.

Katherine Sandifer

Yield: 5 dozen

Cherry Pecan Bars

2 cups flour
½ cup sugar
¾ cup butter, cut in pieces
¼ teaspoon salt

½ teaspoon vanilla
½ cup chopped pecans
1 (10-ounce) jar cherry preserves

Preheat oven to 350 degrees. In a medium mixing bowl combine flour, sugar, butter, salt, and vanilla. Beat at low speed for 1 to 2 minutes, scraping bowl often until well combined and mixture resembles small peas. Combine pecans with ¾ cup of mixture and set aside. Press remaining crumb mixture in a 9-inch square baking pan. Spread preserves over crumb mixture; sprinkle with pecan mixture. Bake for 35 to 40 minutes or until crumb mixture is lightly browned and preserves are bubbly. Cool completely. Cut into 36 squares.

Variation: Blueberry or strawberry may be substituted for cherry preserves.

Carol Ann Hardy

Yield: 3 dozen

Almond Bars

2 eggs
1 cup sugar
1 cup self-rising flour
1 cup butter, melted
½ cup butter

½ cup sugar
½ cup sliced almonds
1 tablespoon flour
1 tablespoon milk

Beat eggs and 1 cup sugar until thick; stir in 1 cup flour and melted butter. Pour into a greased and floured 9x13-inch pan and bake at 350 degrees for 30 minutes. Combine in a saucepan the remaining ingredients and cook on low heat until sugar dissolves and thickens. Pour over cake and broil 3 to 5 minutes. Watch closely. Cut into bars.

Anna Speir   Yield: 3 dozen

Almond Coconut Bars

¾ cup margarine
1½ cups flour
2 teaspoons sugar
5 eggs, beaten

2 cups sugar
3 tablespoons almond extract
2 cups coconut

Mix margarine, flour, and sugar. Press into a 9x13-inch pan. Bake at 350 degrees for 15 minutes. Mix the remaining ingredients and spread over pastry. Bake at 350 degrees for 25 minutes. Cool and cut into bars.

Melanie Culpepper   Yield: 2 dozen

Oatmeal Bars

2½ cups quick cooking oats
1 (18½-ounce) box yellow
  cake mix
¾ cup margarine, melted

1 (16-ounce) jar preserves,
  your choice
1 tablespoon water

Preheat oven to 350 degrees. Combine oats and dry cake mix with melted margarine (will be crumbly). Put ½ of this mixture into a greased 9x13-inch pan. Press down. Combine preserves with 1 tablespoon water and spread over mixture. Put remaining ½ of dry cake mixture over this and press down firmly. Bake for 25 to 35 minutes or until golden brown. Cool completely, then cut into squares.

Laura Wallace   Yield: 2 dozen

Magic Cookie Bars

½ cup butter
1½ cups graham cracker crumbs
1 (14-ounce) can sweetened
  condensed milk
1 (6-ounce) package semi-sweet
  chocolate chips
1 (3½-ounce) can coconut
1 cup chopped pecans

Melt butter in a 9x13-inch baking dish that has been greased with vegetable spray. Sprinkle graham cracker crumbs over butter. Then add the following in the order listed: condensed milk, chocolate chips, coconut, and pecans. Press down. Bake at 325 degrees for 25 to 30 minutes.

Ginger Wilson   Yield: 2 dozen

Caramel Crunchies

½ cup butter
1 (16-ounce) box dark brown
  sugar
4 eggs, beaten
1½ cups flour
⅛ teaspoon salt
1 teaspoon baking powder
1 teaspoon vanilla
1 cup finely chopped nuts

Preheat oven to 300 degrees. Cream butter and sugar together; add beaten eggs. Sift flour, salt, and baking powder together; add to creamed mixture. Add vanilla; fold in nuts. Pour into a 9x13-inch pan. Bake for 30 minutes.

Mary McDavid   Yield: 2 dozen

Chocolate Brownies

1 cup self-rising flour
2 cups sugar
6 tablespoons cocoa
1 cup margarine, melted
4 large eggs
1 teaspoon vanilla
1 cup chopped pecans

Preheat oven to 325 degrees. Mix flour, sugar, and cocoa and add to margarine slowly. Add eggs and vanilla. Stir in pecans. Bake in a greased and floured 9x13-inch pan for 25 minutes or until done.

Tammy Harris Mason   Yield: 2 dozen
  Class of 1981
Fran Pearce

Mama's Brownies

1 (23½-ounce) box brownie mix
½ cup chopped nuts
2 cups tiny marshmallows
1 (6-ounce) package semi-sweet
  chocolate chips

1 cup peanut butter
1½ cups crispy rice cereal

Bake brownie mix with nuts according to package directions in a 9x13-inch pan. While warm add marshmallows on top of brownies and return to oven until marshmallows are slightly melted. In saucepan combine chocolate chips and peanut butter. Heat and stir until melted. Stir in rice cereal and spread mixture on brownies. Chill to set.

Ellen Traylor   Yield: 2 dozen

German Chocolate Cheesy Brownies

1 (18½-ounce) box German
  chocolate cake mix
1 (8-ounce) package cream cheese,
  softened

1 egg
1 cup sugar
1 (6-ounce) package semi-sweet
  chocolate chips

Prepare cake mix according to directions. Pour into a greased 9x13-inch pan. Cream with a mixer: cream cheese, egg, and sugar; add chocolate chips. Drop by tablespoon onto cake batter. Swirl through with a knife. Bake at 350 degrees for about 35 minutes.

Joanne Dillingham   Yield: 2 dozen
Gail Browning

Ooey-Gooey Bars

1 (18½-ounce) box yellow
  cake mix
½ cup margarine, melted
3 eggs

1 cup chopped nuts
1 (8-ounce) package cream cheese
1 (16-ounce) box powdered sugar

Preheat oven to 350 degrees. Combine cake mix, margarine, 1 egg, and nuts. Mix with fork and press into a 9x13-inch pan. Cream with mixer: cream cheese, 2 eggs, and powdered sugar. Pour over first mixture. Bake 45 minutes. Let cool and cut in squares.

Vickie Baldwin   Yield: 3 dozen

Turtle Cake Squares

1 (14-ounce) bag caramels
²⁄₃ cup evaporated milk, divided
1 (18½-ounce) box German
  chocolate cake mix

¾ cup margarine, melted
1 (6-ounce) package semi-sweet
  chocolate chips
1 cup chopped nuts

In double boiler over medium heat, combine caramels and ⅓ cup evaporated milk, stirring until melted and smooth. Remove from heat and set aside. Combine cake mix, margarine, and remaining ⅓ cup milk in a mixing bowl. Mix until well blended. Press half of the mixture in a greased 9x13-inch pan. Bake at 350 degrees for 6 minutes. Remove from oven, sprinkle chocolate chips and nuts over crust. Pour caramel mixture evenly over chips and nuts. Drop remainder of cake mixture over caramel. Return to oven and bake 15 to 18 minutes. Remove from oven; chill for 30 minutes. Cut into small bars, store at room temperature or freeze.

Anne Williamson   Yield: 5 to 6 dozen

Lemon Squares

Crust:
1 cup butter, melted
½ cup powdered sugar

2 cups flour

Mix all ingredients together. Press into bottom and up the sides of a greased 9x13-inch pan. Bake at 350 degrees for 20 minutes.

Filling:
4 eggs
2 cups sugar

4 tablespoons lemon juice
Powdered sugar to taste

Beat eggs; stir in sugar and lemon juice. Pour over the cooked crust and bake at 350 degrees for 20 minutes. Sprinkle with powdered sugar, cool, and cut.

Ginger Wilson   Yield: 3 dozen

Cinnamon Flats

2 cups butter
2 cups sugar
4 cups flour

2 tablespoons cinnamon
2 egg yolks

Cream ingredients together. When blended, press lightly into a 12x15-inch jelly roll pan.

Topping:
2 egg whites
1 cup sugar

1 tablespoon cinnamon
2 cups chopped nuts

Beat egg whites until frothy and brush over creamed mixture. Mix sugar and cinnamon and sprinkle over egg whites. Sprinkle nuts on top and press in lightly. Bake at 350 degrees for 20 to 25 minutes. Cut in small squares while hot. Cool in pan.

Melanie Culpepper   Yield: 8 dozen

English Buttercreams

½ cup salted butter,
  NO SUBSTITUTE
1 tablespoon shortening
1 tablespoon milk

1 (16-ounce) box powdered sugar,
  sifted
1½ teaspoons peppermint extract

Cream butter, shortening, and milk together until light and fluffy. Gradually add sifted sugar, beating each addition in fully. Stir in extract. Continue until all sugar is mixed well and you are not able to feel any grains of sugar when you test a tiny bit with your tongue. Roll out onto aluminum foil in ¾-inch diameter ropes. Slice each rope into ¼-inch slices. Cover lightly and store overnight to set.

Note: Mixture may be divided and tinted with food color. Easier when made in a food processor.

Cookbook Committee   Yield: 5 to 6 dozen

Butterscotch Candy

4 (6-ounce) packages butterscotch
  morsels
1½ cups Spanish peanuts

1 (5-ounce) can chow mein
  noodles

Melt morsels over lot heat. Stir in peanuts and noodles. Drop by teaspoon onto waxed paper.

Helen S. Stewart
    Yield: 3 to 4 dozen

Peanut Butter Candy

2 cups sugar
1 cup dark corn syrup
2 cups peanut butter

½ teaspoon vanilla
8 cups cornflakes

Bring sugar and corn syrup to a boil; add peanut butter and vanilla. Stir until melted; remove from heat. Put a small amount of cornflakes in a separate bowl and pour some of the peanut butter mixture over the cornflakes; stir well and repeat until all the cereal and peanut butter mixture is used. This will be thick. Pat out on cookie sheet and cut into squares while warm.

Lillian Riddle Gilley
  Class of 1972
    Yield: 3 dozen

Ron's Fudge

3 cups sugar
⅔ cup cocoa
⅛ teaspoon salt
1½ cups milk

¼ cup butter
1 teaspoon vanilla extract
⅔ cup pecans or walnut pieces

Combine sugar, cocoa, and salt in heavy saucepan. Add milk and bring to a boil, stirring until sugar dissolves. Do not stir again. Cover and cook 1 minute. Uncover and cook to soft ball stage (238 degrees). Add butter; place in pan of cold water and cool quickly to lukewarm (110 degrees). Add vanilla and beat until it is creamy and loses its gloss. Add nuts and pour into buttered 9-inch square pan. When firm, cut into squares.

Ron Pugh
    Yield: 3 to 4 dozen

Christmas Fudge

3 cups sugar
1 cup light corn syrup
1½ cups evaporated milk
½ teaspoon vanilla or rum
   flavoring

½ cup candied cherries
½ cup candied pineapple
1 cup chopped walnuts
1 cup chopped Brazil nuts
1 cup chopped pecans

Boil sugar, syrup, and milk until soft ball stage (238 degrees). Cool. Stir in vanilla and beat until it begins to thicken. Add fruits and nuts. Pour in greased 9x13-inch pan.

Note: Mixture must be cool before adding nuts and fruit, or it will not harden.

Elsie Randall   Yield: 4 dozen

Microwave Divinity

2 cups sugar
⅓ cup water
⅓ cup light corn syrup
¼ teaspoon salt

2 egg whites
1 teaspoon vanilla
½ cup chopped nuts

Combine sugar, water, syrup, and salt in a 3-quart mixing bowl; stir thoroughly. Microwave on HIGH for 5 minutes or until mixture is clear; stir. Microwave on 70% power for 5 to 7 minutes, or until a small amount of syrup dropped in water forms a hard ball. (This is 260 degrees on a candy thermometer but do NOT use a conventional candy thermometer in the microwave oven). After removing the bowl from the microwave oven, quickly check temperature of the syrup. It should be 260 degrees F. While syrup is cooking, beat egg whites in a large mixing bowl until stiff peaks form. When syrup is ready, pour a thin, slow stream into egg whites, beating constantly with electric mixer. Add vanilla, beat 6 to 8 minutes or until stiff and loses its shine. Fold in nuts. Drop by teaspoon onto waxed paper or spread in a buttered 8x10-inch pan; cool. Cut into squares.

Kay Foster   Yield: 3 dozen

Honey Divinity

¼ cup honey
2½ cups sugar
⅔ cup water

¼ teaspoon salt
2 egg whites
1 teaspoon vanilla

In 2-quart saucepan, mix honey, sugar, water, and salt. Stir over low heat until sugar is dissolved. Continue cooking slowly, without stirring to 265 degrees on candy thermometer (brittle stage). In a large mixing bowl beat egg whites at high speed until very stiff. Slowly pour hot syrup on egg whites, beating at high speed until mixture loses its gloss and when dropped from a spoon it holds its shape. Add vanilla. Drop by teaspoon onto waxed paper.

Terry Hunter   Yield: 3½ dozen

Orange Balls

1 (12-ounce) box vanilla wafers
½ cup margarine
1 (6-ounce) can orange juice
    concentrate

½ cup chopped pecans
1 cup coconut, optional
1 (16-ounce) box powdered sugar

Crush wafers; melt margarine and orange juice. Mix all ingredients. Roll into small balls and may coat with additional powdered sugar. Store in refrigerator.

Fran Pearce   Yield: 2 dozen
Betty Clower

Creamy Pralines

3 cups sugar
½ pint whipping cream
3 tablespoons butter

1 teaspoon vanilla
1 cup chopped pecans

Place 2 cups sugar, whipping cream, and butter in a saucepan; cook slowly and stir well. Place remaining sugar in a small cast iron skillet to melt the sugar, being careful not to burn. Slowly add melted sugar to boiling cream mixture. Continue boiling mixture until it reaches soft ball stage. Remove from heat and allow to cool. Add vanilla and pecans. Beat until ready to drop by teaspoon onto waxed paper.

Note: This is an old New Orleans recipe and it is delicious.

Millie Thomas   Yield: 3 dozen

Chocolate Peanut Butter Squares

1 cup margarine, melted
1 (18-ounce) jar crunchy
    peanut butter
1½ cups graham crackers,
    finely crushed

1 (16-ounce) box powdered sugar
½ cup margarine
1 (12-ounce) package semi-sweet
    chocolate bits

Melt 1 cup margarine in a medium saucepan. Remove from heat and stir in peanut butter. Gradually add graham crackers and sugar. Press into a jelly roll pan. Melt ½ cup margarine and chocolate bits and pour over top. Chill and cut in very small squares to serve. Wonderful!

Suzie Kirkpatrick
Rosemary Harris

Yield: 4 dozen

Chocolate Liqueur Candies

1¼ cups butter or margarine,
    divided
½ cup cocoa
3½ cups powdered sugar, divided
1 egg, beaten
1 teaspoon vanilla

2 cups graham cracker crumbs
⅓ cup Crème de menthe, Grand
    Marnier, or other liqueur
Few drops food coloring, optional
1½ cups semi-sweet chocolate
    chips

In a saucepan melt ½ cup butter. Stir in cocoa, blending well. Remove from heat and mix in ½ cup powdered sugar, egg and vanilla. Combine with graham cracker crumbs and press into greased 9x13-inch pan. Melt ½ cup butter and combine with liqueur and food coloring. Beat in remaining powdered sugar. Carefully spread over first layer. Chill for 1 hour. Melt remaining ¼ cup butter with chocolate chips. Cool slightly and pour in ribbons over liqueur layer. Carefully spread with a knife. Chill 1 to 2 hours. Let stand at room temperature for 1 hour before cutting into small squares. Store in refrigerator.

Peggy Striplin

Yield: 8 dozen

German Chocolate Delights

1 (4-ounce) package German
  Chocolate, grated
2 cups sugar
1 (5-ounce) can evaporated milk
2 tablespoons light corn syrup

½ cup butter
1 (3½-ounce) can coconut
1 cup chopped pecans
1 teaspoon vanilla

Blend chocolate, sugar, milk, syrup and butter. Cook to soft ball stage. Add coconut, pecans, and vanilla. Beat until right consistency to be dropped by teaspoon onto waxed paper.

Millie Thomas   Yield: 3 dozen

Buckeyes

1 (16-ounce) box powdered sugar
1 cup margarine, softened
1 (12-ounce) jar crunchy peanut
  butter

1 (6-ounce) package chocolate
  chips
1 (1-ounce) block paraffin

Mix powdered sugar, margarine, and peanut butter; roll into bite-size balls. Melt chocolate and paraffin in double boiler. Use a toothpick and dip peanut butter balls in chocolate mixture and place on waxed paper. Refrigerate.

Anne Blackwell Stinson   Yield: 3 dozen
Madolyn Oxford
Diane Chappell

Almond Butter Crunch

1½ cups butter,
  NO SUBSTITUTE
2 cups sugar
1 (2-ounce) package slivered
  almonds

6 to 7 milk chocolate candy bars
2 tablespoons shaved paraffin

Cook butter and sugar in an iron skillet to 260 degrees on candy thermometer (a flat metal candy thermometer is recommended rather than a glass bulb type). Add almonds and cook to 300 degrees stirring constantly. Pour into a shallow pan (pizza pan is a good size). Let cool completely. Melt chocolate and paraffin in top of double boiler over low heat. Spread over candy and let harden. Turn candy out and crack into small pieces.

Milly Noah   Yield: 3 dozen

Chocolate Truffles

½ pound hazelnuts or almonds,
  pulverized
10 ounces sweet chocolate
½ pound butter, softened

2 tablespoons instant coffee
4 tablespoons white rum
⅔ cup powdered bitter cocoa

Spread finely grated or pulverized nuts on cookie sheet and brown under pre-heated broiler, being very careful not to let them burn. Set bowl of chocolate over hot water to melt. Add nuts and when almost cool, add butter bit by bit, mixing well. Dissolve coffee in rum and add to the mixture. Refrigerate until firm. Form into balls and roll in powdered cocoa. These may be refrigerated or frozen.

Brian Kittrell   Yield: 75 small balls

Microwave Munchy Peanut Brittle

1 cup raw peanuts
1 cup sugar
½ cup light corn syrup
⅛ teaspoon salt

1 teaspoon butter or margarine
1 teaspoon vanilla
1 teaspoon baking soda

Stir together peanuts, sugar, syrup, and salt in 1½-quart casserole. Microwave on HIGH for 7 to 8 minutes, stirring well after 3 minutes. Add butter and vanilla to syrup, blending well. Microwave on HIGH for 1 to 2 minutes more. Peanuts will be lightly browned and syrup very hot. Add baking soda and gently stir until light and foamy. Pour mixture onto lightly greased cookie sheet; let cool 30 minutes to 1 hour. When cool, break into small pieces and store in airtight container.

Note: If roasted salted peanuts are used, omit salt and add peanuts after first four minutes of cooking.

Kay Foster   Yield: 1 pound

Microwave Caramel Nut Rolls

½ pound caramel candies,
 about 28 pieces
¼ cup butter or margarine
2 tablespoons half and half
 or milk

1½ cups powdered sugar
1 cup salted peanuts
2 cups miniature marshmallows
1 cup flaked coconut

In 2-quart casserole or mixing bowl, place caramels, butter, and half and half.
Microwave at 50% (MEDIUM) for 3 to 5 minutes, or until melted and smooth,
stirring after 2 minutes, then every minute. Stir in sugar until smooth, add peanuts.
Stir in marshmallows, using as few strokes as possible. Sprinkle 2 large sheets of
waxed paper with coconut. Spoon half the caramel mixture in strips on each.
Shape in 10 or 12 rolls, using waxed paper to help shape in jelly roll fashion;
coat well with coconut. Wrap and refrigerate. To serve, cut into ½-inch pieces.

Kay Foster   Yield: 2 pounds (48 pieces)

English Taffá–Marble Candy

2 pounds sweet chocolate,
 27 small bars
1 cup water
2 cups sugar

¾ pound butter
1 pound or 4 cups nuts
½ pound nuts, coarsely chopped

Melt the chocolate in oven on warm. Combine water, sugar, and butter in heavy
saucepan and cook over low heat until it reaches 280 degrees. Add 1 pound of
nuts and stir constantly until it reaches 310 degrees. Pour onto marble slab and
spread with half the melted chocolate and sprinkle with half the chopped nuts.
Turn taffá over and repeat with chocolate and nuts. Let stand for 12 hours.
Break into small pieces or whatever size you like.

Note: A sideless cookie sheet is ideal to turn the taffá with.

Katherine Stoddard   Yield: 4 pounds

Bourbon Balls

2½ cups crushed vanilla wafers
2 tablespoons cocoa
1 cup powdered sugar
1 cup finely chopped pecans

3 tablespoons light corn syrup
¼ cup bourbon
Powdered sugar

Mix dry ingredients. Then add nuts, corn syrup, and bourbon. Using a teaspoon, make into balls and roll in additional powdered sugar. If mixture dries out while making balls, add a few drops of water to hold together. Place in tins that have been lined with plastic wrap. Seal tins with tape.

Note: These are best when left sealed for 3 weeks.

Betsy Pearce   Yield: 3 to 4 dozen

Date Balls

½ cup margarine
¾ cup sugar
1 (8-ounce) box pitted dates,
   chopped
1 egg
1 tablespoon milk

1 teaspoon vanilla
½ teaspoon salt
2 cups crispy rice cereal
½ cup chopped nuts
1 cup coconut

Cook margarine, sugar, and dates over low heat until it boils and melts the sugar. Beat together the egg, milk, vanilla, and salt. Add to the first mixture and cook for 2 minutes. Let cool; add the rice cereal and nuts. Form into bite-size balls and roll in grated coconut. Refrigerate in airtight container.

Carolyn Weissinger   Yield: 3 dozen
Rose Mary DeRamus
Joanne Dillingham

Honey Popcorn Balls

4 quarts popcorn, popped   **1 cup sugar**
1 cup honey   **Pinch of salt**

Pop the corn and measure correct amount into a large bowl. Cook honey, sugar and salt in a saucepan over medium heat until syrup reaches 245 degrees on a candy thermometer or until a few drops tested in cold water form a firm ball which does not flatten when removed from the water. Pour over popcorn in a very thin steady stream. (Fork the syrup through the popcorn thoroughly while you pour.) When mixture is cool enough to handle, butter your hands and shape it into balls, pressing together firmly.

Amy Breeman   Yield: 2½ dozen

Microwave Copy Pop

1 cup butter   **1½ to 2 cups nuts, walnuts,**
½ cup light corn syrup   **pecans, almonds, or peanuts**
1¼ cups sugar   **1 teaspoon vanilla**
2 quarts salted popped corn

In 2 or 2½-quart mixing bowl or casserole, combine butter, syrup, and sugar. Microwave at HIGH power 9 to 15 minutes (stirring every 3 minutes) or until brittle threads form when small amount is dropped in cold water. In a buttered 5-quart or larger container, combine corn and nuts. Stir vanilla into cooked syrup and immediately pour over corn mixture. Stir until well coated. Spread mixture in single layer on 2 large sheets of waxed paper. Let stand until firm. Break into small pieces and store in airtight container.

Kay Foster   Yield: 12 cups

Easy Sherbet

2 (14-ounce) cans sweetened
   condensed milk
1 package orange or lemon-lime
   flavored drink mix

2 (32-ounce) bottles lemon-lime
   carbonated beverage

In ice cream freezer container pour milk, drink mix, and carbonated beverage. Use only enough carbonated beverage to bring liquid up to full line. Freeze.

Adrienne Campbell DeRamus
   Class of 1985

Yield: 1 gallon

Banana Ice Cream

2 quarts milk
2 cups sugar
2 tablespoons cornstarch
8 eggs

2 teaspoons vanilla
2 (14-ounce) cans condensed milk
8 ripe bananas, mashed

Heat milk in double boiler. When hot, add sugar, cornstarch, and eggs. Cook until mixture thickens, stirring often. Cool; add vanilla, condensed milk, and bananas. Freeze in ice cream freezer and let sit 30 minutes before serving.

Paula Vardaman

Yield: 1 gallon

Billy's Favorite Ice Cream

5 cups milk
1 (14-ounce) can sweetened
   condensed milk
1 cup sugar
1 (5-ounce) can evaporated milk

1 pint whipping cream
3 tablespoons vanilla
3 cups mashed fruit of your choice
3/4 cup sugar

Mix all ingredients together and pour in ice cream freezer container. Freeze.

Note: Omit 3/4 cup sugar if fruit is already sweetened.

Terri Till
   Class of 1981

Yield: 1 gallon

Ice Cream Brownies

1 (14-ounce) box brownie mix
½ gallon vanilla ice cream,
   softened

Whipped cream

Prepare brownie mix according to package directions. Cool; crumble and mix in ice cream. Freeze until firm. Cut into squares and serve with whipped cream, if desired.

Peggy Williamson

Yield: 6 to 8 servings

Quick Tortoni Ice Cream

12 almond macaroons
¼ cup cherries, candied or
   maraschino

½ cup salted, toasted almonds
1 quart vanilla ice cream, softened

Crumble two day old (or older) almond macaroons, making about ¾ cup crumbs. Dice cherries and chop almonds. Add crumbs, cherries, and almonds to one quart vanilla ice cream. Refreeze. Sprinkle with additional macaroon crumbs on top of each serving.

Variation: May substitute the cherries and almonds with ¾ cup sherry.

Margaret Wilson
Sarah James

Yield: 6 to 8 servings

Homemade Ice Cream

6 regular candy bars, your favorite
1 (14-ounce) can sweetened
   condensed milk

5 eggs
1½ cups sugar
Milk

Melt candy in condensed milk over low heat. Add eggs and sugar; mix well. Pour into 1-gallon ice cream maker and fill to ¾ full with whole milk. Run ice cream maker until ice cream is frozen.

Deborah Moon

Yield: 1 gallon

Girdle Buster Dessert

25 crushed Oreo cookies
⅓ cup margarine, melted
½ gallon vanilla ice cream,
    softened
2 squares baking chocolate

1 tablespoon margarine
½ cup sugar
1 (5½-ounce) can evaporated milk
1 (8-ounce) carton whipped
    topping

Crush cookies in blender. Mix with margarine and press into a 9x13-inch pan. Place in refrigerator while preparing other ingredients. Spread ice cream over crumb mixture and freeze. In a saucepan melt chocolate, 1 tablespoon margarine, sugar, evaporated milk, and cook until thick, stirring constantly. Cool completely, fold in whipped topping and spread on top of ice cream. Return to freezer.

Variation: 1 (4-ounce) package of instant chocolate pudding prepared according to directions on package can be substituted for chocolate layer.

Rosemary Harris
Laura Wallace

Yield: 15 servings

Milky Way Bar Ice Cream

12 Milky Way candy bars,
    cut into pieces
1 (14-ounce) can sweetened
    condensed milk

3 quarts milk
1 (5½-ounce) can chocolate syrup

Combine candy and condensed milk in a saucepan over low heat. Stir until candy melts; cool, stirring occasionally. Add 1 quart of milk to candy mixture and beat until well blended. Pour into ice cream freezer and stir in chocolate syrup. Add enough milk to fill container until about 4 inches from top. Freeze.

Note: Milky Way is a registered trademark of Mars, Incorporated.

Nellie Kate Tepper

Yield: 1 gallon

Hazelnut and Caramel Ice Cream Dessert

2/3 cup amaretto macaroon crumbs
    or graham cracker crumbs
1/3 cup chopped hazelnuts or
    almonds, toasted

2 tablespoons unsalted butter,
    softened
1/2 gallon pralines and cream ice
    cream, softened

Combine cracker crumbs, nuts, and butter to make crust. Pat into bottom of oiled 10-inch springform pan. Freeze 20 minutes. Then pour in softened ice cream. Refreeze.

Icing:
3 tablespoons frangelica or
    amaretto liqueur or 1/2 teaspoon
    almond flavoring

1 cup heavy cream, whipped
2 teaspoons sugar

Combine ingredients.

Caramel Sauce:
1 1/4 cups sugar
3/4 cup water

1 cup whipping cream, heated

Combine sugar and water; bring to a boil and brown until caramel colored, using a deep boiler and long handled spoon. Reduce heat. Add heated cream carefully for mixture really bubbles up. When bubbling stops, mix well. When ready to serve, remove band of springform and top with icing. Serve with warm sauce and top with extra toasted almonds if desired.

Milly Noah   Yield: 10 to 12 servings

Fried Ice Cream

1/2 cup caramel syrup
6 ounces corn flakes
1/2 gallon vanilla ice cream
Vegetable oil

1 (12-ounce) carton whipped
    topping
12 cherries

Mix caramel with corn flakes until sticky. Scoop out ice cream and apply corn flake coating to cover ice cream. Store any left over coating in refrigerator. Drop ice cream balls in hot oil (enough to cover ice cream ball) for 15 to 20 seconds. Place in a dish; top with whipped topping and a cherry.

Joy Beers   Yield: 12 servings

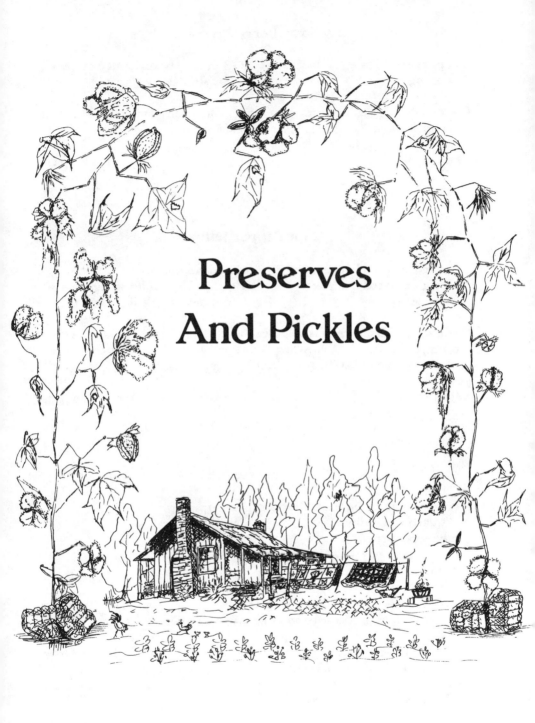

Preserves
And Pickles

Fig Strawberry Preserves

3 cups mashed figs
3 cups sugar

2 (3-ounce) boxes or 1 (6-ounce)
box strawberry gelatin

Cook mashed figs and sugar for 10 to 15 minutes. Add gelatin and boil until it dissolves. Pour into hot sterilized pint jars and seal.

Elma Spurlin

Yield: 3 pints

Hot Pepper Jelly

½ cup ground red hot pepper
¾ cup ground red and green
   bell pepper

6½ cups sugar
1½ cups apple cider vinegar
1 (6-ounce) bottle liquid pectin

Wash, seed, and grind peppers. Dissolve sugar in vinegar in a large saucepan and add peppers. Bring to a full rolling boil. Remove from heat and cool for 10 minutes stirring occasionally. Add pectin. Seal in hot jars.

Sarita DeRamus

Yield: 6 half-pints

Muscadine Jelly

4 cups muscadine juice, about
   2 quarts muscadines
1 tablespoon lemon juice
1 (1¾-ounce) box powdered
   fruit pectin

5½ cups sugar
Paraffin for sealing

Wash muscadines, place in deep pot, cover with water, and simmer for 20 minutes covered. Mash fruit, place in colander lined with two thicknesses of cheese cloth, and save juice. To 4 cups of fruit juice, add lemon juice, and stir in fruit pectin and sugar; bring quickly to full boil for 1 minute (no longer). Remove from heat, skim off foam, and ladle into hot sterilized jars to within ½ inch from top. Seal by spooning hot paraffin onto jelly surface. Prick any air bubbles with a toothpick before paraffin cools.

Joy Beers

Yield: 4 pints

No-Cook Strawberry Jam

2 quarts fully ripe strawberries
1 (1³/₄-ounce) box powdered light
fruit pectin

2³/₄ cups sugar, divided

Wash, stem, and thoroughly crush strawberries, one layer at a time, measuring 4 cups into a large bowl. Combine pectin with ¼ cup sugar. Gradually add pectin mixture to fruit, stirring vigorously. Set aside for 30 minutes, stirring frequently. Gradually stir in 2½ cups sugar until dissolved. Ladle quickly into scalded containers, filling to within ½ inch of top. Cover at once with tight lids. Let stand at room temperature overnight, then store in freezer. Small amount may be covered and stored in the refrigerator for up to 3 weeks.

Eleanor Gantt Scales
 Class of 1981

Yield: 2 pints

Spiced Orange Slices

8 seedless oranges, washed and
 dried
4 cups sugar

1 cup vinegar
10 whole cloves
2 sticks cinnamon

Slice the oranges about ½-inch thick. Discard the end pieces. Cover the oranges with water and simmer in covered pan until they are tender. Do not overcook. Drain the oranges. Boil all other ingredients together for 5 minutes. Add the oranges and simmer until the slices are well glazed. Pack oranges in sterilized jars. Fill with syrup. Cool and seal with paraffin.

Kay Traylor

Yield: 2 pints

Watermelon Jelly

4 cups watermelon
3½ cups sugar

2 tablespoons lemon juice

Purée watermelon in food processor to equal 2 cups of purée. Combine sugar, lemon juice, and purée in 6 to 8-quart pan. Bring to full rolling boil that cannot be stirred down. Using high heat, stir constantly with wooden spoon and boil hard 1 minute; remove from heat. Skim off foam; pour in clean, hot half-pint jars. Leave ¼-inch headspace. Wipe rims. Seal.

Jackie Hines

Yield: 4 half-pints

Pear Relish

1 peck pears	5 medium onions
5 green bell peppers, chopped	5 cups cider vinegar
5 red bell peppers, chopped	5 cups sugar
3 hot peppers, chopped	1 teaspoon salt

Wash, peel, and core pears. Remove seeds and stems from peppers. Put through food grinder or chop fine in food processor fitted with steel blade the pears, peppers, and onions. In a large stainless or enamel pot combine all ingredients. Bring to a boil and cook 25 minutes, stirring occasionally. Pack in hot sterilized jars leaving ¼-inch head space. Seal.

Elaine Walton   Yield: 10 to 12 pints

Squash Relish

8 cups sliced squash	Ice water
4 cups sliced onion	3 cups vinegar
2 green peppers, chopped	3 cups sugar
2 red bell peppers, chopped	2 tablespoons mustard seed
½ cup salt	2 teaspoons celery seed

Combine vegetables, sprinkle with salt, and allow to stand in ice water for 3 hours. Drain. Mix vinegar, sugar, mustard seed, and celery seed; bring to a boil and boil for 1 minute. Pack in jars and seal.

Ruth Newsome   Yield: 4 pints

Refrigerator Pickles

6 cups thinly sliced cucumber	½ teaspoon salt
2 cups thinly sliced onion	½ teaspoon mustard seed
1½ cups sugar	½ teaspoon celery seed
1½ cups apple cider vinegar	½ teaspoon ground turmeric

Alternate layers of cucumber and onion. Combine sugar, vinegar, salt, mustard seed, celery seed, and turmeric. Bring to a boil. Stir until sugar is dissolved. Pour over cucumber and onion. Cover tightly in a 2-quart container and refrigerate for at least 24 hours before serving. The flavor improves with age.

Elma Spurlin   Yield: 2 quarts

Dill Pickles

Cucumbers
Dill seed
Clove garlic
Hot pepper

1 quart vinegar
1 cup salt
3 quarts water

Wash and slice cucumbers vertically or leave whole. To each quart jar add 2 teaspoons dill seed, 1 clove garlic, 1 hot pepper, and cucumbers. Do not let the cucumbers touch the jar lid. Boil vinegar, salt, and water. Pour hot mixture over cucumbers and seal. Set in the sun for 9 days. Let season for 3 weeks. Refrigerate before serving.

Variation: Small whole pods of okra may be substituted for cucumbers.

Elma Spurlin   Yield: 4 quarts

Pickled Okra

4 to 5 pounds small pods of
    tender okra
1 quart vinegar
2 quarts water
1 cup salt

½ teaspoon alum
Fresh dill
Garlic cloves
Red pepper pods

Wash okra thoroughly. Trim stems, but not too short. Soak in ice water 24 hours. Before putting in jars, rinse in cold water. Bring vinegar, water, salt and alum to an active boil. Boil for 3 to 4 minutes. In each sterilized jar, place a generous clump of dill, pod of garlic, and a piece of red pepper. Pack okra, alternating ends of pods to make it fit better. Stand jars in pan of warm water. Keep water in pan hot enough that jars can be handled with bare hands. Fill jars to brim with hot, not boiling, vinegar solution. Allow to stand uncapped for an hour or until okra has absorbed all the solution it will. Fill jars to brim with vinegar solution. With moist cloth, wipe salt and dill seeds off rim of jar and threads where cap fits. Cap tightly. Should be ready to eat in two weeks. Any unused solution can be saved and used at a future pickling, but reboil before using.

Note: Wonderful hors d'oeuvre.

Cookbook Committee   Yield: 8 to 10 pints

301

Crispy Pickle

1 (32-ounce) jar hamburger slice
   dill pickle

1¼ cups sugar
½ cup tarragon vinegar

Drain pickles in colander and rinse. Mix sugar and vinegar. This will be rather dry. Combine with pickle slices in a glass container and stir once a day for 5 days. When mixture becomes liquid, repack in quart jars and refrigerate.

Note: Must use tarragon vinegar. These are easy, tasty, crispy pickles with a different taste.

Millie Thomas

Yield: 2 quarts

Crispy Bread and Butter Pickles

½ cup salt
25 or 30 medium cucumbers,
   thinly sliced
8 medium onions, thinly sliced
2 bell peppers, chopped

5 cups cider vinegar
5 cups sugar
2 tablespoons mustard seed
1 tablespoon turmeric
½ teaspoon whole cloves

Sprinkle ½ cup salt over cucumbers, onions, and bell peppers in a large pan and let stand for 3 hours. Drain the water that forms and wash off any remaining salt. Bring vinegar, sugar, and spices to a boil; add cucumbers, onions, and peppers and let barely come to a boil (just until bubbles appear). Place in sterilized jars and seal. Serve with cheese and crackers.

Elma Spurlin

Yield: 6 to 8 pints

Chili Sauce

25 tomatoes, chopped
3 onions, chopped
⅛ cup chopped hot pepper
4 cups vinegar

3 cups sugar
4 tablespoons salt
1 tablespoon cinnamon
1 tablespoon allspice

Combine all ingredients in a 6-quart saucepan and boil until preferred thickness is reached. Pack in jars and seal.

Linda Thompson

Yield: 7 pints

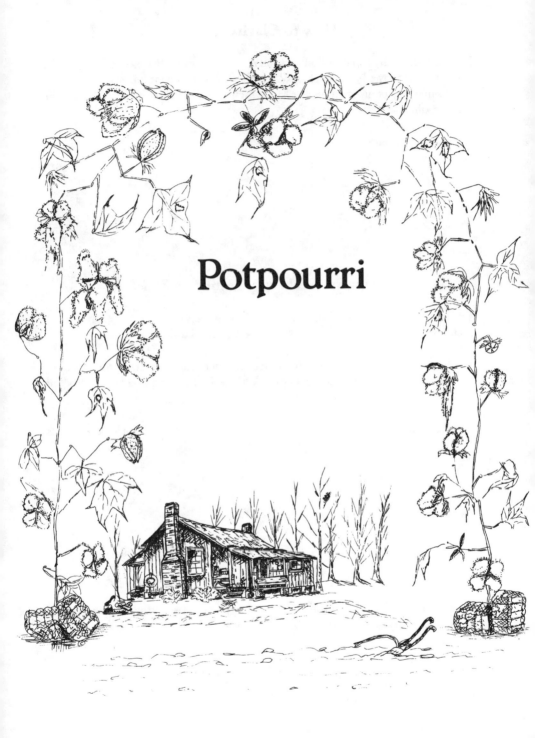

Potpourri

How to Clarify Butter

Place butter in the top of a double boiler over hot water. Place over heat and let stand just until the butter melts. When the milky sediment has separated from the melted fat, pour off the clear fat, which is the clarified butter. Discard the milky sediment.

Cookbook Committee

Mama vonSeeberg's Cranberry Sauce

1 quart or 1 pound cranberries	**2 cups sugar**
1 cup water	**4 ½-pint jars**

Wash cranberries; mix berries and water together. Stew for 20 minutes. Cranberries may be strained or leave whole. Add sugar and bring to a boil. Cook for 5 minutes, pour into jars, and seal.

Lois Sanford   Yield: 4½ pints

Sweetened Condensed Milk

4 cups instant powdered milk	**4 tablespoons margarine or butter,**
1 cup hot water	**melted**
2 cups sugar	

Mix in blender or a food processor and store in refrigerator.

Note: Costs ½ that of a commercial brand.

Cookbook Committee   Yield: 3 cups

Toasted Pumpkin Seeds

2 cups fresh pumpkin seeds
Salted water
1 tablespoon vegetable oil

2 teaspoons salt
1 teaspoon curry powder
1/3 cup grated Parmesan cheese

Clean fibers from seeds. Wash seeds and dry on paper towels. Soak overnight in salted water. Drain. Preheat oven to 350 degrees. Rub oil on hands and coat seeds. Place seeds in shallow pan. Bake approximately 15 minutes, stirring occasionally. Combine salt, curry powder, and cheese; sprinkle on seeds, tossing to coat evenly. Bake five to ten minutes longer until crisp and golden brown.

Sherie Sherrer

Yield: 2 cups

Strawberry Butter

1 (10-ounce) package frozen
  strawberries, thawed

1 cup butter, softened
1 cup powdered sugar

Combine in blender until smooth; chill.

Janice Stapp

Yield: 2 to 3 cups

Ice Cream Cone Cupcakes

1 (18 1/2-ounce box cake mix)

24 to 28 flat bottomed ice cream
cones

Prepare batter according to directions on box. Fill cones 3/4 full with batter. To bake, place cones in muffin tins to prevent toppling. Cook 20 minutes at 350 degrees. Remove from oven and cool.

Frosting:
1 (16-ounce) box powdered sugar
1/2 cup shortening
1 teaspoon vanilla
1 teaspoon almond flavoring,
  optional

1/4 cup milk
Food coloring, optional

Cream together all ingredients until frosting is smooth. Decorate cooled cupcakes.

Ashley Delp

Yield: 24 to 28 servings

Potpourri

3 cups dried flowers and leaves
1 tablespoon allspice
1 tablespoon orrisroot
Citrus peel of 3 oranges
Citrus peel of 3 limes

Citrus peel of 3 lemons
7 drops rose oil
6 drops gardenia oil
Cinnamon sticks

Spread on paper and dry flowers at least 1 week. They should be dry to touch but not crumbly. Add remaining ingredients and store in a large covered container 6 to 8 weeks. Shake weekly. Makes a wonderful gift.

Note: Not edible.

Cookbook Committee

Christmas Ornament Dough

1 cup cornstarch
½ cup cold water

2 cups salt
⅔ cup water

Mix cornstarch and ½ cup cold water in bowl. Mix salt and ⅔ cup water in an electric skillet or saucepan on low heat. Stir 3 to 4 minutes. Remove from heat and immediately add the cornstarch and cold water mixture to the hot salt water. This forms an easy-to-handle dough. This dough will harden to a rock-like consistency. Great for rolling out and cutting into ornaments for all occasions!

Cookbook Committee

Play Dough

1 cup flour
½ cup salt
2 teaspoons cream of tartar
1 tablespoon vegetable oil

1 cup water
Food coloring, optional
¼ teaspoon peppermint extract, optional

Mix ingredients in saucepan. If colored play dough is desired, add color to water before mixing. If scented play dough is desired, add peppermint extract. Heat over medium heat, stirring until mixture comes away from side of pan. Let cool and have children knead until smooth. Add a little more flour while kneading if it is sticky. Store in airtight container.

Betty Clower

Yield: 2 cups

Finger Paint

5 cups hot water
2 cups flour
½ cup soap flakes,
   NOT DETERGENT

½ cup salt
16 tablespoons dry tempera,
   colors of your choice

Combine the water and flour. Cook these two ingredients about 15 minutes, stirring constantly. Remove from heat; add soap flakes and salt. This makes four pints. Add 4 tablespoons dry tempera to each pint while hot.

Note: Although this consistency works well for finger painting, add liquid starch to the mixture for easel painting.

Cookbook Committee   Yield: 4 pints

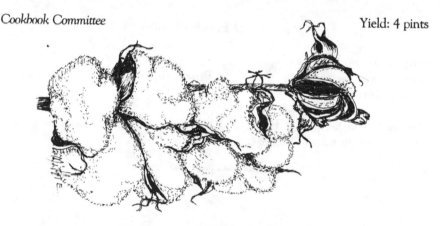

Halloween Magic Makeup

2 tablespoons shortening
5 tablespoons cornstarch
5 drops liquid dishwashing
   detergent

4 to 6 drops food coloring

Mix shortening and cornstarch until creamy. Add dishwashing detergent and mix. Add food coloring and mix until color is even. The detergent keeps the food coloring from staining the skin and clothes.

Note: Color ratios:
   Army green–1 drop red to 3 drops green
   Orange–3 drops yellow to 1 drop red
   Purple–3 drops red to 1 drop blue
   Grey–3 drops blue to 2 drops red

Alice Landham Jones   Yield: ¼ cup

Bubble Solution

½ cup water
½ cup liquid detergent

1 tablespoon glycerine

Mix the water with the liquid detergent. Add the glycerine to the bubble mixture to make the bubbles more durable. Use wire loops, empty thread spools, or straws to make bubbles.

Cookbook Committee　　　　　　　　　　　　　　　　　　　　　Yield: 1 cup

Bird Feeders

1 cup cornmeal
1 cup peanut butter
1¼ cups bird seed

String
Pine cones

Combine cornmeal, peanut butter, and bird seed. Tie a string on pine cones. Smear cones with mixture and hang up outside for birds.

Note: *May be decorated with red ribbon and given as Christmas gifts.*

Mary Drue Wheeler　　　　　　　　　　　　　　　　　　　　　Yield: 3 cups

Bird Food Balls

2 pounds ground suet
2 cups peanut butter
⅓ cup molasses
¼ cup bacon grease

1 pound regular oatmeal
1¼ cups cornmeal
Bird feed with sunflower seeds

Place suet in a pan and melt over medium heat. Strain into a large bowl. Add peanut butter, molasses, bacon grease, oatmeal, and cornmeal. Add enough seeds until mixture can be rolled into balls. Roll into 2-inch balls and coat with bird feed while warm. Chill. Place outside for the birds. If using as a gift, wrap individual balls in plastic wrap, and decorate. Attach a label indicating it is for the birds!

Terry Austin　　　　　　　　　　　　　　　　　　　　Yield: 24 2-inch balls

Homemade Doggie Biscuits

3½ cups flour
2 cups whole wheat flour
1 cup rye flour
1 cup cornmeal
2 cups cracked wheat, bulgar
½ cup nonfat dry milk
4 teaspoons salt

1 envelope yeast
¼ cup warm water
2 cups chicken stock or other
    liquid
1 egg
1 tablespoon milk

Preheat oven to 300 degrees. Combine all the dry ingredients except the yeast. In a separate bowl, dissolve the yeast in ¼ cup warm water. To this, add the chicken stock. Add the liquid to the dry ingredients. Knead mixture for about 3 minutes. (Dough will be quite stiff. If too stiff, add extra liquid or an egg.) Roll the dough out on a floured board to ½-inch thickness, then immediately cut into shapes with cookie cutters. Place on an ungreased cookie sheet. Combine egg and milk to brush dough. Bake in oven 45 minutes, turn oven off, and leave biscuits in oven overnight to get bones hard.

Peggy Watts   Yield: 5 dozen

Quantities To Serve 50 People

Coffee . . . . 1½ pounds
Lump Sugar . . . . 1½ pounds
Cream . . . . 1½ quarts
Milk . . . . 3 gallons
Tomato Juice . . . . 5 (46-ounce) cans
Soup . . . . 2½ gallons
Oysters . . . . 9 quarts
Meat Loaf . . . . 12 pounds
Ham . . . . 20 pounds
Beef . . . . 20 pounds
Roast Pork . . . . 20 pounds
Hamburger . . . . 13 pounds
Potatoes . . . . 17 pounds
Vegetables . . . . 13 pounds
Cakes 4
Ice Cream . . . . 2½ gallons
Cheese . . . . 1½ pounds
Olives . . . . 1 pound
Pickles . . . . 1½ quarts
Nuts . . . . 2 pounds
Baked Beans . . . . 2½ gallons
Bread . . . . 5 loaves
Potato Salad . . . . 6 quarts
Fruit Salad . . . . 10 quarts
Lettuce . . . . 10 heads
Salad Dressing . . . . 1½ quarts

When You Come Up Short

1 tablespoon arrowroot

2 tablespoons all-purpose flour plus
1 tablespoon cornstarch

1 teaspoon baking powder

¼ teaspoon baking soda plus
½ teaspoon cream of tartar

1 cup bread crumbs

¾ cup cracker crumbs

1 cup canned broth, beef or chicken

1 bouillon cube or 1 teaspoon
powdered broth plus 1 cup
boiling water

1 cup butter

1 cup margarine or ⅞ cup vegetable
shortening plus ½ teaspoon salt
or ⅞ cup lard

1 cup buttermilk or sour milk

1 tablespoon vinegar or lemon juice
plus sweet milk added to make
1 cup

1 cup chili sauce

1 cup tomato sauce, ½ cup sugar plus
2 tablespoons vinegar

6 ounces semi-sweet chocolate

2 ounces unsweetened chocolate,
7 tablespoons sugar plus
2 tablespoons butter, margarine,
or vegetable shortening

1 ounce semi-sweet chocolate

3 tablespoons cocoa,
1 tablespoon butter, margarine, or
vegetable shortening plus
3 tablespoons sugar

1 ounce unsweetened chocolate

3 tablespoons cocoa plus 1 tablespoon
butter, margarine, or vegetable
shortening

corn syrup

1 cup sugar plus ¼ cup water or liquid
called for in recipe

1 tablespoon cornstarch

2 tablespoons all-purpose flour or
4 teaspoons quick cooking tapioca

1 cup light cream	3 tablespoons butter plus ⅞ cup milk
1 cup half and half	1½ tablespoons butter plus ⅞ cup milk
1 cup heavy cream	⅓ cup butter plus ¾ cup milk
1 cup sour cream	3 tablespoons butter plus ⅞ cup sour milk or 1 tablespoon lemon juice plus evaporated milk to make 1 cup
1 medium egg	2 egg yolks
1 large egg	3 small eggs
1 cup all-purpose flour	1 cup cake flour plus 2 tablespoons
1 teaspoon baking powder	½ teaspoon cream of tartar plus ¼ teaspoon soda
1 cup cake flour	1 cup sifted all-purpose flour minus 2 tablespoons
1 cup self-rising flour	1 cup all-purpose flour plus 1 teaspoon baking powder and ½ teaspoon salt
1 clove garlic	⅛ teaspoon garlic powder or 1 teaspoon garlic salt or ⅛ teaspoon instant minced garlic
1 tablespoon minced ginger or grated ginger root	⅛ teaspoon powdered ginger
1 tablespoon fresh herbs	1 teaspoon dried
1 cup honey	1¼ cups sugar plus ¼ cup water or liquid called for in recipe
1 teaspoon lemon juice	½ teaspoon vinegar
1 teaspoon mace	1 teaspoon nutmeg

1 cup skim milk	¼ cup dry skim milk powder in measuring cup and water added to make 1 cup
1 cup sweet milk	1 cup sour milk or buttermilk plus ½ teaspoon baking soda
1 cup whole milk	½ cup evaporated milk plus ½ cup water
1 (15-ounce) can sweetened condensed milk	1⅓ cups dry skim milk powder, ½ cup sugar, 3 tablespoons butter, plus ½ cup boiling water
8 ounces fresh, raw, sliced mushrooms	1 cup cooked or 6 ounces canned, drained
1 tablespoon prepared mustard	1 teaspoon dry mustard plus 1 tablespoon vinegar
¼ cup chopped or 1 small onion	1 tablespoon instant chopped, minced, or flaked dehydrated onion
1 cup sour cream	1 tablespoon lemon juice plus evaporated milk to make 1 cup or 3 tablespoons butter plus ⅞ cup sour milk
1 cup granulated sugar	1 cup firmly packed brown sugar or 1 cup molasses plus ¼ to ½ teaspoon baking soda; omit any baking powder in the recipe or combine ½ cup maple syrup and ¼ cup corn syrup
1 tablespoon tapioca	1½ tablespoons all-purpose flour
1 tablespoon tomato paste	1 tablespoon tomato ketchup
1 cup canned tomatoes	Simmer 1⅓ cups chopped fresh tomatoes ten minutes
1 tablespoon active dry yeast	1¼-ounce package active dry yeast or 1 cake compressed yeast
1 cup unflavored yogurt	1 cup buttermilk or sour milk

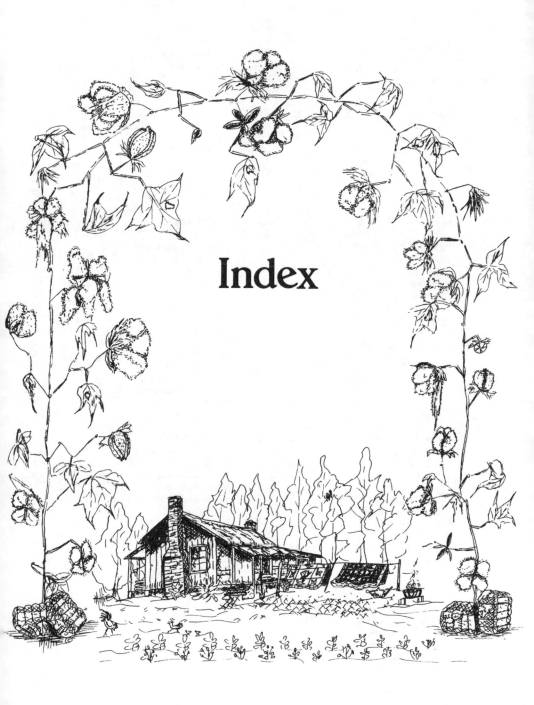

Index

6
60 Minute Hamburger Buns 201

9
9-Boy Indian Curry 136

A
Alabama's Pepper Steak 102
ALMOND(S)
   Almond Bars 279
   Almond Butter Crunch 288
   Almond Coconut Bars 279
   Almond Pound Cake 227
Amaretto Frappé 37
Amaretto Trifle 249
Angel Biscuits 200
Angel Food Cakes 258
Angel Pie 234
APPETIZERS
  Chafing Dish
     Beef Hors d'oeuvres 6
     Bourbon Franks 9
     Broccoli Dip, Hot 25
     Cocktail Meatballs 8
     Picadillo Dip 7
  Dips
     Artichoke Spread, Hot 24
     Bacon and Tomato Spread 10
     Broccoli Dip, Hot 25
     Cream Cheese-Olive Dip 19
     Creamy Beef Cheese Dip 8
     Cucumber Dip 24
     Fondue Cheese Dip 16
     Guacamole Dip 25
     Hot Shrimp Dip I 12
     Hot Shrimp Dip II 12
     Oriental Dip 28
     Pizza Dip 9
     Raw Vegetable Dip 25
     Second Lady Spinach Dip 22
     South of the Border Appetizer Platter 28
     Spinach Dip 21
  Finger Foods
     Beef Rolls 7
     Cheese Rolls 18
     Cheese Straws I 16
     Cheese Straws II 17
     Cheese Wafers 16
     Cherry Tomato Appetizers 23
     Garlic Rounds 27
     Marinated Oyster Crackers 27
     Mushroom Sandwiches 23
     Orange Sugar Pecans 26
     Pecans Worcestershire 26
     Shrimp Celery Stuffing 13
     Stuffed Snow Pea Pods 20
     Toasted Pecans 27
  Hot Hors d'oeuvres
     Artichoke Hearts, Crispy Fried 24
     Beef Knishes 6

Cheese and Olive Croquettes 20
Cheese Puffs 17
Chicken Nut Bites 11
Corndog Bites 10
Curried Crab Meatballs 14
Delicious Chicken Wings 11
Greek Spinach Triangles 21
Ham and Cheese Puffs 9
Holladay's Cream Cheese Puffs 19
Mushroom Turnovers 22
Oysters in Mexican Blankets 15
Sausage Balls 7
Stuffed Mushrooms 23
Spreads and Molds
   Artichoke Spread, Hot 24
   Bacon and Tomato Spread 10
   Baked Brie 19
   Cheese Ball 18
   Cream Cheese-Crabmeat Log 13
   Famous Cheese Ring 17
   Nut Roll 26
   Olive Pimento Cheese Spread 15
   Oyster Roll 15
   Party Crab Mold 14
   Salmon Spread 13
   Shrimp Mold 12
APPLE(S)
Fresh Apple Cake 214
Fresh Apple Salad 74
Glazed Apple Cookies 268
Mother's Applesauce Cake 214
Spiced Apple Rings 192
Apricot Nectar Cake 215
Apricots, Baked 190
ARTICHOKE(S)
Artichoke Hearts, Crispy Fried 24
Artichoke Rice 170
Artichoke Spread, Hot 24
Poulet d'Artichoke 125
Shrimp and Artichoke Salad 86
ASPARAGUS
Asparagus Casserole 170
Asparagus Sandwiches, Puff-Topped 49
Aunt Jean's Lasagna 107
Autumn Fruitcake 217
AVOCADO(S)
Guacamole Dip 25
South of the Border Appetizer Platter 28

B
Bacon and Tomato Spread 10
Bacon Sandwiches 53
Baked Apricots 190
Baked Beans 172
Baked Brie 19
Baked Cheese Squash 179
Baked Chicken Reuben 131
Baked Corn with Sour Cream 175
Baked Cranberry Casserole 190

Baked Creamed Cabbage 182
Baked Oysters 157
Baked Oysters Alabama 156
Baked Sandwiches 51
Baked Tuna 157
Baked Vidalia Onions 180
Baklava 262
BANANA(S)
Banana Ice Cream 293
Banana Muffins 212
Banana Nut Bread 204
Banana Split Cake 258
Bananas Foster 263
Blu-Bana Bread 204
Very Easy Banana Pudding 253
Whole Wheat Banana Bread 203
Barbecue Corn 177
Barbecue Meat Loaf 104
Barbecue Sauce 164
Barbecued Shrimp 151
Bay Salad 88
BEANS
Baked Beans 172
Green Bean Casserole 173
Red Beans and Rice 172
Three Bean Casserole 173
Béarnaise Sauce 168
BEEF (Also see LAMB and VEAL)
Alabama's Pepper Steak 102
Beef Burgundy Stroganoff 103
Beef Hors d'oeuvres 6
Beef Piquant 100
Beef Rolls 7
Beef Scraps 98
Beef Teriyaki Marinade 162
Best Steak in Alabama 98
Calves' Liver with Sherry 114
Chateaubriand 98
Chinese Beef in Oyster Sauce 102
Creamy Beef Cheese Dip 8
Filet of Beef Wellington 99
Ground Beef
Aunt Jean's Lasagna 107
Barbecue Meat Loaf 104
Beef Bonaparte 108
Beef Knishes 6
Cheeseburger Pie 110
Cherokee Casserole 111
Coal Miner's Pie 109
Cocktail Meatballs 8
Family Supper Casserole 109
Got It All Together 111
Hamburger Stroganoff 103
Hamburger-Can-Be-Heaven Casserole 110
Meat Loaf 105
Mexican Casserole 114
Mexican Cornbread Casserole 113
Mexican Salad 85
Oriental Green Casserole 112
Picadillo Dip 7

Quick Manicotti 106
Stuffed Green Peppers 105
Taco Casserole 113
Tagganocci 108
Three Way Meat Loaf 104
World Famous Spaghetti 106
Hearty Steak and Onions 101
Herb Marinated Tenderloin 99
Hole-In-One Peppers 114
Old-Time Beef Stew 48
Real Texas Chili 49
Reuben Casserole 115
Sausage Rice Bake 112
Stir-Fry Beef and Vegetables 101
Sunday Dinner Roast Beef 100
V-8 Beef Stew 48
Beer Biscuits 199
Beets, Southern 189
Best Gingerbread Cookie 269
Best Steak in Alabama 98
Bev's Fruitcake 217
BEVERAGES
Alcoholic
Amaretto Frappé 37
Eggnog 38
Homemade Kahlúa 39
Hot Buttered Rum 39
Margaritas 37
Milk Punch 40
Mimosa 37
Mint Julep 39
Never Fail Blackberry Wine 38
Peach Fuzz Buzz 40
Southern Comfort Punch 38
Stan's Bloody Marys 36
Cold
Citrus Cooler 30
Easy Punch 30
Fruit Crush Punch 30
Mint Drink Frappé 33
Mother's Fruit Icee 32
Orange Blend 33
Orange Blush 33
Party Punch 31
Purple Cow 34
Rita Boyd's Fruit Punch 31
Sarah's Fruit Tea Punch 32
Slush Fruit Punch 31
Tomato Juice Cocktail 32
Tropical Tea 34
Hot
Cafe Viennese 35
Guaranteed Good Coffee 35
Hot Chocolate Mix 34
Percolator Hot Punch 35
Russian Tea I 36
Russian Tea II 36
Bill's Barbecued Catfish Sauce 166
Billy's Favorite Ice Cream 293
Bird Feeders 308

Bird Food Balls 308
Biscuits 199
Black Bottom Pie 243
Blender Mayonnaise 91
Bleu Cheese Salad Dressing 93
Blow Your Diet Cinnamon Rolls 209

BLUEBERRY(IES)
Blu-Bana Bread 204
Blueberry Salad 76
Blueberry Sweet Rolls 210
Bourbon Balls 291
Bourbon Franks 9
Brandied Caramel Flan 253
Bread Pudding with Whiskey Sauce 254

BREADS
Biscuits
  Angel Biscuits 200
  Beer Biscuits 199
  Biscuits 199
  Lemonade Biscuits 198
  Mayonnaise Biscuits 199
Cornbread
  Cornbread Dressing 196
  Cracklin' Bread 195
  Hush Puppies 196
  Mexican Cornbread I 194
  Mexican Cornbread II 194
  Specialty of the House Cornbread 194
  Spoon Bread 195
Miscellaneous
  60 Minute Hamburger Buns 201
  Cream Cheese Pie Crust 241
  Dilly Casserole Bread 205
  French Toast 197
  Garlic Rounds 27
  Judy's Honey and Cracked Wheat Bread . 201
  Marinated Oyster Crackers 27
  Old Fashioned Honey Wheat Bread 202
  Onion-Cheese Supper Bread 206
  Parmesan Croutons 198
  Paw Paw's Pancakes 198
  Pie Crust 232
  Poppy Seed Bread 206
  Potato Bread 202
  Rodney's Rapjacks for a Crowd 197
  Royal Bread Pudding 254
  Spicy Italian Bread 206
  Tasty Italian Bread Strips 195
Muffins
  Easy Wheat Muffins 211
  Onion Cheese Muffins 211
  Pecan Muffins 212
  Quick Muffins 210
  Six Week Bran Muffins 211
  Sour Cream Muffins 212
Rolls
  Monkey Bread 207
  Potato Bread 202
  Refrigerator Rolls 200
  Sourdough Starter 207

Spoon Rolls 200
Sweet Breads
  Banana Muffins 212
  Banana Nut Bread 204
  Blow Your Diet Cinnamon Rolls 209
  Blu-Bana Bread 204
  Blueberry Sweet Rolls 210
  Cranberry-Cheese Bread 205
  Graham Nut Bread 203
  Orange Cream Cheese Coffee Cake 208
  Quick Monkey Bread 208
  Whole Wheat Banana Bread 203
Breakfast Sausage Casserole 60

BROCCOLI
Broccoli and Rice Casserole 171
Broccoli Casserole 172
Broccoli Dip, Hot 25
Broccoli Salad 79
Broccoli Soup 43
Broccoli-Corn Casserole 171
Chicken and Broccoli 130
Ham Dumbbells and Broccoli Casserole 119
Hurry-Up-Broccoli Soup 43
Marinated Broccoli Ring 80
Nutty Broccoli Salad 80
Brown Rice 66
Brown Sugar Cookies 271
Brunch Eggs Supreme 57
Brussels Sprouts Oriental 174
Bubble Solution 308
Buckeyes 288
Butter Pecan Cookies 270
Butterscotch Candy 284

C

CABBAGE
Baked Creamed Cabbage 182
Cabbage Patch Soup 43
Cabbage Salad Dressing 96
Kraut Salad-Relish 91
Marinated Slaw 90
Cafe Viennese 35
Cahawba Chicken 132

CAKES
Almond Pound Cake 227
Angel Food Cakes 258
Apricot Nectar Cake 215
Autumn Fruitcake 217
Banana Split Cake 258
Bev's Fruitcake 217
Caramel Cake 220
Carrot Cake 215
Chocolate Mound Cake 222
Chocolate Pound Cake 228
Cinnamon Pound Cake 229
Coconut Pound Cake 227
Coconut Sour Cream Dream Cake 225
Coffee Chiffon Cake 226
Cream Cheese Pound Cake 228
Creole Cake 221

Easy Chocolate Cake 223
Fig Cake 216
Fresh Apple Cake 214
Fruit Cocktail Cake 216
Grandma's Buttermilk Pound Cake 229
Happy Birthday Cake 225
Hummingbird Cake 218
Ice Cream Cone Cupcakes 305
Mandarin Orange Cake 220
Million Dollar Pound Cake 229
Mother's Applesauce Cake 214
Old Fashioned Sour Cream Pound Cake . . . 231
Pecan Cake 219
Plum Cake 219
Punch Bowl Cake 250
Red Velvet Cake 221
Seven Up Cake 224
Strawberry Cake 219
Swedish Pound Cake 230
Tasty Finger Length Cake 256
Triple Fudge Cake 226
Vanilla Wafer Cake 224
Whipping Cream Pound Cake 230
White Chocolate Cake 223
White Fruitcake 218
Calves' Liver with Sherry 114
Calypso Pie 244
Campfire Chicken 141

CANDY(IES)
Almond Butter Crunch 288
Bourbon Balls 291
Buckeyes 288
Butterscotch Candy 284
Chocolate Liqueur Candies 287
Chocolate Peanut Butter Squares 287
Chocolate Truffles 289
Christmas Fudge 285
Creamy Pralines 286
Date Balls 291
English Buttercreams 283
English Taffa'—Marble Candy 290
German Chocolate Delights 288
Honey Divinity 286
Honey Popcorn Balls 292
Microwave Caramel Nut Rolls 290
Microwave Copy Pop 292
Microwave Divinity 285
Microwave Munchy Peanut Brittle 289
Orange Balls 286
Peanut Butter Candy 284
Ron's Fudge 284
Caramel Cake 220
Caramel Cake Icing 231
Caramel Crunchies 280
Caramel Icing 220

CARROT(S)
Carrot Cake 215
Carrot Casserole 182
Carrot Salad 77
Mom Bryant's Carrot Salad 77

Catfish in Beer Batter 161
Cauliflower Salad 79
Charlotte 251
Chateaubriand 98

CHEESE (Also see QUICHE)
Baked Brie 19
Bleu Cheese Salad Dressing 93
Breakfast Sausage Casserole 60
Cheese and Olive Croquettes 20
Cheese Ball 18
Cheese Puffs 17
Cheese Rolls 18
Cheese Sandwich Casserole 60
Cheese Straws I 16
Cheese Straws II 17
Cheese Wafers 16
Cheeseburger Pie 110
Cheesy Vegetable Chowder 44
Chicken-Cheese Soup 44
Chili Cheese Rolls 52
Famous Cheese Ring 17
Fondue Cheese Dip 16
Ham and Cheese Puffs 9
Macaroni and Cheese 64
Macaroni and Cheese Deluxe 65
Never Fail Cheese Souffle 61
Olive Pimento Cheese Spread 15
Pimento Sandwiches 50
Scalloped Cheese Tomatoes 178

CHEESECAKE (See DESSERTS: Cheesecake)
Cheesy Vegetable Chowder 44
Cherokee Casserole 111
Cherry Pecan Bars 278
Cherry Tomato Appetizers 23
Chess Pie 233

CHICKEN
9-Boy Indian Curry 136
Baked Chicken Reuben 131
Cahawba Chicken 132
Campfire Chicken 141
Chicken and Wild Rice Casserole 140
Chicken and Broccoli 130
Chicken and Dumplings 137
Chicken Casserole 139
Chicken-Cheese Soup 44
Chicken Cordon Bleu 128
Chicken Cottage Pie 132
Chicken Crêpes with Mushrooms 125
Chicken Morgan 124
Chicken Nut Bites 11
Chicken Parisienne 123
Chicken Roll-Ups 134
Chicken Salad 85
Chicken Skillet 138
Chicken Spaghetti 135
Chicken Strips 129
Chicken Supreme 138
Chicken Teriyaki 133
Chinese Chicken 124
Chinese Veggies 129

Index

Crunchy Chicken Pie 133
Crunchy Party Chicken 135
Delicious Chicken Wings 11
Don's Chicken and Rice Salad 86
Easy Baked Chicken 128
Easy Barbecued Chicken 137
Foiled-Up Fowl 134
Hot Chicken Salad I 126
Hot Chicken Salad II 127
Italian Drumsticks 127
King Ranch Casserole 130
Mama's Fried Chicken 136
Mexican Chicken 131
Oven Barbecued Chicken 137
"Paul M's" Charcoal Chicken 138
Pop's Chicken Curry 126
Poulet d'Artichoke 125
Quick and Easy Chicken Casserole 140
Ritzy Chicken Pie 133
Skewered Chicken Livers 135
Stuffed Cornish Hens 141
Sweet and Sour Chicken 139
Swiss Chicken 139
Chili Cheese Rolls 52
Chili Sauce 302
Chinese Beef in Oyster Sauce 102
Chinese Chicken 124
Chinese Veggies 129
CHOCOLATE
Black Bottom Pie 243
Calypso Pie 244
Chocolate Brownies 280
Chocolate Chip Pie 247
Chocolate Eclair Dessert 251
Chocolate Leaves 267
Chocolate Liqueur Candies 287
Chocolate Meringue Pie 246
Chocolate Mound Cake 222
Chocolate Peanut Butter Squares 287
Chocolate Pound Cake 228
Chocolate Trifle 249
Chocolate Truffles 289
Christmas Fudge 285
Easy Chocolate Cake 223
Easy Chocolate Cheesecake 266
Easy Chocolate Icing 223
Easy Never Fail Chocolate Icing 231
Famous Chocolate Chip Cookies 277
Frozen Chocolate Crêpes with
    Custard Sauce 259
German Chocolate Cheesy Brownies 281
German Chocolate Delights 288
Granny's Chocolate Cookies 276
Hot Chocolate Mix 34
Hot Fudge Pie 245
Hot Fudge Pudding 255
Hot Fudge Sauce 267
Libbett's Black Bottom Ice Cream Pie 244
Mama's Brownies 281
Milky Way Bar Ice Cream 295

Milky Way No Bake Cheesecake 266
"Quickie" Chocolate Pie 247
Ritz Cracker Cookies 278
Ron's Fudge 284
Sweet Angel Chocolate Pie 245
Triple Fudge Cake 226
Turtle Cake Squares 282
White Chocolate Cake 223
White Chocolate Frosting 223
Christmas Fudge 285
Christmas Ornament Dough 306
Christmas Pies 238
Cinnamon Cookies 271
Cinnamon Flats 283
Cinnamon Pound Cake 229
Citrus Chiffon Pie 235
Citrus Cooler 30
Clam Chowder 46
Coal Miner's Pie 109
Cocktail Meatballs 8
COCONUT
Almond Coconut Bars 279
Coconut Pie I 238
Coconut Pie II 238
Coconut Pound Cake 227
Coconut Sour Cream Dream Cake 225
Coffee Chiffon Cake 226
COOKIES
Almond Bars 279
Almond Coconut Bars 279
Best Gingerbread Cookie 269
Brown Sugar Cookies 271
Butter Pecan Cookies 270
Caramel Crunchies 280
Cherry Pecan Bars 278
Chocolate Brownies 280
Cinnamon Cookies 271
Cinnamon Flats 283
Date Tarts 277
Eugenia's Sugar Cookies 273
Famous Chocolate Chip Cookies 277
First Prize Tea Cakes 274
Fruitcake Cookies 269
German Chocolate Cheesy Brownies 281
Glazed Apple Cookies 268
Graham Cracker Crisps 274
Granny's Chocolate Cookies 276
Ice Box Cookies 272
Ice Cream Brownies 294
Ice Water Cookies 272
Jewish Prune Cookies 268
Lemon Squares 282
Magic Cookie Bars 280
Mama's Brownies 281
Oatmeal Bars 279
Oatmeal Cookie Crisp 276
Oatmeal Cookies 275
Oatmeal Crispies 275
Ooey-Gooey Bars 281
Peanut Blossoms 270

Peanut Butter Drop Cookies 271
Pineapple Cookies 267
Potato Chip Cookies 278
Ritz Cracker Cookies 278
Sand Tarts 274
Snickerdoodles 272
Toffee Cookies 273
Turtle Cake Squares 282

CORN
Baked Corn with Sour Cream 175
Barbecue Corn 177
Broccoli-Corn Casserole 171
Corn Custard Casserole 175
Corn Oysters 174
Cornbread Casserole 177
Creamy Shoe Peg Corn 177
Easy Corn Salad 77
Golden Corn Casserole 176
Parmesan Hominy 184
Shoe Peg Corn Casserole 176
Spicy Corn-On-The-Cob 174
Cornbread Casserole 177
Cornbread Dressing 196
Cornbread Salad 90
Corndog Bites 10
Country Ham and Red Eye Gravy 118

CRAB
Crab "Blue Moon" 149
Crab Gumbo 46
Crab Louis Salad 89
Crabmeat au Gratin 149
Crabmeat Casserole 148
Cream Cheese-Crabmeat Log 13
Curried Crab Meatballs 14
Marinated Crabmeat 150
Party Crab Mold 14
West Indies Salad 88
Cracklin' Bread 195

CRANBERRY(IES)
Baked Cranberry Casserole 190
Cranberry-Cheese Bread 205
Mama vonSeeberg's Cranberry Sauce 304
Mama's Cranberry Salad 69
Cream Cheese Icing 215
Cream Cheese Pie Crust 241
Cream Cheese Pound Cake 228
Cream Cheese-Crabmeat Log 13
Cream Cheese-Olive Dip 19
Creamy Baked Cheesecake 265
Creamy Beef Cheese Dip 8
Creamy Peanut Butter Pie 242
Creamy Pralines 286
Creamy Shoe Peg Corn 177
Crème de Menthe Salad 74
Creole Cake 221
Crispy Bread and Butter Pickles 302
Crispy Pickle 302
Crunchy Chicken Pie 133
Crunchy Party Chicken 135

CUCUMBER(S)
Crispy Bread and Butter Pickles 302
Crispy Pickle 302
Cucumber Dip 24
Dill Pickles 301
Refrigerator Pickles 300
Savory Cucumbers 190
Curried Crab Meatballs 14
Curried Fruit 191

D
Daddy's Tender Turkey 142
Date Balls 291
Date Tarts 277
David's Vegetable Surprise 188
Day-Of-The-Wedding Sausage Casserole 122
Delicious Boiled Custard 252
Delicious Chicken Wings 11
Delicious Shrimp Batter 160
Deluxe Waldorf Salad 71

DESSERTS
Angel Food Cakes 258
Baklava 262
Banana Split Cake 258
Bananas Foster 263
Charlotte 251
Cheesecake
  Cheesecake 265
  Coconut Cream Cheesecake 263
  Creamy Baked Cheesecake 265
  Easy Chocolate Cheesecake 266
  Mac's Cheesecake 264
  Milky Way No Bake Cheesecake 266
  Praline Cheesecake 264
Chocolate Eclair Dessert 251
Chocolate Leaves 267
Chocolate Trifle 249
Custard
  Amaretto Trifle 249
  Brandied Caramel Flan 253
  Delicious Boiled Custard 252
  Frozen Chocolate Crêpes with
    Custard Sauce 259
  Jamie's Egg Custard 252
  Microwave Boiled Custard 252
  Trifle 248
Finger Gelatin 261
Four Layer Lemon Dessert 261
French Strawberry Mousse 250
Granny Bobo's Trillby 248
Heavenly Grapes 260
Hot Fudge Sauce 267
Nut Roll Extraordinaire 257
Panic 260
Pavlova Meringue 260
Peach Crisp 255
Pudding
  Bread Pudding with Whiskey Sauce 254
  Hot Fudge Pudding 255
  Pugh's Ozark Pudding 255
  Royal Bread Pudding 254

Very Easy Banana Pudding 253
Punch Bowl Cake 250
Swedish Pastry 256
Tasty Finger Length Cake 256
Deviled Eggs 56
Deviled Turkey 143
Diane's Marinated Ham Slice 118
Dill Pickles 301
Dilly Casserole Bread 205
Don's Chicken and Rice Salad 86

DRESSINGS
Blender Mayonnaise 91
Bleu Cheese Salad Dressing 93
Cabbage Salad Dressing 96
French Dressing 95
Granny's Salad Dressing for Green Salad 94
Kay's Famous Birmingham Slaw Dressing . . . 95
Lemon Dressing 92
Mother's Honey Dressing 92
Mr. B's House Dressing 94
Mrs. Baen's Ranch Dressing 94
Poppy Seed Dressing 93
Sherry Mayonnaise 91
Sweet and Sour Dressing 93
Thousand Island Dressing 95
Tomato Honey Dressing 92
Duck Breasts 147

E
Easy Baked Chicken 128
Easy Barbecued Chicken 137
Easy Brunswick Stew 47
Easy Chocolate Cake 223
Easy Chocolate Cheesecake 266
Easy Chocolate Icing 223
Easy Corn Salad 77
Easy Miracle Pie 232
Easy Never Fail Chocolate Icing 231
Easy Peach Cobbler 237
Easy Punch 30
Easy Sausage Rice Casserole 121
Easy Sherbet 293
Easy Wheat Muffins 211
Eggnog 38

EGGPLANT
Eggplant Creole 178
Seafood Stuffed Eggplant 153
Shrimp and Eggplant Casserole 153

EGGS (Also see QUICHE)
Brunch Eggs Supreme 57
Deviled Eggs 56
Egg Pie 233
Glorified Eggs 56
Jamie's Egg Custard 252
Scotch Eggs 56
Shrimp and Deviled Egg Casserole 154
Elephant Stew 49
English Buttercreams 283
English Pea Casserole 181
English Pea Salad 81

English Taffa'—Marble Candy 290
Eugenia's Sugar Cookies 273

F
Family Supper Casserole 109
Famous Cheese Ring 17
Famous Chocolate Chip Cookies 277
Fettuccini Supreme 62
Fig Cake 216
Fig Strawberry Preserves 298
Filet of Beef Wellington 99
Finger Gelatin 261
Finger Paint 307
Fire and Ice Tomatoes 178
First Prize Tea Cakes 274

FISH
Catfish in Beer Batter 161
Fish Florentine 160
Flounder Meuniere 159
"Poor Man's" Lobster 159
Flounder Meuniere 159
Fluffy Coffee Icing 226
Foiled-Up Fowl 134
Fondue Cheese Dip 16
Four Layer Lemon Dessert 261
French Dressing 95
French Fried Okra 189
French Fried Onion Rings 180
French Onion Soup 42
French Pecan Pie 241
French Strawberry Mousse 250
French Toast 197
Fresh Apple Cake 214
Fresh Apple Salad 74
Fresh Fruit Compote 71
Fresh or Frozen Black-Eyed Peas 181
Fresh Tartar Sauce 167
Fried Duck Breast 146
Fried Ice Cream 296
Frozen Chocolate Crêpes with
  Custard Sauce 259

FRUIT(S)
Baked Apricots 190
Baked Cranberry Casserole 190
Curried Fruit 191
Deluxe Waldorf Salad 71
Fresh Fruit Compote 71
Fruit Salad 68
Here's Lookin' At Ya Kid 69
Hot Fruit Casserole 191
Hot Pineapple Casserole 192
Magnolia Room Frozen Fruit Salad 70
Paradise Salad 68
Pineapple Casserole 191
Rosie Pink Salad 69
Snow Ball Salad 68
Spiced Apple Rings 192
Thanksgiving Salad 72

FRUITCAKE
Autumn Fruitcake 217

Bev's Fruitcake 217
Fruitcake Cookies 269
Japanese Fruitcake Pie 239
White Fruitcake 218

G
GAME
Duck Breasts 147
Fried Duck Breast 146
Hardy Eating 145
Louisiana Duck 145
Marinated Dove 148
Mike's Venison Jerkey 144
Smothered Dove or Quail 147
Southern Quail 148
Tew's Duck Casserole 146
Garlic Grits 66
Garlic Rice 65
Garlic Rounds 27
German Chocolate Cheesy Brownies 281
German Chocolate Delights 288
Girdle Buster Dessert 295
Glazed Apple Cookies 268
Glorified Eggs 56
Golden Corn Casserole 176
Golden Parmesan Potatoes 184
Got It All Together 111
Gourmet Hamburger Sauce 166
Governor's Seafood Gumbo 45
Graham Cracker Crisps 274
Graham Nut Bread 203
Grandma's Buttermilk Pound Cake 229
Granny Bobo's Trillby 248
Granny's Buttermilk Pie 233
Granny's Chocolate Cookies 276
Granny's Salad Dressing for Green Salad 94
Greek Spinach Triangles 21
Green Bean Casserole 173
GREEN PEPPER(S)
Hole-In-One Peppers 114
Stuffed Green Peppers 105
Grilled Ham with Sauce 118
GRITS (See PASTA)
Guacamole Dip 25
Guaranteed Good Coffee 35

H
Halloween Magic Makeup 307
HAM
Country Ham and Red Eye Gravy 118
Diane's Marinated Ham Slice 118
Grilled Ham with Sauce 118
Ham and Cheese Puffs 9
Ham and Scalloped Potatoes 119
Ham Dumbbells and Broccoli Casserole 119
Ham Loaf 117
Ham-Pita-Wiches 52
Pasta with Cream, Ham and Mushrooms . . . 63
Three Way Meat Loaf 104
Hamburger-Can-Be-Heaven Casserole 110

Hamburger Stroganoff 103
Happy Birthday Cake 225
Hardy Eating 145
Hazelnut and Caramel Ice Cream Dessert 296
Healthy Pasta Primavera 63
Hearty Steak and Onions 101
Heavenly Grapes 260
Herb Fettuccini 62
Herb Marinated Tenderloin 99
Here's Lookin' At Ya Kid 69
Hole-In-One Peppers 114
Holladay's Cream Cheese Puffs 19
Hollandaise Sauce 167
Homemade Doggie Biscuits 309
Homemade Ice Cream 294
Homemade Kahlúa 39
Honey Divinity 286
Honey Popcorn Balls 292
Hot Buttered Rum 39
Hot Chicken Salad I 126
Hot Chicken Salad II 127
Hot Chocolate Mix 34
Hot Fruit Casserole 191
Hot Fudge Pie 245
Hot Fudge Pudding 255
Hot Fudge Sauce 267
Hot Pepper Jelly 298
Hot Pineapple Casserole 192
Hot Shrimp Dip I 12
Hot Shrimp Dip II 12
How to Clarify Butter 304
Hummingbird Cake 218
Hurry-Up-Broccoli Soup 43
Hush Puppies 196

I
Ice Box Cookies 272
ICE CREAM
Banana Ice Cream 293
Billy's Favorite Ice Cream 293
Easy Sherbet 293
Fried Ice Cream 296
Girdle Buster Dessert 295
Hazelnut and Caramel Ice Cream Dessert . . . 296
Homemade Ice Cream 294
Ice Cream Brownies 294
Libbett's Black Bottom Ice Cream Pie 244
Milky Way Bar Ice Cream 295
Quick Tortoni Ice Cream 294
Ice Cream Cone Cupcakes 305
Ice Water Cookies 272
ICINGS
Caramel Cake Icing 231
Caramel Icing 220
Cream Cheese Icing 215
Easy Chocolate Icing 223
Easy Never Fail Chocolate Icing 231
Fluffy Coffee Icing 226
Mother's White Icing 232
White Chocolate Frosting 223

Italian Drumsticks 127

J

Jamie's Egg Custard 252
Jamie's Mustard Sauce 161
JAMS & JELLIES
    Fig Strawberry Preserves 298
    Hot Pepper Jelly 298
    Mama vonSeeberg's Cranberry Sauce 304
    Muscadine Jelly 298
    No-Cook Strawberry Jam 299
    Spiced Orange Slices 299
    Watermelon Jelly 299
Japanese Fruitcake Pie 239
JELLY (See JAMS & JELLIES)
Jewish Prune Cookies 268
Jill's Pasta Salad 85
Johnnie's Barbecue Sauce 165
Judy's Honey and Cracked Wheat Bread 201

K

Kay's Famous Birmingham Slaw Dressing 95
King Ranch Casserole 130
Kraut Salad-Relish 91

L

LAMB
    Lamb Casserole 116
    Leg of Lamb 116
    Marinated Lamb 117
Layered Salad 81
LEMON(S)
    Four Layer Lemon Dessert 261
    Lemon Dressing 92
    Lemon Squares 282
    Lemonade Biscuits 198
Libbett's Black Bottom Ice Cream Pie 244
Lots O' Macaroni Salad 84
Louisiana Duck 145

M

Mac's Cheesecake 264
Macaroni and Cheese 64
Macaroni and Cheese Deluxe 65
Madras Tuna Sandwiches 50
Magic Cookie Bars 280
Magnolia Room Frozen Fruit Salad 70
Make Ahead Breakfast Casserole 61
Mama vonSeeberg's Cranberry Sauce 304
Mama vonSeeberg's Sauce 162
Mama's Brownies 281
Mama's Cranberry Salad 69
Mama's Fried Chicken 136
Mandarin Orange Cake 220
Mandarin Orange Salad 75
Mandarin Orange-Almond Salad 83
Margaritas 37
MARINADES
    Beef Teriyaki Marinade 162
    Marinade for Chicken or Beef 164
    Meat Marinade Sauce 164
    Southern Flavor Marinade and Seasoning . . 163

Marinated Broccoli Ring 80
Marinated Crabmeat 150
Marinated Dove 148
Marinated Lamb 117
Marinated Oyster Crackers 27
Marinated Slaw 90
Mariners' Salad 89
Mayonnaise Biscuits 199
Meat Loaf 105
Meat Marinade Sauce 164
Mexican Casserole 114
Mexican Chicken 131
Mexican Cornbread Casserole 113
Mexican Cornbread I 194
Mexican Cornbread II 194
Mexican Salad 85
MICROWAVE
    Baked Vidalia Onions 180
    Creamy Beef Cheese Dip 8
    Microwave Boiled Custard 252
    Microwave Caramel Nut Rolls 290
    Microwave Copy Pop 292
    Microwave Divinity 285
    Microwave Munchy Peanut Brittle 289
    Microwave Scalloped Potatoes 186
    Microwave Stuffed Zucchini 180
    Microwave Vegetable-Rice 189
    Spiced Apple Rings 192
Mike's Venison Jerkey 144
Mile High Pie 236
Milk Punch 40
Milk, Sweetened Condensed 304
Milky Way Bar Ice Cream 295
Milky Way No Bake Cheesecake 266
Million Dollar Pound Cake 229
Mimosa 37
Mini Pizzas 54
Mint Drink Frappé 33
Mint Julep 39
Mom Bryant's Carrot Salad 77
Monkey Bread 207
Mother's Applesauce Cake 214
Mother's Fruit Icee 32
Mother's Honey Dressing 92
Mother's White Icing 232
Mr. B's House Dressing 94
Mrs. Baen's Ranch Dressing 94
Muscadine Jelly 298
MUSHROOM(S)
    Chicken Crêpes with Mushrooms 125
    Mushroom Sandwiches 23
    Mushroom Turnovers 22
    Sautéed Mushrooms 183
    Stuffed Mushrooms 23
Mystery Salad 78

N

Nassau Grits 66
Never Fail Blackberry Wine 38
Never Fail Cheese Soufflé 61

New Orleans Shrimp Salad 87
New Orleans Style Shrimp 151
No-Cook Strawberry Jam 299
Noodle Ring 64
Nut Roll 26
Nut Roll Extraordinaire 257
Nutty Broccoli Salad 80

O

OATMEAL
Oatmeal Bars 279
Oatmeal Cookie Crisp 276
Oatmeal Cookies 275
Oatmeal Crispies 275
OKRA
French Fried Okra 189
Pickled Okra 301
Old Fashioned Honey Wheat Bread 202
Old Fashioned Sour Cream Pound Cake 231
Old-Time Beef Stew 48
Olive Mold 76
Olive Pimento Cheese Spread 15
ONION(S)
Baked Vidalia Onions 180
French Fried Onion Rings 180
French Onion Soup 42
Onion Cheese Muffins 211
Onion-Cheese Supper Bread 206
Ooey-Gooey Bars 281
ORANGE(S)
Citrus Chiffon Pie 235
Mandarin Orange Cake 220
Mandarin Orange Salad 75
Mandarin Orange-Almond Salad 83
Orange Balls 286
Orange Blend 33
Orange Blush 33
Orange Chiffon Pie 235
Orange Cream Cheese Coffee Cake 208
Orange Sherbet Salad 72
Orange Sugar Pecans 26
Spiced Orange Slices 299
Oriental Dip 28
Oriental Green Casserole 112
Oriental Salad 82
Original "Twix and Tween" Barbecue Sauce . . . 165
Oven Barbecued Chicken 137
OYSTERS
Baked Oysters 157
Baked Oysters Alabama 156
Oyster Roll 15
Oysters and Wild Rice 156
Oysters in Mexican Blankets 15
Oysters on Toast 155

P

Panic 260
Paradise Salad 68
Parmesan Croutons 198
Parmesan Hominy 184

Party Crab Mold 14
Party Pear Salad 70
Party Punch 31
PASTA
Aunt Jean's Lasagna 107
Beef Bonaparte 108
Beef Burgundy Stroganoff 103
Chicken Spaghetti 135
Family Supper Casserole 109
Fettuccini Supreme 62
Garlic Grits 66
Healthy Pasta Primavera 63
Herb Fettuccini 62
Jill's Pasta Salad 85
Lots O' Macaroni Salad 84
Macaroni and Cheese 64
Macaroni and Cheese Deluxe 65
Nassau Grits 66
Noodle Ring 64
Pasta Prima 61
Pasta Salad with Parmesan Mayonnaise 84
Pasta with Cream, Ham and Mushrooms . . . 63
Quick Manicotti 106
Shrimp Fettucini 150
Tagganocci 108
World Famous Spaghetti 106
"Paul M's" Charcoal Chicken 138
Pavlova Meringue 260
Paw Paw's Pancakes 198
PEA(S)
English Pea Casserole 181
English Pea Salad 81
Fresh or Frozen Black-Eyed Peas 181
Split Pea Soup 42
PEACH(ES)
Easy Peach Cobbler 237
Peach Crisp 255
Peach Fuzz Buzz 40
Peach Pickle Salad 75
Peanut Blossoms 270
PEANUT BUTTER
Buckeyes 288
Chocolate Peanut Butter Squares 287
Creamy Peanut Butter Pie 242
Peanut Blossoms 270
Peanut Butter Candy 284
Peanut Butter Drop Cookies 271
PEAR(S)
Party Pear Salad 70
Pear Relish 300
PECAN(S)
Cherry Pecan Bars 278
French Pecan Pie 241
Nut Roll 26
Orange Sugar Pecans 26
Pecan Cake 219
Pecan Muffins 212
Pecan Pie I 240
Pecan Pie II 240
Pecan Pie with Cream Cheese Crust 241

Pecans Worcestershire 26
Teresa's Butter Pecan Pie 240
Toasted Pecans 27
Percolator Hot Punch 35
Picadillo Dip 7
Pickled Okra 301

PICKLES & RELISHES
Chili Sauce 302
Crispy Bread and Butter Pickles 302
Crispy Pickle 302
Dill Pickles 301
Pear Relish 300
Pickled Okra 301
Refrigerator Pickles 300
Squash Relish 300
Picnic Potato Salad 83

PIES
Angel Pie 234
Black Bottom Pie 243
Calypso Pie 244
Chess Pie 233
Chocolate Chip Pie 247
Chocolate Meringue Pie 246
Christmas Pies 238
Citrus Chiffon Pie 235
Coconut Pie I 238
Coconut Pie II 238
Creamy Peanut Butter Pie 242
Easy Miracle Pie 232
Easy Peach Cobbler 237
Egg Pie 233
French Pecan Pie 241
Granny's Buttermilk Pie 233
Hot Fudge Pie 245
Japanese Fruitcake Pie 239
Libbett's Black Bottom Ice Cream Pie 244
Mile High Pie 236
Orange Chiffon Pie 235
Pecan Pie I 240
Pecan Pie II 240
Pecan Pie with Cream Cheese Crust 241
Pie Crust 232
"Quickie" Chocolate Pie 247
Raisin Pie 239
Strawberry Pie 236
Sugarless Strawberry Pie 237
Sweet Angel Chocolate Pie 245
Sweet Potato Pie 239
Teresa's Butter Pecan Pie 240
Toffee Shortbread Pie 234
Walnut Pie 242
Pimento Sandwiches 50

PINEAPPLE
Hot Pineapple Casserole 192
Pineapple Casserole 191
Pineapple Cookies 267
Pineapple Glaze for Ham 161
Pineapple Sauce 162
Pizza Dip 9
Play Dough 306

Plum Cake 219
"Poor Man's" Lobster 159
Pop's Chicken Curry 126
Poppy Seed Bread 206
Poppy Seed Dressing 93

PORK
Pork Chops 120
Pork Chops and Rice 120
Quick Barbecued Pork Chops 120
Smoked Country Style Backbones 122
Sweet and Pungent Spareribs 123
Three Way Meat Loaf 104

POTATO(ES)
Golden Parmesan Potatoes 184
Ham and Scalloped Potatoes 119
Microwave Scalloped Potatoes 186
Picnic Potato Salad 83
Potato Bread 202
Potato Casserole 185
Potato Chip Cookies 278
Refrigerator Mashed Potatoes 186
Senator Russell's Sweet Potatoes 187
Sloppy Potato Skins 183
Sow's Ears and Silver Purses 185
Sweet Potato Pecan Balls 187

POTPOURRI
Bird Feeders 308
Bird Food Balls 308
Bubble Solution 308
Christmas Ornament Dough 306
Finger Paint 307
Halloween Magic Makeup 307
Homemade Doggie Biscuits 309
How to Clarify Butter 304
Ice Cream Cone Cupcakes 305
Mama vonSeeberg's Cranberry Sauce 304
Play Dough 306
Potpourri 306
Strawberry Butter 305
Sweetened Condensed Milk 304
Toasted Pumpkin Seeds 305
Poulet d'Artichoke 125

POULTRY (See CHICKEN and TURKEY)
Praline Cheesecake 264
Pretzel Congealed Salad 73
Puff-Topped Asparagus Sandwiches 49
Pugh's Ozark Pudding 255
Punch Bowl Cake 250
Purple Cow 34

Q
Quantities to Serve 50 310

QUICHE
Quiche Lorraine 58
Sausage Quiche I 59
Sausage Quiche II 59
Spinach Pie Parma 57
Spinach Quiche 58
Quick and Easy Chicken Casserole 140
Quick Barbecued Pork Chops 120

Quick Manicotti 106
Quick Monkey Bread 208
Quick Muffins 210
Quick Tortoni Ice Cream 294
"Quickie" Chocolate Pie 247

R

Raisin Pie 239
Raw Vegetable Dip 25
Real Texas Chili 49
Red Beans and Rice 172
Red Velvet Cake 221
Refrigerator Mashed Potatoes 186
Refrigerator Pickles 300
Refrigerator Rolls 200
RELISH (See PICKLES & RELISHES)
Reuben Casserole 115
Reuben Turnovers 53
RICE
  Artichoke Rice 170
  Broccoli and Rice Casserole 171
  Brown Rice 66
  Cherokee Casserole 111
  Chicken and Wild Rice Casserole 140
  Day-Of-The-Wedding Sausage Casserole 122
  Don's Chicken and Rice Salad 86
  Easy Sausage Rice Casserole 121
  Garlic Rice 65
  Hamburger Stroganoff 103
  Hamburger-Can-Be-Heaven Casserole 110
  Microwave Vegetable-Rice 189
  Oysters and Wild Rice 156
  Pork Chops and Rice 120
  Red Beans and Rice 172
  Sausage Rice Bake 112
  Shrimp Fried Rice 152
  Sour Cream Rice Casserole 65
  St. Paul's Sausage and Rice 121
Rita Boyd's Fruit Punch 31
Ritz Cracker Cookies 278
Ritzy Chicken Pie 133
Rodney's Rapjacks for a Crowd 197
Ron's Fudge 284
Rosie Pink Salad 69
Royal Bread Pudding 254
Russian Tea I 36
Russian Tea II 36

S

SALADS (Also see DRESSINGS)
  Bay Salad 88
  Blueberry Salad 76
  Broccoli Salad 79
  Carrot Salad 77
  Cauliflower Salad 79
  Chicken Salad 85
  Cornbread Salad 90
  Crab Louis Salad 89
  Créme de Menthe Salad 74
  Deluxe Waldorf Salad 71

  Don's Chicken and Rice Salad 86
  Easy Corn Salad 77
  English Pea Salad 81
  Fresh Apple Salad 74
  Fresh Fruit Compote 71
  Fruit Salad 68
  Here's Lookin' At Ya Kid 69
  Hot Chicken Salad I 126
  Hot Chicken Salad II 127
  Jill's Pasta Salad 85
  Kraut Salad-Relish 91
  Layered Salad 81
  Lots O' Macaroni Salad 84
  Magnolia Room Frozen Fruit Salad 70
  Mama's Cranberry Salad 69
  Mandarin Orange Salad 75
  Mandarin Orange-Almond Salad 83
  Marinated Broccoli Ring 80
  Marinated Crabmeat 150
  Marinated Slaw 90
  Mariners' Salad 89
  Mexican Salad 85
  Mom Bryant's Carrot Salad 77
  Mystery Salad 78
  New Orleans Shrimp Salad 87
  Nutty Broccoli Salad 80
  Olive Mold 76
  Orange Sherbet Salad 72
  Oriental Salad 82
  Paradise Salad 68
  Party Pear Salad 70
  Pasta Salad with Parmesan Mayonnaise 84
  Peach Pickle Salad 75
  Picnic Potato Salad 83
  Pretzel Congealed Salad 73
  Rosie Pink Salad 69
  Seafood Salad 87
  Shrimp and Artichoke Salad 86
  Shrimp Salad 87
  Snow Ball Salad 68
  Spinach Salad 81
  Suttles "Church" Salad 72
  Tea Room Salad 73
  Thanksgiving Salad 72
  Tomato Soup Salad 78
  Vegetable Salad 82
  West Indies Salad 88
SALMON
  Salmon Loaf 159
  Salmon Mousse 158
  Salmon Pie 158
  Salmon Spread 13
Sand Tarts 274
SANDWICHES
  Bacon and Tomato Spread 10
  Bacon Sandwiches 53
  Baked Sandwiches 51
  Chili-Cheese Rolls 52
  Cucumber Dip 24
  Got It All Together 111

Ham-Pita-Wiches 52
Madras Tuna Sandwiches 50
Mini Pizzas 54
Mushroom Sandwiches 23
Olive Pimento Cheese Spread 15
Pimento Sandwiches 50
Puff-Topped Asparagus Sandwiches 49
Reuben Turnovers 53
Shrimp Burgers 51
Tuna Puffs 50
Yumbos 54
Sarah's Fruit Tea Punch 32

SAUCES
Barbecue Sauce 164
Bearnaise Sauce 168
Bill's Barbecued Catfish Sauce 166
Chili Sauce 302
Crab Cocktail Sauce 166
Fresh Tartar Sauce 167
Gourmet Hamburger Sauce 166
Hollandaise Sauce 167
Hot Fudge Sauce 267
Jamie's Mustard Sauce 161
Johnnie's Barbecued Sauce 165
Mama vonSeeberg's Cranberry Sauce 304
Mama vonSeeberg's Sauce 162
Original "Twix and Tween" Barbecue Sauce 165
Pineapple Glaze for Ham 161
Pineapple Sauce 162
Steak Sauce Alano 165
White Sauce 167

SAUSAGE
Breakfast Sausage Casserole 60
Day-Of-The-Wedding Sausage Casserole . . . 122
Easy Sausage Rice Casserole 121
Make Ahead Breakfast Casserole 61
Sausage Balls 7
Sausage Quiche I 59
Sausage Quiche II 59
Sausage Rice Bake 112
St. Paul's Sausage and Rice 121
Sautéed Mushrooms 183
Savory Cucumbers 190
Scalloped Cheese Tomatoes 178
Scotch Eggs 56

SEAFOOD (See Individual Listings)
Baked Oysters 157
Baked Oysters Alabama 156
Baked Tuna 156
Barbecued Shrimp 151
Bay Salad 88
Clam Chowder 46
Crab "Blue Moon" 149
Crab Gumbo 46
Crab Louis Salad 89
Crabmeat au Gratin 149
Crabmeat Casserole 148
Cream Cheese-Crabmeat Log 13
Curried Crab Meatballs 14
Delicious Shrimp Batter 160

Fish Florentine 160
Flounder Meuniere 159
Governor's Seafood Gumbo 45
Hot Shrimp Dip I 12
Hot Shrimp Dip II 12
Marinated Crabmeat 150
New Orleans Shrimp Salad 87
New Orleans Style Shrimp 151
Oyster Roll 15
Oysters and Wild Rice 156
Oysters in Mexican Blankets 15
Oysters on Toast 155
Party Crab Mold 14
"Poor Man's" Lobster 159
Salmon Loaf 159
Salmon Mousse 158
Salmon Pie 158
Salmon Spread 13
Seafood Casserole 155
Seafood Delight 155
Seafood Stuffed Eggplant 153
Seafood Thermidore 154
Shrimp and Artichoke Salad 86
Shrimp and Deviled Egg Casserole 154
Shrimp and Eggplant Casserole 153
Shrimp Burgers 51
Shrimp Casserole 151
Shrimp Celery Stuffing 13
Shrimp Creole 152
Shrimp Fettucini 150
Shrimp Fried Rice 152
Shrimp Mold 12
Shrimp Salad 87
Tuna Puffs 50
West Indies Salad 88

SHRIMP
Barbecued Shrimp 151
Bay Salad 88
Delicious Shrimp Batter 160
Hot Shrimp Dip I 12
Hot Shrimp Dip II 12
New Orleans Shrimp Salad 87
New Orleans Style Shrimp 151
Seafood Thermidore 154
Shrimp and Artichoke Salad 86
Shrimp and Deviled Egg Casserole 154
Shrimp and Eggplant Casserole 153
Shrimp Burgers 51
Shrimp Casserole 151
Shrimp Celery Stuffing 13
Shrimp Creole 152
Shrimp Fettucini 150
Shrimp Fried Rice 152
Shrimp Mold 12
Shrimp Salad 87
Six Week Bran Muffins 211
Skewered Chicken Livers 135
Sloppy Potato Skins 183
Slush Fruit Punch 31
Smoked Country Style Backbones 122

Smoked Turkey 144
Smothered Dove or Quail 147
Snickerdoodles 272
Snow Ball Salad 68
SOUPS
   Broccoli Soup 43
   Cabbage Patch Soup 43
   Cheesy Vegetable Chowder 44
   Chicken-Cheese Soup 44
   Clam Chowder 46
   Crab Gumbo 46
   Easy Brunswick Stew 47
   Elephant Stew 49
   French Onion Soup 42
   Governor's Seafood Gumbo 45
   Hurry-Up Broccoli Soup 43
   Old-Time Beef Stew 48
   Real Texas Chili 49
   Split Pea Soup 42
   Uncle Clifford's Brunswick Stew 47
   V-8 Beef Stew 48
Sour Cream Muffins 212
Sour Cream Rice Casserole 65
Sourdough Starter 207
South of the Border Appetizer Platter 28
Southern Beets 189
Southern Comfort Punch 38
Southern Flavor Marinade and Seasoning . . . 163
Southern Quail 148
Sow's Ears and Silver Purses 185
Specialty of the House Cornbread 194
Spiced Apple Rings 192
Spiced Orange Slices 299
Spicy Corn-On-The-Cob 174
Spicy Italian Bread 206
SPINACH
   Greek Spinach Triangles 21
   Second Lady Spinach Dip 22
   Spinach Casserole 184
   Spinach Dip 21
   Spinach Pie Parma 57
   Spinach Quiche 58
   Spinach Salad 81
Split Pea Soup 42
Spoon Bread 195
Spoon Rolls 200
SQUASH
   Baked Cheese Squash 179
   Microwave Stuffed Zucchini 180
   Squash Casserole 179
   Squash Patties 179
   Squash Relish 300
St. Paul's Sausage and Rice 121
Stan's Bloody Marys 36
Steak Sauce Alano 165
STEW (See SOUPS)
Stir-Fry Beef and Vegetables 101
STRAWBERRY(IES)
   Fig Strawberry Preserves 298
   French Strawberry Mousse 250

Mile High Pie 236
No-Cook Strawberry Jam 299
   Strawberry Butter 305
   Strawberry Cake 219
   Strawberry Pie 236
   Sugarless Strawberry Pie 237
Stuffed Cornish Hens 141
Stuffed Green Peppers 105
Stuffed Mushrooms 23
Stuffed Snow Pea Pods 20
Substitutions 311
Sugarless Strawberry Pie 237
Sunday Dinner Roast Beef 100
Suttles "Church" Salad 72
Swedish Pastry 256
Swedish Pound Cake 230
Sweet and Sour Chicken 139
Sweet and Pungent Spareribs 123
Sweet and Sour Dressing 93
Sweet Angel Chocolate Pie 245
SWEET POTATO(ES) (Also see POTATOES)
   Senator Russell's Sweet Potatoes 187
   Sweet Potato Pecan Balls 187
   Sweet Potato Pie 239
Sweetened Condensed Milk 304
Swiss Chicken 139

T

Taco Casserole 113
Tagganocci 108
Tasty Finger Length Cake 256
Tasty Italian Bread Strips 195
Tea Room Salad 73
Teresa's Butter Pecan Pie 240
Tew's Duck Casserole 146
Thanksgiving Salad 72
Thousand Island Dressing 95
Three Bean Casserole 173
Three-Way Meat Loaf 104
Toasted Pecans 27
Toasted Pumpkin Seeds 305
Toffee Cookies 273
Toffee Shortbread Pie 234
TOMATO(ES)
   Bacon and Tomato Spread 10
   Cherry Tomato Appetizers 23
   Fire and Ice Tomatoes 178
   Scalloped Cheese Tomatoes 178
   Tomato Honey Dressing 92
   Tomato Juice Cocktail 32
   Tomato Soup Salad 78
Trifle 248
Triple Fudge Cakes 226
Tropical Tea 34
TUNA
   Baked Tuna 157
   Madras Tuna Sandwiches 50
   Mariners' Salad 89
   Mystery Salad 78
   Tuna Puffs 50

TURKEY
Daddy's Tender Turkey 142
Deviled Turkey 143
Smoked Turkey 144
Turkey Almondine 143
Turkey Noodle Casserole 142
Turnip Greens 181
Turtle Cake Squares 282

U
Uncle Clifford's Brunswick Stew 47

V
V-8 Beef Stew 48
Vanilla Wafer Cake 224
VEAL
Veal Congealed Loaf 115
Veal Cordon Bleu 115
Veal Parmesan 116
VEGETABLE(S) (See Individual Listings)
Artichoke Rice 170
Asparagus Casserole 170
Baked Beans 172
Baked Cheese Squash 179
Baked Corn with Sour Cream 175
Baked Creamed Cabbage 182
Baked Vidalia Onions 180
Barbecue Corn 177
Broccoli and Rice Casserole 171
Broccoli Casserole 172
Broccoli-Corn Casserole 171
Brussels Sprouts Oriental 174
Carrott Casserole 182
Cornbread Casserole 177
Corn Custard Casserole 175
Corn Oysters 174
Creamy Shoe Peg Corn 177
David's Vegetable Surprise 188
Eggplant Creole 178
English Pea Casserole 181
Fire and Ice Tomatoes 178
French Fried Okra 189
French Fried Onion Rings 180

Fresh or Frozen Black-Eyed Peas 181
Golden Corn Casserole 176
Golden Parmesan Potatoes 184
Green Bean Casserole 173
Microwave Scalloped Potatoes 186
Microwave Stuffed Zucchini 180
Microwave Vegetable-Rice 189
Parmesan Hominy 184
Potato Casserole 185
Refrigerator Mashed Potatoes 186
Red Beans and Rice 172
Sautéed Mushrooms 183
Savory Cucumbers 190
Scalloped Cheese Tomatoes 178
Senator Russell's Sweet Potatoes 187
Shoe Peg Corn Casserole 176
Sloppy Potato Skins 183
Southern Beets 189
Sow's Ears and Silver Purses 185
Spicy Corn-On-The-Cob 174
Spinach Casserole 184
Squash Casserole 179
Squash Patties 179
Sweet Potato Pecan Balls 187
Three Bean Casserole 173
Turnip Greens 181
Vegetable Casserole 188
Vegetable Salad 82
Very Easy Bannana Pudding 253

W
Walnut Pie 242
Watermelon Jelly 299
West Indies Salad 88
Whipping Cream Pound Cake 230
White Chocolate Cake 223
White Chocolate Frosting 223
White Fruitcake 218
White Sauce 167
Whole Wheat Banana Bread 203
World Famous Spaghetti 106

Y
Yumbos 54

Notes

Notes

* * WORLD'S FINEST SEASONING * *

LAND OF COTTON
P.O. BOX 1587
SELMA, AL 36702

**SOUTHERN FLAVOR
SEASONING**
delicious on
beef, deer and chicken
produced in
Selma, Alabama

SEND THE FOLLOWING: (Price includes shipping)

_____ ea. – 3 oz. cannister of Southern Flavor @ $3.50 ea.

_____ ea. – 16 oz. cannister of Southern Flavor @ $9.50 ea.

Please find enclosed my check for: $ _____ , or charge to:

☐ MasterCard ☐ Visa

Acct. No. _____ Date expires _____

Name _____

Address _____

City _____ State _____ Zip _____

Make check payable to Land of Cotton – Allow 4-5 weeks

-------------------------------- Cut along dotted line --------------------------------

GIFT CERTIFICATE
* * WORLD'S FINEST SEASONING * *

LAND OF COTTON
P.O. BOX 1587
SELMA, AL 36702

**SOUTHERN FLAVOR
SEASONING**
delicious on
beef, deer and chicken
produced in
Selma, Alabama

SEND THE FOLLOWING: (Price includes shipping)

_____ ea. – 3 oz. cannister of Southern Flavor @ $3.50 ea.

_____ ea. – 16 oz. cannister of Southern Flavor @ $9.50 ea.

Please find enclosed my check for: $ _____ , or charge to:

☐ MasterCard ☐ Visa

Acct. No. _____ Date expires _____

Name _____

Address _____

City _____ State _____ Zip _____

Message to friend: _____

_____

ADDITIONAL PRINTS

"AT ROW'S END"

Limited Edition Print, signed and numbered by artist, depicted on cover of "Land of Cotton", may be obtained from:

Mrs. Millie Thomas
400 Battery Avenue
Selma, Alabama 36701

Send _____ prints, 16x20 double matted and wrapped,
         by color: Indicate light or dark
         Blues _____
         Greens _____
         Browns_____   Amount:
         Neutrals____
         .@ $35.00 each. $ _____

Send _____ prints, 8x10 double matted and wrapped.
         Color indicated above, @$15.00 each. $ _____

Please snd $1.25 for postage on 16x20 and $.75 for 8x10. $ _____

                                      Total $ _____

Prints are suitable for framing and may be either rustic or nostalgic.
Enquiries regarding custom matting and/or framing are welcome.
Call Millie Thomas: 334-872-9995.

Original painting is in the private collection of R.D. Ralph, Huntsville, Alabama. Book cover and prints are offered with permission. All rights reserved.

Name _____

Address _____

City _____ State _____ Zip _____

LAND OF COTTON
P.O. Box 1587
Selma, Alabama 36702-1587

Phone (334) 875-4464
(334) 875-4465

Please send me_____copies of LAND OF COTTON at $16.95 per copy. Please include $2.00 per copy for postage. Alabama residents please add $1.53 per copy for sales tax.

Enclosed check for $_____. Make check payable to LAND OF COTTON.

Charge to Visa ☐ or MasterCard ☐ #_____ Exp. Date_____

Signature:_____

Mail to: Name_____

Address_____

City_____ State_____ Zip_____

- -

LAND OF COTTON
P.O. Box 1587
Selma, Alabama 36702-1587

Phone (334) 875-4464
(334) 875-4465

Please send me_____copies of LAND OF COTTON at $16.95 per copy. Please include $2.00 per copy for postage. Alabama residents please add $1.53 per copy for sales tax.

Enclosed check for $_____. Make check payable to LAND OF COTTON.

Charge to Visa ☐ or MasterCard ☐ #_____ Exp. Date_____

Signature:_____

Mail to: Name_____

Address_____

City_____ State_____ Zip_____

Reorder Additional Copies